ADVANCES IN
DATA MINING
AND MODELING

ADVANCES IN DATA MINING AND MODELING

Hong Kong   27 – 28 June 2002

Editors

Wai-Ki Ching
Michael Kwok-Po Ng
University of Hong Kong, China

World Scientific
New Jersey • London • Singapore • Hong Kong

Published by

World Scientific Publishing Co. Pte. Ltd.

5 Toh Tuck Link, Singapore 596224

USA office: Suite 202, 1060 Main Street, River Edge, NJ 07661

UK office: 57 Shelton Street, Covent Garden, London WC2H 9HE

British Library Cataloguing-in-Publication Data
A catalogue record for this book is available from the British Library.

ADVANCES IN DATA MINING AND MODELING

ISBN 981-238-354-9

Printed in Singapore by World Scientific Printers (S) Pte Ltd

CONTENTS

Data Modeling

Preface

Data mining and data modeling are hot topics and are under fast development. Because of its wide applications and rich research contents, a lot of practitioners and academics are attracted to work on these areas. In the view of promoting the communications and collaborations among the practitioners and researchers in Hong Kong, a two-day workshop on data mining and modeling was held on 27–28 June 2002. Prof. Ngaiming Mok, the Director of the Institute of Mathematical Research, The University of Hong Kong and Prof. Tze Leung Lai, Stanford University and the C.V. Starr Professor of the University of Hong Kong initialized the workshop. The workshop was organized by Dr. Michael Kwok-Po Ng, Department of Mathematics, The University of Hong Kong, and supported by the Institute of Mathematical Research and Hong Kong Mathematical Society. The two-day workshop is the first workshop on data mining and modeling in Hong Kong. It aims at promoting research interest in mathematical, statistical and computational methods and models in data mining for computer scientists, mathematicians, engineers and statisticians to foster contacts and inter-flow.

This book contains selected papers presented in the workshop. The papers fall into two main categories: data mining and data modeling. Data mining papers contain pattern discovery, clustering algorithms, classification and practical applications in stock market. Data modeling papers deal with neural network models, time series models, statistical models and practical applications. In the following, we give brief summaries for individual paper.

The problem of mining frequent sequences is to extract frequently occurring subsequences in a sequence database. Many algorithms have been proposed to solve the problem efficiently. Kao and Zhang survey several notable algorithms for mining frequent sequences, and analyze their characteristics.

Feng *et al.* discuss the gene selection problem which is an important issue in microarray data analysis and has critical implications for the discovery of genes related to serious diseases. They propose a Fisher optimization model in gene selection and uses Fisher linear discriminant in classification. They also demonstrated the validity of this method by using public data.

In the real applications of clustering, one has to perform two important tasks: partitioning data sets into clusters and validating the clustering results. Various clustering algorithms have been designed for the first task. Few techniques are available for cluster validation in data mining. Huang *et al.* present a number of techniques for the first two tasks. They first discuss the family of the k-means type algorithms, which are mostly used in data mining. A visual method for cluster validation is also presented. The method is based on the Fastmap data projection algorithm and its enhancement. Finally, they present a method to combine a clustering algorithm and the visual cluster validation method to interactively build classification models.

Leung *et al.* present a new method for cluster analysis based on Uni-Dimensional Scaling (UDS). UDS is a technique to find the coordinates of n objects on a real line so that the interpoint distances can best approximate the observed dissimilarities between pairs of objects. They first propose a simple and effective way to find the coordinates of the objects by minimizing the squared error function. Then the coordinates of these n objects are used to detect the hidden clusters. Large jumps or gaps in the coordinate indicate possible boundaries of two clusters. They also give real and simulated examples to illustrate and to compare their method with the k-means clustering.

Mining textual document and time series concurrently, such as predicting the movements of stock prices based on news articles, is definitely an emerging topic in data mining society nowadays. Previous research has already suggested that relationships between news articles and stock prices do exist. Fung *et al.* explore such an opportunity and propose a systematic framework for predicting the movement of stock trends by analyzing the influence of news articles. In particular, they investigate the immediate impacts of news articles onto the stock market based on the Efficient Markets Hypothesis (EMH). Several data mining and text mining techniques are used in a novel way. They present extensive experiments using real-life data and encouraging results are obtained.

Current attempts to analyze international financial markets include the use of financial technical analysis and data mining techniques. These efforts, however, do not make a clear distinction between the local and global perspectives of inter-market actions. Tse and Liu propose a new approach that incorporates implication networks, i.e., a variation of probabilistic network, and association rules to form an associated network structure. The proposed approach explicitly addresses the issue of local vs. global influences in knowledge domains. They found from the validation experiments that their approach can adequately model different international markets based on the discovered associated network structure when some real-world market data is given. The associated network structure can be used for financial analysis purposes, yielding satisfactory and stable analysis results.

Systematic approach of detecting chart patterns and their trading signals are important in technical analysis of financial data. Yu *et al.* suggest using the filter rule to identify the local extrema. They apply the proposed method to the daily stock price data of Hong Kong in the period from 1980 to 1999. They offer an alternative algorithm to automatically identify chart patterns. Instead of using sophisticated techniques unfamiliar to technical analysts, they use methods popular among technical analysts to identify peaks and troughs in a time series of stock prices. Other than using a new algorithm to automatically identify chart patterns, they also test whether the chart patterns can help in improving trading performances.

Huang *et al.* present a new divide-and-conquer learning approach to radial basis function networks (DCRBF). The DCRBF network is a hybrid system consisting of several sub-RBF networks, each of which takes a sub-input space as its input. Since this system divides a high-dimensional modeling problem into several low-dimensional ones, it can considerably reduce the structural complexity of a RBF network, whereby the net's learning is much faster. They have experimentally shown its outstanding learning performance on forecasting two real time series as well as synthetic data in comparison with a conventional RBF one.

Sunspot series is a record of the activities of the surface of the sun. It is chaotic and is a well-known challenging task for time series analysis. Li shows that one can approximate the transformed sequence with a discrete-time recurrent neural network. He then applies a new smoothing technique to integrate the original sequence twice with mean correction and also normalize the smoothened sequence to $[-1,1]$. The smoothened sequence is divided into a few segments and each segment is approximated by a neuron of a discrete-time fully connected neural network. His approach is based on the universal approximation property of discrete-time recurrent neural network. The relation between the least square error and the network size are discussed. The results are compared with the linear time series models.

The one-bit-matching conjecture in independent component analysis (ICA) is usually stated as "all the sources can be separated as long as there is a one-to-one same-sign-correspondence between the kurtosis signs of all source probability density functions (pdf's) and the kurtosis signs of all model pdf's". Liu *et al.* prove it under the assumption of zero skewness for source and model pdf's. Based on the theorem, a simplified LPM-ICA algorithm with only one free parameter is suggested with experimental demonstrations.

Ching *et al.* proposed an higher-order Markov chain model for modeling categorical data sequences. They also propose an efficient estimation method based on solving a linear programming problem for the model parameters. Data sequences such as DNA and sales demand are used to illustrate the predicting power of their proposed models.

The Mixture Auto-Regressive (MAR) model has been introduced in the literature recently. The MAR model possesses certain nice features which other time series models do not enjoy. Wong and Wong apply the MAR models to the yearly sunspot numbers and made comparison with other competing models.

Fan studied a bond risk and return problem. The yield term structures implied in bond prices in the SSE are given, and two typical yield curves are found: inverted yield curves from January 1994 to March 1996, and rising yield curves from April 1996 to October 2001. The traditional expectation hypothesis is tested and it does not hold in the SSE. With all the forward rates in the term structure, it is found that bond excess returns have strong predictability, and the predictability is absorbed by two predicting factors. Risk analysis finds that bond risk premium come from three risk sources: level factor, slope factor, and curvature factor.

E-retailing and database marketing are two emerging industries that require strong support from the customer relationship management (CRM) system. For a website, it is important to keep customers interested and come back frequently to visit. As for a database marketing company, the selection of potential customers to mail an offer or catalog is of key importance. Who should receive which catalogs and when to send out the catalogs are difficult questions constantly challenging the management. As web data and direct marketing data are available in huge volumes, data mining is an important and popular tool for both industries to develop good CRM systems to target loyal customers. Since most of these data are genuine purchasing data, one could even go one step further to develop models to describe and predict behaviors of customers. Lo *et al.* proposed two statistical models from the theory of repeat buying, the logarithmic series distribution and the negative binomial distribution. They used the models to fit the data from two large databases: One is obtained from a popular website in Hong Kong and the other is a publicly available database from a direct marketing company. Both models provide very good fit to the data and useful predictions are obtained.

We would like to thank the Institute of Mathematical Research, University of Hong Kong and the Hong Kong Mathematical Society for their support in the workshop. Finally it is a pleasure to thank all the speakers and contributors for their contributions to both the workshop and the proceedings.

Wai-Ki Ching
Michael Kwok-Po Ng

Author Index

ALGORITHMS FOR MINING FREQUENT SEQUENCES

BEN KAO AND MINGHUA ZHANG

Department of Computer Science and Information System,
The University of Hong Kong, Hong Kong.
E-mail: {kao,mhzhang}@csis.hku.hk

The problem of mining frequent sequences is to extract frequently occurring sub-sequences in a sequence database. It was first put forward in [1]. Since then, many algorithms have been proposed to solve the problem efficiently [6,9,7,4]. This paper surveys several notable algorithms for mining frequent sequences, and analyze their characteristics.

1. Introduction

Data mining has recently attracted considerable attention from database practitioners and researchers because of its applicability in many areas such as decision support, market strategy and financial forecasts. Combining techniques from the fields of machine learning, statistics and databases, data mining enables us to find out useful and invaluable information from huge databases.

One of the many data mining problems is the extraction of frequent sequences from transactional databases. The goal is to discover frequent sequences of events. Sequence mining finds its application in many different areas. For example, by examining a medical database, researchers may discover that the occurrence of certain symptom sequence would likely lead to certain illness; by analyzing its web log, a web site could discover the most popular web page visiting order; DNA sequence analysis, an extremely important research area in bio-informatics, allows the discovery of hereditary illness, which helps predict whether a person is vulnerable to certain diseases; an on-line bookstore may analyze the purchase sequences of its customers to deduce their purchase patterns, which helps the store in designing sale and promotional strategies.

The problem of mining frequent sequences was first introduced by Agrawal and Srikant [1]. In their model, a database is a collection of transactions. Each transaction is a set of items (or an itemset) and is associated with a customer ID and a time ID. If one groups the transactions by their customer IDs, and then sorts the transactions of each group by their time IDs in increasing value, the database is transformed into a number of customer sequences. Each customer sequence shows the order of transactions a customer has conducted. Roughly speaking, the problem of mining frequent sequences is to discover "subsequences" (of itemsets) that occur frequently enough among all the customer sequences. Many works have been published on the problem and its variations recently [1,6,7,3,9,8,2,4].

Among them, GSP is a multi-phase iterative algorithm. It scans the database a number of times. Very similar to the structure of the Apriori algorithm [5] for mining association rules, GSP starts by finding all frequent length-1 sequences[a] by scanning the database. This set of length-1 frequent sequences is then used to generate a set of candidate length-2 sequences. The supports, or occurrence frequencies, of the candidate sequences are counted by scanning the database again. Those length-2 sequences that are frequent are used to generate candidate sequences of length 3, and so on. This process is repeated until no more frequent sequences are discovered during a database scan, or no candidates are generated. GSP is efficient. However, the number of iterations (and hence database scans) required by GSP is dependent on the length of the longest frequent sequences in the database. Therefore, if the database is huge and if it contains very long frequent sequences, the I/O cost of GSP is high.

To improve the I/O performance of GSP, an algorithm called MFS is devised [9]. MFS first finds an *approximate solution*, S_{est}, to the set of frequent sequences. One way to obtain S_{est} is to mine a sample of the database using, for example, GSP. MFS then scans the database once to verify and to retain those sequences in S_{est} that are frequent w.r.t. the whole database. After that, MFS enters a loop. In each iteration, it first generates a set of candidate sequences of various lengths using the frequent sequences known so far (also of various lengths) as input. Then it scans the database once to find out new frequent sequences from the candidates, and refine the frequent sequence set it keeps. The candidate-generation-refinement process is repeated until no more candidates can be generated. MFS is much more I/O efficient than GSP, because long sequences can be generated early and processed early.

Neither GSP nor MFS assumes the database is memory-resident. With a memory-abundant system, data can be stored in main memory for efficient random accesses. Some algorithms have been proposed that try to achieve efficiency by keeping valuable information of the database in memory. One of such algorithms is SPADE [7]. SPADE requires a *vertical represen-*

---

[a] A length-i sequence is one that contains i items.

tation of the database. In this representation, each item is associated with an id-list. The id-list of an item a is a list of records that show which customer transactions the item a appears in. The concept is similar to that of *inverted lists* used in traditional document retrieval systems. Similarly, a sequence can also be associated with an id-list. With the help of the id-lists, the support counts of sequences can be easily obtained. SPADE is a very efficient algorithm if the memory size is relatively large compared with the database size.

Another efficient algorithm that takes advantage of memory availability is PrefixSpan[4]. It discovers frequent sequences by database projection. In the process, a number of intermediate databases are generated. Similar to SPADE, PrefixSpan is very efficient if the database is small relative to the amount of available memory.

The goal of this paper is to survey different algorithms available for sequence mining, and to analyze their characteristics and applicable environment.

The rest of this paper is organized as follows. In Section 2 we give a formal definition of the problem of mining frequent sequences. In Section 3 we describe four important sequence mining algorithms, namely, GSP, MFS, SPADE, and PrefixSpan. Finally, we conclude the paper in Section 4.

2. Problem Definition and Model

In this section, we give a formal definition of the problem of mining frequent sequences.

Let $I = \{i_1, i_2, \ldots, i_m\}$ be a set of literals called items. An itemset X of the universe I is a set of items (hence, $X \subseteq I$). A sequence $s = \langle t_1, t_2, \ldots, t_n \rangle$ is an ordered set of transactions, where each transaction t_i $(i = 1, 2, \ldots, n)$ is an itemset.

The length of a sequence s is defined as the number of items contained in s. If an item occurs several times in different itemsets of a sequence, the item is counted for each occurrence. For example, the sequence $\langle \{A, B\}, \{A, C\}, \{C, D, E\} \rangle$ consists of three transactions and its length is 7. We use $|s|$ to represent the length of s.

Given two sequences $s_1 = \langle a_1, a_2, \ldots, a_n \rangle$ and $s_2 = \langle b_1, b_2, \ldots, b_l \rangle$, we say s_1 contains s_2 (or equivalently s_2 is a subsequence of s_1) if there exist integers $j_1, j_2, \ldots, j_l$, such that $1 \leq j_1 < j_2 < \ldots < j_l \leq n$ and $b_1 \subseteq a_{j_1}, b_2 \subseteq a_{j_2}, \ldots, b_l \subseteq a_{j_l}$. We represent this relationship by $s_2 \sqsubseteq s_1$.

In a sequence set V, a sequence $s \in V$ is *maximal* if s is not a subsequence of any other sequence in V.

Given a database D of sequences, the *support count* of a sequence s, denoted by δ_D^s, is defined as the number of sequences in D that contain s. The *fraction* of sequences in D that contain s is called the *support* of s. If we use the symbol $|D|$ to denote the number of sequences in D (or the size of D), then support of $s = \delta_D^s/|D|$.

If the support of s is not less than a user specified support threshold, ρ_s, s is a frequent sequence. We use the symbol L_i to denote the set of all frequent length-i sequences. Also, we use L to denote the set of all frequent sequences. That is $L = \bigcup_{i=1}^{\infty} L_i$. The problem of mining frequent sequences is to find all *maximal* frequent sequences in a database D (i.e., $Max(L)$).

For reference, Table 1 summarizes the notations used in our definitions.

Table 1.   Notations

Symbol	Description
s	a sequence
D	a database
$|D|$	number of sequences in database D (the size of D)
δ_D^s	support count of sequence s in database D
ρ_s	support threshold
L_i	the set of frequent length-i sequences
L	the set of all frequent sequences

3. Algorithms

In this section we describe some notable algorithms for mining frequent sequences, namely, GSP, MFS, PrefixSpan, and SPADE. We also discuss their characteristics and under which conditions they are most efficient.

3.1. *GSP*

Agrawal and Srikant first studied the problem of mining frequent sequences [1] and they proposed an algorithm called AprioriAll. Later, they improved AprioriAll and came up with a more efficient algorithm called GSP [6]. GSP can also be used to solve other generalized versions of the frequent-sequence mining problem. For example, a user can specify a sliding time window. Items that occur in itemsets that are within the sliding time window could be considered as to occur in the same itemset.

Similar to the structure of the Apriori algorithm [5] for mining association rules, GSP starts by finding all frequent length-1 sequences from the database. A set of candidate length-2 sequences are then generated. The support counts of the candidate sequences are then counted by scanning the database once. Those frequent length-2 sequences are then used to generate candidate sequences of length 3, and so on. In general, GSP uses a function GGen to generate candidate sequences of length $k + 1$ given the set of all frequent length-k sequences. The algorithm terminates when no more frequent sequences are discovered during a database scan.

The candidate generation function GGen works as follows. Given the set of all frequent length-k sequences, L_k, as input, GGen considers every pair of sequences s_1 and s_2 in L_k. If the sequence obtained by deleting the first item of s_1 is equal to the sequence obtained by deleting the last item of s_2, then a candidate is generated by appending the last item of s_2 to the end of s_1. For example, consider $s_1 = \langle\{A, B\}, \{C\}\rangle$ and $s_2 = \langle\{B\}, \{C, D\}\rangle$. Since removing the leading item A from s_1 gives the same sequence ($\langle\{B\}, \{C\}\rangle$) as that obtained by removing the trailing item D from s_2, a candidate sequence $\langle\{A, B\}, \{C, D\}\rangle$ is generated by GGen. After a candidate sequence s is generated, GGen checks whether all subsequences of s are frequent. If not, the candidate is thrown away.

As an example, consider the database shown in Table 2. If the support threshold is 75%, then a sequence is frequent if it is contained in at least 3 customer sequences. In this case, the candidates (C_i's) generated by GGen and the frequent sequences (L_i's) discovered by GSP for each iteration (i) are listed in Table 3.

Table 2.   Database

Customer ID	Sequence
1	$\langle\{A, B, C\}, \{E, G\}, \{C, D\}\rangle$
2	$\langle\{A, B\}, \{A, D, E\}\rangle$
3	$\langle\{A, F\}, \{B, E\}\rangle$
4	$\langle\{A, B, F\}, \{C, E\}\rangle$

Table 3.   Mining process of GSP

C_1	$\{\langle\{A\}\rangle, \langle\{B\}\rangle, \langle\{C\}\rangle, \langle\{D\}\rangle, \langle\{E\}\rangle, \langle\{F\}\rangle, \langle\{G\}\rangle\}$
L_1	$\{\langle\{A\}\rangle, \langle\{B\}\rangle, \langle\{E\}\rangle\}$
C_2	$\{\langle\{A, B\}\rangle, \langle\{A, E\}\rangle, \langle\{B, E\}\rangle, \langle\{A\}, \{A\}\rangle, \langle\{A\}, \{B\}\rangle, \langle\{A\}, \{E\}\rangle,$ $\langle\{B\}, \{A\}\rangle, \langle\{B\}, \{B\}\rangle, \langle\{B\}, \{E\}\rangle, \langle\{E\}, \{A\}\rangle, \langle\{E\}, \{B\}\rangle, \langle\{E\}, \{E\}\rangle\}$
L_2	$\{\langle\{A, B\}\rangle, \langle\{A\}, \{E\}\rangle, \langle\{B\}, \{E\}\rangle\}$
C_3	$\{\langle\{A, B\}, \{E\}\rangle\}$
L_3	$\{\langle\{A, B\}, \{E\}\rangle\}$
C_4	$\emptyset$

GSP is an efficient algorithm. However, the number of database scans it requires is determined by the length of the longest frequent sequences. Consequently, if there are very long frequent sequences and if the database is huge, the I/O cost of GSP could be substantial.

6

3.2. *MFS*

To improve the I/O efficiency of GSP, the algorithm MFS was proposed [9]. Similar to GSP, MFS is an iterative algorithm. MFS first requires an initial estimate, S_{est}, of the set of frequent sequences of the database be available. (We will discuss how to obtain this estimate shortly.) In the first iteration of the algorithm, the database is scanned to obtain the support counts of all length-1 sequences as well as those of the sequences in the estimated set, S_{est}. Sequences that are found frequent are collected into a set *MFSS*. Essentially, *MFSS* captures the set of frequent sequences that MFS has known so far. Typically, the set *MFSS* contains frequent sequences of various lengths. MFS then applies a candidate generation function MGen on *MFSS* to obtain a set of candidate sequences. The database is then scanned to determine which candidate sequences are frequent. Those that are frequent are added to the set *MFSS*. MFS then again applies the generation function MGen on the *refined MFSS* to obtain a new set of candidate sequences, whose supports are then counted by scanning the database, and so on. MFS executes this candidate-generation-verification-refinement iteration until the set *MFSS* cannot be refined further.

The heart of MFS is the candidate generation function MGen. MGen can be considered as a generalization of GGen (used in GSP) in that MGen takes as input a set of frequent sequences of various lengths and generates a set of candidate sequences of various lengths. (For GSP, all the candidates generated in an iteration are of the same length.)

The idea of MGen goes as follows. For every pair of frequent sequences s_1 and s_2 in *MFSS* that have a common subsequence, MGen generates candidates by prepending an item i_1 from s_1 to the beginning of a common subsequence and appending an item i_2 from s_2 to the same subsequence. For example, if $s_1 = \langle \{A, B\}, \{C\}, \{D, E, F\} \rangle$ and $s_2 = \langle \{B\}, \{C, G\}, \{H\} \rangle$, then a common subsequence would be $\langle \{B\}, \{C\} \rangle$. By the above generation rule, MGen would generate the candidates $\langle \{A, B\}, \{C, G\} \rangle$ and $\langle \{A, B\}, \{C\}, \{H\} \rangle$. Note that, unlike GGen, the generating sequences s_1 and s_2 have different lengths. After generating a candidate, MGen also examines whether all subsequences of the candidate are frequent. If not, the candidate is discarded.

Recall that MFS requires that an initial estimate (S_{est}) of the set of frequent sequences be available. If the set S_{est} is a reasonably good estimate of the true set of frequent sequences, then it is shown that MFS will generate long candidate sequences early (compared with GSP). As a result, in many cases, MFS requires fewer database scans and less data processing than GSP does. This reduces both CPU and I/O costs.

One method to obtain a good estimate is to mine a small sample of the database, and use the frequent sequences of the sample as S_{est}. If the database is updated regularly, MFS can use the frequent sequences in the previous mining exercise as S_{est} directly.

3.3. *PrefixSpan*

PrefixSpan is a newly devised efficient algorithm for mining frequent sequences [4]. PrefixSpan mines frequent sequences by intermediate database generation instead of the tradition approach of candidate sequence generation. PrefixSpan is shown to be efficient if a large amount of memory is available.

In [4], it is assumed without loss of generality that all items within an itemset are listed in alphabetical order. Before we review the algorithm, let us first introduce several terminologies defined in [4].

- **prefix.** Given two sequences $s_1 = \langle t_1, t_2, \ldots, t_n \rangle$, $s_2 = \langle t'_1, t'_2, \ldots, t'_m \rangle$ $(m \leq n)$, s_2 is called a prefix of s_1 if (1) $t_i = t'_i$ for $i \leq m - 1$; (2) $t'_m \subseteq t_m$; and (3) all items in $(t_m - t'_m)$ are alphabetically ordered after those in t'_m.

  For example, if $s_1 = \langle \{a\}, \{b, c, d\}, \{e\} \rangle$, $s_2 = \langle \{a\}, \{b\} \rangle$, $s_3 = \langle \{a\}, \{d\} \rangle$, then s_2 is a prefix of s_1, but s_3 is not.

- **projection.** Given a sequence s_1 and one of its subsequences s_2 (i.e., $s_2 \sqsubseteq s_1$), a sequence p is called the projection of s_1 w.r.t. prefix s_2, if (1) $p \sqsubseteq s_1$; (2) s_2 is a prefix of p; (3) p is the "maximal" sequence that satisfies conditions (1) and (2), that is, $\nexists p'$, s.t. $(p \sqsubseteq p' \sqsubseteq s_1) \wedge (p \neq p') \wedge (s_2 \text{ is a prefix of } p')$.

  For example, if $s_1 = \langle \{a\}, \{b, c, d\}, \{e\}, \{f\} \rangle$, $s_2 = \langle \{a\}, \{c, d\} \rangle$, then $p = \langle \{a\}, \{c, d\}, \{e\}, \{f\} \rangle$ is the projection of s_1 w.r.t. prefix s_2.

- **postfix.** If p is the projection of s_1 w.r.t. prefix s_2, then s_3 obtained by removing the prefix s_2 from p is called the postfix of s_1 w.r.t. prefix s_2.

  For example, if $s_1 = \langle \{a\}, \{b, c, d\}, \{e\}, \{f\} \rangle$, $s_2 = \langle \{a\}, \{c, d\} \rangle$, then $p = \langle \{a\}, \{c, d\}, \{e\}, \{f\} \rangle$, is the projection of s_1 w.r.t. prefix s_2, and the postfix of s_1 w.r.t. prefix s_2 is $\langle \{e\}, \{f\} \rangle$.

  If s_2 is not a subsequence of s_1, then both the projection and the postfix of s_1 w.r.t. s_2 are empty.

There are three major steps of PrefixSpan.

- Find frequent length-1 sequences.

  In this step, PrefixSpan scans the database D once to find all frequent items. The set of frequent length-1 sequences is $L_1 = \{\langle\{i\}\rangle | i \text{ is a frequent item}\}$. For example, given the database shown in Table 2, and a support count threshold of 3, the set of frequent items is $\{A, B, E\}$.

- Divide search space into smaller subspaces.

  The set of all frequent sequences can be divided into several groups, such that the sequences within a group share the same prefix item.

  For example, if $\{A, B, E\}$ is the set of frequent items discovered in the first step, then all the frequent sequences can be divided into three groups, corresponding to the three prefixes $\langle\{A\}\rangle$, $\langle\{B\}\rangle$, and $\langle\{E\}\rangle$.

- Discover frequent sequences in each subspace.

  In this step, PrefixSpan finds frequent sequences in each subspace. We use an example to illustrate the procedure.

  Using the running example, to find the frequent sequences with prefix $\langle\{A\}\rangle$, PrefixSpan first projects the database D to get an intermediate database $D_{\langle\{A\}\rangle}$. For every sequence s in D, $D_{\langle\{A\}\rangle}$ contains the postfix of s w.r.t. $\langle\{A\}\rangle$. The projected database $D_{\langle\{A\}\rangle}$ of our example is shown in Table 4. In the table, an underscore '_' preceding an item x indicates that x is contained in the same itemset of the last item in the prefix. For example, w.r.t. the prefix $\langle\{A\}\rangle$, the postfix sequence $\langle\{\_B, \_C\}, \{E, G\}, \{C, D\}\rangle$ indicates that the items B and C are contained in the same itemset of A in an original database sequence.

Table 4. Projected database

Customer ID	Postfix sequence
1	$\langle\{\_B, \_C\}, \{E, G\}, \{C, D\}\rangle$
2	$\langle\{\_B\}, \{A, D, E\}\rangle$
3	$\langle\{\_F\}, \{B, E\}\rangle$
4	$\langle\{\_B, \_F\}, \{C, E\}\rangle$

After $D_{\langle\{A\}\rangle}$ is obtained, PrefixSpan scans $D_{\langle\{A\}\rangle}$ once to get all frequent items in $D_{\langle\{A\}\rangle}$. In our example, the frequent items are $\{\_B, E\}$. So there are in total two length-2 frequent sequences with prefix $\langle\{A\}\rangle$, namely, $\langle\{A, B\}\rangle$ and $\langle\{A\}, \{E\}\rangle$. Then recursively, the database $D_{\langle\{A\}\rangle}$ is projected w.r.t. the prefixes $\langle\{\_B\}\rangle$ and

$\langle\{E\}\rangle$ to obtain $D_{\langle\{A,B\}\rangle}$ and $D_{\langle\{A\},\{E\}\rangle}$. Each one is recursively mined to obtain frequent sequences with the corresponding prefix.

Very different from GSP, PrefixSpan discovers frequent sequences by projecting databases and counting items' supports. This implies that only the supports of sequences that actually occur in the database are counted. In contrast, a candidate sequence generated by GSP may not appear in the database at all. The time for generating such a candidate sequence and checking whether such a candidate is a sub-sequence of database sequences is wasted. This factor contributes to the efficiency of PrefixSpan over GSP.

The major cost of PrefixSpan is that of generating projected databases. It can be shown that for every frequent sequence discovered, a projected database has to be computed for it. Hence, the number of intermediate databases is very large if there are many frequent sequences. If the database D is large, then PrefixSpan requires substantial amount of memory. For example, if there are n frequent items in D, then in order to generate all "level 1" projections, D has to be scanned n times. To avoid a high I/O cost, D has to be stored in memory. Therefore, PrefixSpan is only efficient for small databases.

3.4. SPADE

The algorithms we have reviewed so far, namely, GSP and PrefixSpan, assume a *horizontal database representation*. In this representation, each row in the database table represents a transaction. Each transaction is associated with a customer ID, a transaction timestamp, and an itemset. For efficient processing, the records are sorted using customer ID as the primary sort key and transaction timestamp as the secondary sort key. Table 5 shows an example of a database in the horizontal representation.

Table 5. Horizontal database

Customer ID	Transaction timestamp	Itemset
1	110	A B C
1	120	E G
1	130	C D
2	210	A B
2	220	A D E
3	310	A F
3	320	B E
4	410	G
4	420	A B F
4	430	C E

In [7], it is observed that a *vertical* representation of the database may be better suited for sequence mining. In the vertical representation, every item in the database is associated with an id-list. For an item a, its id-list is a list of (customer ID, transaction timestamp) pairs. Each such pair identifies a unique transaction that contains a. A vertical database is composed of the id-lists of all items. Table 6 shows the vertical representation of the database shown in Table 5.

Table 6.   Vertical database

Item	Customer ID	Transaction timestamp
A	1	110
	2	210
	2	220
	3	310
	4	420
B	1	110
	2	210
	3	320
	4	420
C	1	110
	1	130
	4	430
D	1	130
	2	220
E	1	120
	2	220
	3	320
	4	430
F	3	310
	4	420
G	1	120
	4	410

In [7], the algorithm SPADE is proposed that uses a vertical database to mine frequent sequences. To understand SPADE, let us first define two terms: *generating subsequences* and *sequence id-list*.

- **generating subsequences.** For a sequence s such that $|s| \geq 2$, the two generating subsequences of s are obtained by removing the first or the second item of s. For example, if $s = \langle \{A, B\}, \{C\}, \{D\} \rangle$ then the two generating subsequences of s are $\langle \{B\}, \{C\}, \{D\} \rangle$ and $\langle \{A\}, \{C\}, \{D\} \rangle$. Note that the two generating subsequences share the same suffix ($\langle \{C\}, \{D\} \rangle$ in the example).
- **sequence id-list.** Similar to the id-list of an item, we can also associate an id-list to a sequence. The id-list of a sequence s is

a list of (Customer ID, transaction timestamp) pairs. If the pair (C, t) is in the id-list of a sequence s, then s is contained in the sequence of Customer C, and that the first item of s occurs in the transaction of Customer C at timestamp t. For example, we see that the sequence $\langle\{B\}, \{E\}\rangle$ is a subsequence of Customer 1 (Table 5), and that its first item B appears in the transaction of Customer 1 with a timestamp of 110. Therefore, (1, 110) is included in the id-list of $\langle\{B\}, \{E\}\rangle$. Table 8 shows the id-list of $\langle\{B\}, \{E\}\rangle$.

Table 8. ID-list of $\langle\{B\}, \{E\}\rangle$

Customer ID	Transaction timestamp
1	110
2	210
4	420

We note that if id-lists are available, counting the supports of sequences is trivial. In particular, the support count of a length-1 sequence can be obtained by inspecting the vertical database. For example, from Table 6, we see that the support count of $\langle\{A\}\rangle$ is four, since there are four distinct customer id's in A's id-list. In general, the support count of a sequence s is given by the number of distinct customer id's in s's id-list. The problem of support counting is thus reduced to the problem of sequence id-list computation.

With the vertical database, only the id-lists of length-1 sequences can be readily obtained. The id-lists of longer sequences have to be computed. Part of the job of SPADE is to compute such id-lists efficiently. In [7], it is shown that the id-list of a sequence s can be computed easily by *intersecting* the id-lists of the two generating subsequences of s. Let us use an example to illustrate the intersecting process. Readers are referred to [7] for further details.

Consider a length-2 sequence $\langle\{B\}, \{E\}\rangle$. Its generating subsequences are $\langle\{B\}\rangle$ and $\langle\{E\}\rangle$. Since these generating subsequences are of length 1, their id-lists can be obtained from the vertical database directly (see Table 6). To compute the id-list of $\langle\{B\}, \{E\}\rangle$, we scan the id-lists of $\langle\{B\}\rangle$ and $\langle\{E\}\rangle$. From the table, we see that Customer 1 occurs in both id-lists and that the timestamp of the record in B's id-list (110) is smaller than that of E's (120). This timestamp ordering thus agrees with the ordering in the sequence $\langle\{B\}, \{E\}\rangle$. Hence, the pair (1, 110) is put into the id-list of $\langle\{B\}, \{E\}\rangle$. After processing the id-lists of $\langle\{B\}\rangle$ and $\langle\{E\}\rangle$, the id-list of $\langle\{B\}, \{E\}\rangle$ is computed (Table 8).

Here, we summarize the key steps of SPADE.

(1) Find frequent length-1 sequences.

As we have explained, the support count of a length-1 sequence can be obtained by simply scanning the id-list of the lone item in the sequence. The first step of SPADE is to discover all frequent length-1 sequences by scanning the vertical database once.

(2) Find frequent length-2 sequences.

Suppose there are M frequent items, then the number of candidate frequent length-2 sequences is $O(M^2)$. If the support counts of these length-2 sequences are obtained by first computing their id-lists using the intersection procedure, we have to access id-lists from the vertical database $O(M^2)$ times.[b] This could be very expensive.

Instead, SPADE solves the problem by building a horizontal database on the fly that involves only frequent items. In the horizontal database, every customer is associated with a list of (item, transaction timestamp) pairs. For each frequent item found in Step 1, SPADE reads its id-list from disk and the horizontal database is updated accordingly. For example, the first record of A's id-list is (1, 110) (Table 6), therefore, SPADE adds a new node (A, 110) in the list for Customer 1. Similarly, the node (A, 210) is added to the list of Customer 2, and so on. If the frequent items of our example database (Table 6) are A, B, E, then the constructed horizontal database is shown in Table 9. After obtaining the horizontal database, the supports of all candidate length-2 sequences are computed from it.

We remark that maintaining the horizontal database might require a lot of memory. This is especially true if the number of frequent items and the vertical database are large.

Table 9. Horizontal database generated for computing L_2

Customer ID	(item, transaction timestamp) pairs
1	(A 110) (B 110) (E 120)
2	(A 210) (A 220) (B 210) (E 220)
3	(A 310) (B 320) (E 320)
4	(A 420) (B 420) (E 430)

(3) Find long frequent sequences.

In step 3, SPADE generates the id-lists of long candidate se-

---

[b]This is because computing the id-list of a length-2 sequence requires accessing the 2 id-lists of the 2 items involved.

quences (those of length ≥ 3) by the intersection procedure. SPADE carefully controls the order in which candidate sequences (and their id-lists) are generated to keep the memory requirement at a minimum. It is shown that the amount of disk access involved in this step should not exceed the cost of one full database scan. For details, readers are again referred to [7].

SPADE is shown to be an efficient algorithm. However, it does suffer from two disadvantages. First, SPADE requires a vertical representation of the database. In many applications, a horizontal database is more natural. Hence, in order to apply SPADE, the database has to be converted to the vertical representation first, which could be computationally expensive. Second, SPADE generates id-lists and a horizontal database, which require a large amount of memory. The memory requirement of SPADE grows with the database. Hence, unless memory is abundant, SPADE is efficient only when applied to small databases.

4. Conclusions

In this paper we surveyed the problem of mining frequent sequences. We described four algorithms, namely, GSP, MFS, PrefixSpan, and SPADE. We discussed the various characteristics of the algorithms, such as their memory requirements, I/O costs, and database representation. We conclude that if the amount of memory is relatively large compared with the database size, PrefixSpan and SPADE are the most efficient ones. For vertical databases, we can choose SPADE; for horizontal representations, PrefixSpan should be considered. If memory is limited, both GSP and MFS are good choices. In such a case, MFS outperforms GSP in terms of I/O cost.

References

1. Rakesh Agrawal and Ramakrishnan Srikant. Mining sequential patterns. In *Proc. of the 11th Int'l Conference on Data Engineering*, Taipei, Taiwan, March (1995).
2. Minos N. Garofalakis, Rajeev Rastogi, and Kyuseok Shim. SPIRIT: Sequential pattern mining with regular expression constraints. In *Proceedings of the 25th International Conference on Very Large Data Bases*, Edinburgh, Scotland, UK, September (1999).
3. S. Parthasarathy, M. J. Zaki, M. Ogihara, and S. Dwarkadas. Incremental and interactive sequence mining. In *Proceedings of the 1999 ACM 8th International Conference on Information and Knowledge Management (CIKM'99)*, Kansas City, MO USA, November (1999).
4. Jian Pei, Jiawei Han, Behzad Mortazavi-Asl, Helen Pinto, Qiming Chen, Umeshwar Dayal, and Mei-Chun Hsu. Prefixspan: Mining sequential patterns

by prefix-projected growth. In *Proc. 17th IEEE International Conference on Data Engineering (ICDE)*, Heidelberg, Germany, April (2001).

5. T. Imielinski R. Agrawal and A. Swami. Mining association rules between sets of items in large databases. In *Proc. ACM SIGMOD International Conference on Management of Data*, page 207, Washington, D.C., May (1993).

6. Ramakrishnan Srikant and Rakesh Agrawal. Mining sequential patterns: Generalizations and performance improvements. In *Proc. of the 5th Conference on Extending Database Technology (EDBT)*, Avignion, France, March (1996).

7. Mohammed J. Zaki. Efficient enumeration of frequent sequences. In *Proceedings of the 1998 ACM 7th International Conference on Information and Knowledge Management(CIKM'98)*, Washington, United States, November (1998).

8. Minghua Zhang, Ben Kao, David Cheung, and Chi-Lap Yip. Efficient algorithms for incremental update of frequent sequences. In *Proc. of the sixth Pacific-Asia Conference on Knowledge Discovery and Data Mining (PAKDD)*, Taiwan, May (2002).

9. Minghua Zhang, Ben Kao, C.L. Yip, and David Cheung. A GSP-based efficient algorithm for mining frequent sequences. In *Proc. of IC-AI'2001*, Las Vegas, Nevada, USA, (June 2001).

HIGH DIMENSIONAL FEATURE SELECTION FOR DISCRIMINANT MICROARRAY DATA ANALYSIS [*]

JUFU FENG, JIANGXIN SHI AND QINGYUN SHI

Center for Information Science, National Key Laboratory on Machine Perception
Peking University, Beijing 100871 P. R. China
E-mail: fjf@cis.pku.edu.cn

Gene selection is an important issue in microarray data analysis and has critical implications for the discovery of genes related to serious diseases. This paper proposes a Fisher optimization model in gene selection and uses Fisher linear discriminant in classification. Experiment result in public data has demonstrated validity of this method.

1. Introduction

With development of the human genome project (HGP), a large number of genes have been found and located, and the study on the functions of genes has become an important issue in the post-genome project [1]. With the rapid development of microarray technology [2] and the great emergence of functional genome data in recent years, microarray data analysis has become an important area of study in bioinformatics. This has also brought about enormous challenge as well opportunities for pattern recognition and machine learning. In the perspective of pattern recognition and machine learning, microarray data analysis mainly covers gene expression pattern clustering, supervised learning, classification, gene selection, etc. [3-6]. An extensive concern and research have been given to these areas. Through discrimination of genes and their functions, mankind will find new ways to take precautions and finally cure serious diseases such as cancer and heart disease.

A human being has around 30 thousand genes [7]. However, only a very small number of them are related to a specific disease. It is the job of gene selection to find out such critical genes from the 30 thousand genes. Gene selection can be reduced to feature selection in pattern recognition and machine learning, i.e., selection of k sets of most effective features from a group of N features. This is a typical combination optimization problem. The total number of combinations is C_N^k. The computation work is gigantic, and it is unrealistic to

---

[*] The work is supported by the National Natural Science Foundation of China (60175004).

compare all possible combinations and select the optimized feature sets. In fact, it is impossible because there are thousands over thousands of genes. The simplest way is scoring of each gene based on a certain criterion and filtering away genes with the lowest scores and selecting genes with the highest scores by various mean, such as individual gene-based scoring method [6, 8], mutual information scoring method [9], Markov Blanket filtering method [10], etc. However, the feature sets selected using such methods may not be the optimal ones, or might even be the worst feature sets [11]. Another strategy is association with a designed classifier and uses various search algorithms or optimization algorithms in feature selection [12]. Bradley and Mangasarian proposed a feature selection method based on linear classifier and mathematical programming [13, 14].Support Vector Machine (SVM) is a learning algorithm developed in recent years based on statistical learning theory. It has very good extended applications when the sample number is small [15, 16]. SVM has been given a large amount of profound studies and has found successful applications in pattern recognition, feature selection and bioinformatics [17-21]. Guyon et al [22] combined SVM and Recursive Feature Elimination (RFE) in gene selection and have attained the best result to date. Good results have also been got by Bayesian Automatic Related Discrimination (ARD) based on Relational Vector Machine (RVM) [23].

Fisher linear discriminant is a classical method in pattern recognition and is verified in many applications. Fisher non-linear discriminant using kernel function has also been studied in recent years, and experiments show its classification effect is better than non-linear SVM in some circumstances [24, 25]. This paper proposes a Fisher optimization model (FOM) based on Fisher linear discriminant for feature selection and uses Fisher linear discriminant in classification. Tests have been done in public data.

2. Introduction of Fisher Linear Discriminant

Gene expression data can be represented in an $N \times M$ matrix $X = (x_{i,j})_{N \times M}$, where N and M are respectively the numbers of genes and samples. Assume that there are two types of cells: normal cells and cancer cells, and normal cells are represented by $\aleph_-$, and cancer cells are represented by $\aleph_+$, the basic idea of Fisher linear discriminant is: project the samples onto a line so that the projection of the samples in this direction is well separated. That is to say, find the direction w so that function J(w) is maximum.

$$J(w) = \frac{w^T S_b w}{w^T S_w w} \tag{1}$$

$$S_b = (m_+ - m_-)(m_+ - m_-)^T = mm^T \qquad (2)$$

$$S_w = S_+ + S_- = \sum_{x \in \aleph_+} (x - m_+)(x - m_+)^T + \sum_{x \in \aleph_-} (x - m_-)(x - m_-)^T \quad (3)$$

where, m_+ is the mean of cancer sample, m_- is the mean of normal cell, $m = m_+ - m_-$. S_w is the within-class scatter matrix, and S_b is the between-class scatter matrix.

Solve the equations with the Lagrange multiplier method, and get

$$S_b w = \lambda S_w w \qquad (4)$$

For a two-class problem, the above equation can be simplified to the following:

$$S_w w = m \qquad (5)$$

However, because N>>M, matrix S_w is singular, we can not solve Equation (5) directly. We propose below a Fisher optimization model to solve this problem.

3. Gene Selection Based on Fisher Optimization Model

Equation (5) is ill-conditioned because matrix S_w is singular. A natural way is to use regularized method, i.e. introducing regularization item $\|w\|_2^2$, and minimize the following function with respect to w:

$$F_1(w) = \|S_w w - m\|_2^2 + \lambda \|w\|_2^2 \qquad (6)$$

Solve Equation (6) and get:

$$w = (S_w^T S_w + \lambda I)^{-1} S_w^T m \qquad (7)$$

But our purpose is gene selection, i.e., what is desired is that w is best if it is made of a small number of non-zero elements. Therefore, we have imported $\sigma(w) = \sum_{k=1}^{N} 1_{[w_k^2 > 0]}$. Minimize the following function with respect to w:

$$F_2(w) = \left\|S_w w - m\right\|_2^2 + \lambda_1 \left\|w\right\|^2 + \lambda_2 \sigma(w) \qquad (8)$$

However, the last item is not continuous and it is not easy to solve the equation. Therefore, we use a continuous function $f(w) = 1 - e^{-\alpha w^2}$ to approximate $\sigma(w)$, and get the following objective function:

$$F(w) = \left\|S_w w - m\right\|_2^2 + \lambda_1 \left\|w\right\|_2^2 + \lambda_2 \sum_{i=1}^{N}(1 - e^{-\alpha w_i^2}) \qquad (9)$$

A global optimal solution can hardly be got because the objective function is composed of two quadratic concave functions (the first two items) and one convex function (the third item). Therefore, we use a linear function to approximate the exponential function and use gradient descent method to get the solution.

$$f(w) \cong f(w_0) + \alpha e^{-\alpha w_0^2}(w^2 - w_0^2) \qquad (10)$$

$$F(w) = \left\|S_w w - m\right\|_2^2 + \lambda_1 \left\|w\right\|_2^2 + \lambda_2 \alpha \sum_{i=1}^{N} e^{-\alpha(w_i^k)^2} w_i^2 \qquad (11)$$

Take $w^i = (w_1^i, w_2^i, \ldots\ldots w_n^i)$ as the iterative result of step i, and w^{i+1} can be solved with Equation (12):

$$(S_w^T S_w + \lambda_1 I + \lambda_2 \alpha D_i) w^{i+1} = S_w^T m \qquad (12)$$

$$D_i = diag\{e^{-\alpha(w_1^i)^2}, e^{-\alpha(w_2^i)^2} \cdots e^{-\alpha(w_N^i)^2}\} \qquad (13)$$

When $w \to \infty$, the two quadratic concave functions go infinite while the convex function is also positive, $F(w)$ will converge to a stable point after a few of iteration (usually 5 to 10).

The regularized solution w got from Equation (7) has many non-zero elements and does not directly fit feature selection. However, it can be used as the initial value w^0 for the above Fisher optimization model. The following is the algorithm of Fisher optimization model:

i) Get the mean and scatter matrix of the sample from Equations (2) and (3);

ii) Initialization: k=0, take parameters λ_1, λ_2, α and threshold T. Get the initial value w^0 from Equation (7);

iii) Get w^{k+1} from Equation (12);

iv) If $\left| F(w^{k+1}) - F(w^k) \right| > T$, then k=k+1, go to 3; or $w = w^{k+1}$;

v) If $f(w_i) < 0.8,$ $w_i = 0$ i=1......N,

or select the gene corresponding to i.

We have not only selected the gene by now, but also give the projection direction w of Fisher linear discriminant, and thus we are able to project the sample to a one-dimension space for discrimination. The mean of the projected means of two classes is selected as the threshold for discrimination. The following is the result of experiments.

4. Experiment Result and Discussion

We have implemented classification programs with Matlab for Fisher optimization model and Fisher linear discriminant on a Pentium III PC (733MHz, 256M). No optimization is done. Experiments have been done on two sets of public data and the results are compared with those of other methods.

4.1. MIT AML/ALL Data

MIT AML/ALL data [6] contains 7129 genes and 72 samples, and 25 of them are acute lymphoid leukemia (ALL), 47 of them are acute myeloid leukemia (AML), 38 of them are training samples and 34 of them are test samples.

First of all, we select the first 800 genes with the method of [6]. This is based on the consideration for calculation. Because $N=7129$, a large RAM and lengthy time is required for inverse of the matrix in equation (12). Initial selecting not only reduces a large amount of calculation but also greatly lowers the requirement for RAM. This step of calculation takes 5.85 seconds. Then we use Fisher optimization model in gene selection. The algorithm converges at the eighth step. Sixteen genes are selected and Fisher linear discriminant is used for classification. All the 38 training samples and 34 test samples are correctly classified. This latter step takes 9.3 seconds.

Golub et al [6] selected the first 50 genes with individual gene scoring method and used weighted voting method in classification, and 36 are correctly classified from the 38 training samples and 29 are correctly classified from the 34 test samples. Furey et al [20] used the same method and respectively selected the first 25, 250 and 500 genes and used SVM in classification, and 38 training samples have all been correctly classified, and 30-32 are correctly classified from the 34 test samples. Guyon et al [22] used SVM and RFE in feature selection and classification. All training samples and test samples have been correctly classified when 8 and 16 genes are selected. When 32 and 64 genes are selected, all training samples are correctly classified and 33 and 32 are correctly classified from the 34 test samples. Campbell el al [23] used Bayesian ARD method in feature selection and classification, and all test samples have been correctly classified. However, the number of genes and the result of training sample have not been given.

4.2. *Colon Cancer Data*

Colon cancer data [5] contains 2000 genes and 62 samples. Among them, 40 are negative and 22 are positive. This set of samples is recognized as more difficult data. Alon el al [5] used non-supervised clustering method and did not distinguish training samples and test samples. For ease of comparison, we have randomly divided them into 31 training samples and 31 test samples as Campbell el al did and repeated 100 times. The average mistaken number among the training samples is 3.01 ± 1.23, and the mistaken number among the test samples is 4.35 ± 1.79. The best case is only 1 mistake. On the average, 29.87 ± 4.83 genes were selected. The algorithm converges at 5-8 steps of iterations. The average of one calculation cycle is around 1.5 minutes. Campbell el al [23] reported their using of Bayesian ARD method in feature selection and classification. The average mistaken number in the test samples is 6.6 ± 1.8 and 7.6 ± 2.6 genes are selected on the average. Using RFE in selection of 71 genes, the smallest mistaken number is 5.9 ± 0.2 in the test samples. The smallest mistaken number is 5.7 ± 0.2 among the test samples using Fisher scoring method and SVM method in selection 1977 genes. However, training sample results have not been given. Guyon el al [22] used SVM and RFE in feature selection and classification. The best result in the test samples is 3 mistakes and 8 genes are selected. No average result is given. Neither is the training sample result. One cycle of calculation is around 15 minutes.

4.3. *Discussion*

It can be seen from the above experiment result that both our method and SVM + RFE [22] have correctly classified all samples for MIT's AML/ALL data. As for Colon cancer data, the test result of Fisher optimization is obviously better than other methods.

There are three parameters in our algorithm: λ_1, λ_2 and α. We have discovered that when the value of parameter λ_1 taken is bigger, the test accuracy will be increased (Figure 1). Parameter λ_2 can regulate the number of genes. Smaller number of genes are selected when λ_2 is bigger, and more genes are selected when λ_2 is smaller (Figure 2).

Our consideration for parameter α is as follows. Assuming that every element $f(w_i)$ of $f(w)$ is distributed around 0.5, i.e.,

$$f(w_i) = 1 - e^{-\alpha w_i^2} = 0.5 \tag{14}$$

We get:

$$\prod_{i=1}^{N} e^{-\alpha(w_0)_i^2} = \frac{1}{2^N} \tag{15}$$

$$\alpha = \frac{N \ln(2)}{\|w_0\|_2^2} \tag{16}$$

5. Conclusion

This paper studies one of the most important issues in microarray data analysis — gene selection. It proposes the use of Fisher optimization model in gene selection and Fisher linear discriminant in classification. Excellent results got from experiments on public data demonstrated validity of the method. Selection of related parameters is also discussed.

Acknowledgement:

The work is supported by the National Natural Science Foundation of China (60175004).

References

1. Lin He (eds.) 《Decoding Life - the Human Genome Project and Post Human Genome Project》, Science Press, 2000. (in Chinese)
2. *Nature Genetics Supplement* Vol. 21, January 1999. *Nucl. Phy*

3. Eisen, M, Spellman, P., Brown, P. & Botstein, D. Cluster analysis and display of genome-wide expression patterns. *Proc. Natl. Acad. Sci. USA,* 95, 14863-14868, 1998.

4. J. Quackenbush, Computational analysis of microarray data. *Nature Genetics* 2:418-427, 2001.

5. Alon, U., Barkai N., Notterman D.A., et al. Broad patterns of gene expression revealed by clustering analysis of tumor and normal colon tissues probed by oligonucleotide arrays. *Proc. Nat. Acad. Sci. USA,* 96:6745-6750, 1999.

6. Golub, T., Slonim D. K., Tamayo P. et al. Molecular classification of cancer: calss discovery and class predication by gene expression monitoring. *Science,* 286:531-537, 1999.

7. Lender E. S. Initial sequencing and analysis of the human genome. *Nature,* 408:860-921 Feb. 15, 2001.

8. Pavlidis P., Weston J., Cai J. and Grundy W. N. Gene functional classification from heterogeneous. In *RECOMB 2001: Proceedings of the fifth International Conference on Computational Molecular Biology.* pp.242-248, April 22-25, 2001, Montreal, Québec, Canada. ACM, 2001.

9. Ben-Dor A., Friedman N. and Yakhini Z. Scoring genes for relevance. *Agilent Technologies Technical Report* AGL-2000-13, 2000.

10. Xing E. P., Jordan M. I. and Karp R. M. Feature selection for high-dimention genomic microarray data. *Proc. of 18th International Conference on Machine Learning (ICML2001),* June 28-July 1, 2001.

11. Duda R. O., Hart P. E. and Stork D. G. Pattern Classification (2nd Edition), Wiley-Interscience, October 2000

12. Kohai R. and John G. H. Wrappers for feature subset selection. *Artificial Intelligence journal,* special issue on relevance, 97:12, pp.273-324, 1997.

13. Bradley P., Mangasarian O., and Street W. Feature selection via mathematical programming, *INFORMS Journal on computing,* 1998.

14. Bradley P. and Mangasarian O. Feature selection via concave minimization and support vector machines, *Proc. of the 15th International Conference on Machine Learning,* pp.82-90, San Francisco, CA, 1998.

15. Burges C. J. C. A tutorial on support vector machines for pattern recognition. *Data Mining and Knowledge Discovery* 2(2), 121-167, 1998.

16. Vapnik, V. P. Statistical learning theory. John Wiley & Sons, Inc. 1998.

17. Weston J., Muckerjee S., Chapelle O., Pontil M., Poggio T., and Vapnik V. Feature Selection for SVMs. *Proceedings of NIPS 2000,* 2000.

18. Mukherjee S., Tamayo P., Slonim D., Verri A., Golub T., Mesirov J.P., and Poggio T. Support vector machine classification of microarray data. *A.I. Memo No.1677, C.B.C.L. Paper No. 182,* MIT, 1998.

19. Brown M. P. S., Grundy W. N., Lin D., Cristianini N., Sugnet C. W., Furey T. S., Ares M. and Haussler Jr. D. Knowledge-based analysis of microarray

gene expression data by using support vector machines. *Proc. Nat. Acad. Sci. USA,* 97, No. 1: 262–267, 2000.

20. Furey T. S., Cristianini N., Duffy N., Bednarski D.W., Schummer and Haussler D. Support vector machine classification and validation of cancer tissue samples using microarray expression data. *Bioinformatics,* 16, 906-914, 2000.

21. Cristianini N. and Shawe-Taylor J. An Introduction to support vector machines and other kernel-based learning methods. Cambridge University Press, 2000.

22. Guyon I., Weston J., Barnhill S., and Vapnik V. Gene Selection for Cancer Classification using Support Vector Machines. *Machine Learning* 46, 389-422, 2002.

23. Campbell C., Li Y. and Tipping M. An Efficient Feature Selection Algorithms for Classification of Gene Expression Data. *NIPS 2001 Workshop on: Machine Learning Techniques for Bioinformatics,* British Columbia, Canada, 2001.

24. Mika S., Ratsch G., Weston J., Scholkopf B. and Muller K.R. Fisher discriminant analysis with kernels. *IEEE Neural Networks for Signal Processing IX*, pp.41-48, 1999.

25. Baudat G. and Anouar F. Generalized discriminant analysis using a kernel approach. *Neural Computation* 12:2385-2404, 2000.

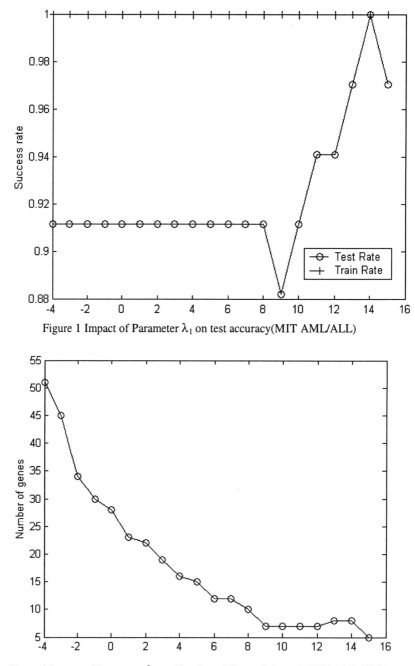

Figure 1 Impact of Parameter λ_1 on test accuracy(MIT AML/ALL)

Figure 2 Impact of Parameter λ_2 on Number of Genes Selected (MIT AML/ALL)

CLUSTERING AND CLUSTER VALIDATION IN DATA MINING

JOSHUA ZHEXUE HUANG, HONGQIANG RONG AND JESSICA TING

E-Business Technology Institute, The University of Hong Kong, Hong Kong, China
E-mail: jhuang@eti.hku.hk

YUNMING YE

Shanghai Jiao Tong University, Shanghai, China
E-mail: yym@sjtu.edu.cn

QIMING HUANG

Beijing University of Post & Telecom, Beijing, China
E-mail: qm_huang@yahoo.com

Clustering is one of the fundamental operations in data mining. Clustering is widely used in solving business problems such as customer segmentation and fraud detection. In real applications of clustering, we are required to perform three tasks: partitioning data sets into clusters, validating the clustering results and interpreting the clusters. Various clustering algorithms have been designed for the first task. Few techniques are available for cluster validation in data mining. The third task is application dependent and needs domain knowledge to understand the clusters. In this paper, we present a few techniques for the first two tasks. We first discuss the family of the k-means type algorithms, which are mostly used in data mining. Then we present a visual method for cluster validation. This method is based on the Fastmap data projection algorithm and its enhancement. Finally, we present a method to combine a clustering algorithm and the visual cluster validation method to interactively build classification models.

1. Introduction

Clustering is a fundamental operation in data mining. Clustering is used to solve many business problems. A typical example is customer segmentation. In direct marketing, sound customer segmentation is a necessary condition for conducting effective marketing campaigns. In telecommunication, customer segmentation is critical in identifying potential churners. Clustering is also used as a common tool to detect fraudulent claims in medical insurance.

In real applications of clustering, we are required to perform three tasks, (1) partitioning data sets into clusters, (2) validating the clustering results and (3) interpreting the clusters. Various clustering algorithms have been developed for the first task. The standard hierarchical clustering methods [2][15] and the k-means algorithm [2][16] are well known clustering techniques not only in data mining but also in other disciplines. To deal with large and complex data often encountered in data mining applications, a number of new clustering algorithms have been developed in recent years, for example, CLIQUE [1], CLARANS [21], BIRCH [25], DBSCAN [7] and the k-means extension algorithms [10]. Although these new algorithms are well known in the research community, the k-means algorithm is still most popular in commercial data mining tools due to its efficiency, reliability and simplicity.

The second task, validating a clustering result, is always tricky in data mining practice. Unlike supervised classification in which a separate data set can be used to validate the models, such approach is not applicable in real world data clustering. A notorious problem of clustering is that different clustering algorithms often impose different clustering structures on data [15][17], even though the data may not contain any cluster at all. A number of cluster validation methods have been developed in the past to tackle this problem [6][15][17][19]. Most methods are based on the statistical framework that one first adopts a null hypothesis of randomness (i.e., no structure in data) and then decides either rejecting or accepting it according to the distribution of a chosen statistical model for a clustering structure. A few employ graphical displays to visually verify the validity of a clustering [22]. Recent surveys on cluster validation methods can be found in [9][18]. The problem of using these cluster validation methods in data mining is that the computational cost is very high when the data sets are large and complex.

The third task is to give explanations on the characteristics of discovered clusters to the cluster users. For example, a cluster of credit card holders in a bank shows a large portion of customers have spent in the last 12 months heavily and frequently on their credit cards. This cluster is interpreted as high and frequent spending customer cluster or segment. With such description, marketing professionals will be able to design particular marketing campaigns to target this group of customers. Cluster interpretation is usually based on simple statistics of some variables and business knowledge. In performing this task, application domain knowledge is important.

In this paper, we present some techniques for the first two tasks. For the first task, we focus on the family of k-means type algorithms, which are mostly used in real data mining projects. We review the basic k-means algorithm [2][16], its extensions to handle categorical data and mixed data types [10], and the new development on its fuzzy versions [3][5][[12][[23]. These new developments have extended the capability of the original k-means algorithm to solve more complex data clustering problems in data mining.

For the second task, we present a visual cluster validation method [11]. This method combines the data projection technique with the fast clustering algorithm to solve cluster validation problem in data mining. We present the Fastmap algorithm [8] and its modification [20] for projection of clusters from high dimensional space to low dimensional space in which the clusters can be visualized. In such a way, a human can visually judge the validity of clusters generated by a clustering algorithm. In the clustering process, we use this method to solve two problems: (1) to verify the separations of clusters and (2) to determine the number of clusters to be generated.

The interactive approach of clustering and cluster validation can be used to build classification models [14]. In the last part of the paper, we present a decision clusters classifier (DCC) for data mining. A DCC model is defined as a set of p decision clusters generated with a clustering algorithm from the training data set. A decision cluster is labeled of one of the classes in data. The DCC model classifies new objects by deciding to which decision clusters these objects belong. In making classification decisions, DCC is very similar to KNN. However, their model building processes are different.

2. The k-means algorithm family

The members of the k-means algorithms family currently include k-means, k-modes and k-prototypes algorithms and their fuzzy versions. The last two are designed to handle categorical data and mixed data with both numeric and categorical variables. The fuzzy versions allow objects to be assigned to more than one cluster. The new members to be developed will be the algorithms, which can automatically calculate the weights of variables. All these algorithms have the same properties and use the same algorithmic process to cluster data.

2.1. The k-means algorithm

The k-means algorithm [2][16], one of the mostly used clustering algorithms in data mining, is classified as a partitional or nonhierarchical clustering method [15]. Given a set of numeric objects X and an integer number k (n), the k-means algorithm searches for a partition of X into k clusters that minimizes the within groups sum of squared errors (WGSS). This process can be formulated as the following mathematical program problem P [4][24]:

$$\text{Minimize} \quad P(W,Q) = \sum_{l=1}^{k} \sum_{i=1}^{n} W_{i,l}\, d(X_i, Q_l) \tag{1}$$

$$\text{Subject to} \quad \sum_{l=1}^{k} W_{i,l} = 1, \quad 1 \quad i \quad n$$

$$W_{i,l} \in \{0,1\}, \quad 1 \quad i \quad n, \quad 1 \quad l \quad k$$

where W is an $n \times k$ partition matrix, $Q = \{Q_1, Q_2, \ldots, Q_k\}$ is a set of objects in the same object domain, and $d(.,.)$ is the squared Euclidean distance between two objects.

Problem P can be solved by iteratively solving the following two sub problems:

1. Problem $P1$: Fix $Q = \hat{Q}$ and solve the reduced problem $P(W, \hat{Q})$

2. Problem $P2$: Fix $W = \hat{W}$ and solve the reduced problem $P(\hat{W}, Q)$

P_1 is solved by

$$q_{l,i} = \frac{\sum_{i=1}^{n} w_{i,l} x_{i,j}}{\sum_{i=1}^{n} w_{i,l}} \qquad (2)$$

For $1 \bullet l \bullet k$, and $1 \bullet j \bullet m$.

The basic algorithm to solve problem P is given as follows [4][24]:

1. Choose an initial Q^0 and solve $P(W, Q^0)$ to obtain W^0. Set $t=0$.

2. Let $\hat{W} = W^t$ and solve $P(\hat{W}, Q))$ to obtain Q^{t+1}. If $P(\hat{W}, Q^t) = P(\hat{W}, Q^{t+1})$, output $\hat{W}, Q^t$ and stop; otherwise, go to 3.

3. Let $Q^t = Q^{t+1}$ and solve $P(W, \hat{Q})$ to obtain $W\{t+1\}$. If $P(W^t, \hat{Q}) = P(W^{t+1}, \hat{Q})$, output $W^t, \hat{Q}$ and stop; otherwise, let $t=t+1$ and go to 2.

Because $P(.,.)$ is non-convex and the sequence $P(.,.)$ generated by the algorithm is strictly decreasing, after a finite number of iterations the algorithm converges to a local minimum point [24]. The computational cost of the algorithm is $O(Tkn)$ where T is the number of iterations and n the number of objects in the input data set.

The k-means algorithm has the following important properties:

1. It is efficient in processing large data sets.
2. It terminates at a local optimum [16][24].
3. The clusters have convex shapes [2].
4. It works only on numeric values.

These properties make the k-means algorithm a good candidate for data mining but also represent limitations, especially in dealing with data with non-numeric values.

2.2. The *k*-modes and *k*-prototypes algorithms

The limitation that the *k*-means algorithm cannot cluster categorical objects is caused by its dissimilarity measure and the method used to solve problem P_2. The *k*-modes algorithm is designed to remove this limitation by:

1. Using a simple matching dissimilarity measure for categorical objects,
2. Replacing means of clusters by modes, and
3. Using a frequency-based method to find the modes to solve problem P_2.

We rewrite the cost function of Eq. (1) as:

$$P(W,Q) = \sum_{l=1}^{k} \sum_{i=1}^{n} \sum_{j=1}^{m} w_{i,l} \delta(x_{i,j}, q_{l,j}) \qquad (3)$$

where $w_{i,l} \in W$, $Q_l = [q_{l,1}, q_{l,2}, ..., q_{l,m}]$ is the mode of cluster l and

$$\delta(x_i, y_j) = \begin{cases} 0 & (x_i = y_j) \\ 1 & (x_i \neq y_j) \end{cases} \qquad (4)$$

Definition 1. Let X be a set of categorical objects. A mode of $X = \{X1, X2, ..., Xn\}$ is a vector $Q = [q_1, q_2, ..., q_m]$ that minimizes $D(X,Q) = \sum_{i=1}^{n} d_l(X_i, Q)$, where Q is not necessarily an element of X.

Let $n_{ck,j}$ be the number of objects having the *k*th category $c_{k,j}$ in attribute A_j and $f_r(A_j = C_{k,j} \mid X) = \dfrac{n_{ck,j}}{n}$ the relative frequency of category $c_{k,j}$ in X.

Theorem 1. The function $D(X,Q)$ is minimized iff $f_r(A_j = q_j \mid X) \geq f_r(A_j = c_{k,j} \mid X)$ for $q_j \neq c_{k,j}$ for all $j = 1...m$.

The proof is given in [10].

If we use Eq. (4) to solve P_1 and Theorem 1 to solve P_2, we can still use the basic algorithm in the above section to minimize Eq. (3).

Now, we can integrate the *k*-means and *k*-modes algorithms into the *k*-prototypes algorithm to cluster the mixed-type objects. The cost function of the *k*-prototypes algorithm is defined as follows:

$$P(W,Q) = \sum_{l=1}^{k} (\sum_{i=1}^{n} w_{i,l} \sum_{j=1}^{p} (x_{i,j} - q_{l,j})^2 + \gamma \sum_{i=1}^{n} w_{i,l} \sum_{j=p+1}^{m} \delta(x_{i,j}, q_{l,j}) \qquad (5)$$

The first term follows the k-means algorithm for numeric attributes and the second term the k-modes algorithm for categorical attributes. The weight γ is used to avoid favoring either type of attribute. The centers of clusters contain both numeric and categorical values so the k vectors of cluster centers are named k prototypes. The basic algorithm can also used to minimize the cost function. In the optimization process, the k-means update method is used to update the numeric values of the prototypes and the k-modes method is used to update the categorical values.

The k-modes and k-prototypes algorithms still hold the first three properties of the k-means algorithm but remove the limitation of the last property. This makes the k-prototypes algorithm more suitable for clustering data from real databases.

2.3. The fuzzy versions of k-means type algorithms

The k-means, k-modes and k-prototypes algorithms are called hard clustering algorithms because they assign each data object into only one cluster. However, objects in different clusters often overlap at boundaries. Instead of assigning each boundary object into only one cluster, the boundary objects can be assigned to more than one cluster with different confidence levels. The fuzzy versions of these algorithms are designed for this purpose.

Let X be a set of n objects described by m attributes. The fuzzy k-means type clustering algorithms to cluster X into k clusters can be stated as the process to minimize the following cost function [3]:

$$\text{Minimize} \quad F(W,Q) = \sum_{l-1}^{k} \sum_{i=1}^{n} w_{l,i}^{\alpha} d(X_i, Q_l) \tag{6}$$

Subject to:

$$0 \leq w_{l,i} \leq 1, \quad 1 \leq l \leq k, \quad 1 \leq i \leq n$$

$$\sum_{l-1}^{k} w_{l,i} = 1, \quad 1 \leq i \leq n$$

and

$$0 < \sum_{i-1}^{n} w_{l,i} < n, \quad 1 \leq l \leq k$$

where W is an $n \times k$ matrix, $Q = \{Q_1, Q_2, \ldots, Q_k\}$ is the set of means, $d(.,.)$ is a dissimilarity measure between two objects and $\alpha > 1$ is a weighting exponent. When $\alpha = 1$, the cost function is same as the hard algorithm.

F is minimized in the same process of the basic k-means algorithm. In each iteration, W is updated by

$$w_{l,i} = \begin{cases} 1 & \text{if } X_i = Q_l \\ \\ 0 & \text{if } X_i = Q_h, \ h \neq l \\ \\ 1/\sum_{h=1}^{k}\left[\dfrac{d(X_i, Q_l)}{d(X_i, Q_h)}\right] & \text{if } X_i \neq Q_l \text{ and } X_i \neq Q_h, \ 1 \leq h \leq k \end{cases} \tag{7}$$

For a numeric variable, the mean of a cluster is calculated by:

$$Q_l = \frac{\sum_{i=1}^{n} w_{l,i}^{\alpha} X_i}{\sum_{i=1}^{n} w_{l,i}^{\alpha}} \qquad 1 \leq l \leq k \tag{8}$$

For a categorical variable, Q_l is the mode of the variable values in cluster l. The integration of the two methods forms the fuzzy k-prototypes algorithm. The detail of the fuzzy k-modes algorithm is discussed in [12] and the fuzzy k-prototypes algorithm is presented in [5].

3. Visual Cluster Validation

Cluster validation refers to the procedures that evaluate clusters created from a data set by a clustering algorithm [15]. Cluster validation is required in data mining because no clustering algorithm can guarantee the discovery of genuine clusters from real data sets. In fact, different clustering algorithms often impose different cluster structures on a data set even though there is no cluster structure present in it [9][18].

In statistics, cluster validation is treated as a hypothesis test problem [9][15][18]. More precisely, let S be a statistic and H_0 a null hypothesis stating that no cluster structure exists in a data set X. Let Prob($\mathbf{B}|H_0$) be the baseline distribution $\mathbf{B}$ under H_0. The event $\mathbf{B}$ could be either $S \geq s_\alpha$ or $S < s_\alpha$, where s_α is a fixed number called a threshold at significance level • and

Prob($S \geq s_\alpha$) = • . Suppose that s_* is the value of S calculated from a clustering result of data set X. If $s_* \geq s_\alpha$, then we reject hypothesis H_0. This is because the probability that H_0 is true is low (•).

Several statistical cluster validation methods are available [9][18]. The problem of using these statistical methods in data mining is the computational cost. In this section, we present a visual cluster validation method for data mining. The visual cluster validation method uses the Fastmap algorithm [8] to project clustered objects onto a low dimensional space (2D or 3D) and allow humans to visually examine the clusters created with a clustering algorithm and determine genuine clusters found. The visual cluster validation method is based on the principle *that if a cluster is separate from other objects in the 2D space, it is also separate from other objects in the original high dimensional space* (the opposite is not true). The comparison studies on some synthetic data have shown that this method can produce results equivalent to those of statistical methods [13]. However, this method is efficient in processing large data sets.

3.1. Fastmap algorithm

Given a set of N objects in an n dimensional space and their mutual distances measured by $d(.,.)$, the Fastmap algorithm projects the N objects onto an m (<< n) dimensional space. The projection is performed in m steps. First, two objects O_a and O_b are selected as 'pivot objects' and a line passing through them is chosen to form the first axis in the projected m dimensional space. For any object O_i, its coordinate x_i on the first axis is calculated as

$$x_i = \frac{d_{a,i}^2 + d_{a,d}^2 - d_{b,i}^2}{2d_{a,b}} \tag{9}$$

Here, $d_{a,b}$ is the distance between O_a and O_b, and $d_{a,i}$ and $d_{b,i}$ the distances between O_i and O_a, O_b, respectively. Because all distances between objects are known, it is straightforward to calculate the coordinates of all objects on the first axis.

To calculate the coordinates of objects on the second axis, we first need to calculate the distances between objects in the reduced ($n - 1$) dimensional space. The distances can be calculated from the distances in the original n dimensional space and the coordinates on the first axis, as follows:

$$(d'_{i,j})^2 = (d_{i,j})^2 - (x_i - x_j)^2 \qquad i,j = 1,...,N \tag{10}$$

where $d'_{i,j}$ is the distance between obejcts O_i and O_j in the reduced $(n - 1)$ dimensional space, $d_{i,j}$ is the distance between obejcts O_i and O_j in the original n dimensional space, x_i, x_j are the coordinates of O_i and O_j on the first axis. After the distances between objects in the reduced $(n - 1)$ dimensional space are calculated, Eq. (9) is used to calculate the coordinates on the second axis. This process is recursively used until the coordinates on the mth axis are calculated.

3.2. Cluster Validation with Fastmap

For cluster validation with Fastmap, we apply a clustering algorithm (one of k-means family members) to cluster data in the original space. Then, we use Fastmap to project clusters onto a 2D space and visualize them. Objects belonging to different clusters are visualized in different colors and/or with different symbols. If a cluster is observed to be separate from other objects on the 2D display, we can claim that it is also separate from other objects in the original space. The objects belonging to this cluster can be removed from the data set. To interactively conduct clustering and cluster validation on a large data set, a series clusters can be gradually identified.

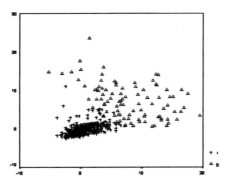

Fig. 1. The 2D display of two clusters from a real data set

Figure 1 shows a real example of the Fastmap projection of two clusters discovered from a telecommunication data set. The symbols "crosses" and "triangles" represent objects in two different clusters. One can see that the cluster in "crosses" is more compact than the cluster in "triangles".

34

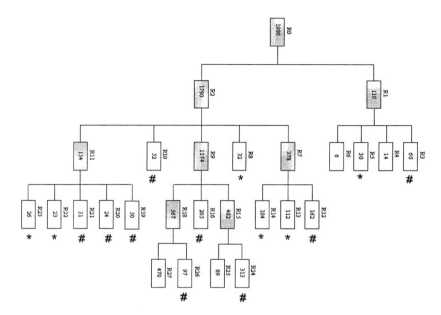

Fig. 2. A cluster tree created by interactive clustering and cluster validation. The symbols "*" and "#" show dominant classes of leaf clusters. Some leaf clusters do not have a dominant class whose frequency is greater than the given threshold.

When dealing with a large complex data set, we use a top-down approach to interactively conducting clustering and cluster validation to build a tree of clusters (see Figure 2). Each node can be considered a cluster. A node containing children is a composite clusters while all leaves are atomic clusters. In practice, by analyzing the node clusters, interesting ones can be identified. This approach can also be used to build classification models, which is discussed in the next section.

To project clusters onto the 2D space, the Fastmap algorithm turns to produce overlapping projections. The improved algorithm called M-Fastmap is designed to solve this problem [20].

4. Classification

Assume a given sample data set X has two classes and the classes of data objects are identified by the target variable y. We use the interactive clustering and cluster validation to partition X into subsets at different levels of a cluster tree. In the clustering process, the target variable y is not used. Instead, at each validated clustering, we calculate the distribution of the two classes in each cluster. We call the class with the highest frequency as the dominant class. If the frequency of the dominant class of a cluster is smaller than a given threshold, the cluster is further partitioned into sub clusters. Otherwise, the cluster becomes a leaf of the cluster tree with its dominant class identified.

After a cluster tree is built and the dominant classes of leaf nodes are identified (see the "*" and "#" symbols for two different classes in Figure 2), we can use a set of leaf clusters with dominant classes to classify new data. The leaf clusters are called decision clusters. The set of decision clusters is called a decision cluster classifier or a DCC model. Given a new data object x, we compute its distance to the centers of the decision clusters. If x is close to the center of decision cluster C_i, then the dominant class of C_i is assigned to x.

Formally, let G be a DCC model with m decision clusters $G = \{C_1, C_2, ..., C_m\}$, and x a new object with unknown class. x is classified into class C_i if

$$d(x, C_i) \le d(x, C_k) \qquad i,k = 1,...,\text{m}.$$

where d is a distance function.

Let χ denote the training data set, Θ the clustering algorithm (e.g., a member of the k-means family) and F the Fastmap algorithm. We summarize the interactive process to build a cluster tree in Figure 3:

After we build a cluster tree from the training data set using this process, we have created a sequence of clusterings. In principle, each clustering is a DCC model. Their classification performances are different. Therefore, we use a test data set (or the tuning data set) to identify the best DCC model from a cluster tree. We start from a top level clustering. First, we select all clusters of the top level clustering as decision clusters, use them to classify the test data set and calculate the classification accuracy. Then we identify the decision clusters, which have classified more objects wrongly than other clusters. We replace these clusters with its sub-clusters in the lower level clustering and test the model again. We continue this process until the best DCC model is found.

---

1. **Begin**: Set χ as the root of the cluster tree. Select the root as the current node S_c.
2. Use $\mathbf{F}$ to project S_c onto 2D. Visually examine the projection to decide k, the number of potential clusters.
3. Apply Θ to partition S_c into k clusters.
4. Use $\mathbf{F}$ and other visual methods to validate the partition.(The tuning data set can also be used here to test the increase of classification accuracy of the new clustering.)
5. If the partition is accepted, go to step 6, otherwise, select a new k and go to step 3.
6. Attach the clusters as the children of the partitioned node. Select one as the current node S_c.
7. Validate S_c to determine whether it is a terminal node or not.
8. If it is not a terminal node, go to step 2. If it is a terminal node, but not the last one, select another node as the current node S_c, which has not been validated, and go to step 7. If it is the last terminal node in the tree, **stop**.

Fig 3. The interactive process to build a cluster tree

Each level of clustering in the cluster tree is a partition of the training data set. However, our final DDC model is not necessarily to be a partition. In the final DDC model, we often drop certain clusters from a clustering. For example, some leaves in Figure 2 do not have class symbols. These clusters contain few objects in several classes. These are the objects, which are located in the boundaries of other clusters. From our experiment, we found that dropping these clusters from the model can increase the classification accuracy.

Table 1 shows four public data sets taken from the UCI machine learning data repository[c], which were used to test the DCC models against some other classifiers. Table 2 gives the accuracies of the DCC models on the four data sets and accuracies of other 5 well-known classifiers. On average, the DCC models performance was slightly better than other classifiers. The results of C5.0 and boosted C5.0 were conducted with the Clementine data mining system. The

---

[c] http://www.ncc.up.pt/liacc/ML/statlog/datasets.html

results of other classifiers were taken from the UCI machine learning website. Detail discussions of these results can be found in [14].

We give the following remarks on the DCC models. If we put a set of classified objects into a high dimensional space formed by the independent variables, we would assume objects in the same classes are close to each other while objects in different classes tend to be separate. In such a case, our interactive clustering and cluster validation process would be able to find clusters significantly dominated by a class. Then, any object falling in such a cluster tends to have the same class. Therefore, the DCC model can give an accurate classification result.

5. Conclusions

In this paper, we have reviewed the family of the *k*-means clustering algorithms, which are mostly used in data mining. Efficiency, easy to implement and easy to use are the most attractive features of the *k*-means algorithm in real data mining applications. Extensions to the original *k*-means algorithm enable the *k*-means paradigm to be used in clustering data in more complex data domains. We have presented a visual cluster validation method for data mining application. This method is based on the Fastmap algorithm to project clusters onto 2D or 3D spaces, which allow humans to visually examine the separation of clusters. The advantage of this method is easy to use and fast in projecting large data sets. In the end, we presented how to use clustering and cluster validation interactively to build DCC classification models. The DCC model is similar to the KNN model but more efficient since it uses the centers of decision clusters rather than individual records in the training data set. The number of decision clusters is much smaller than the number of data records in the training data set.

Table 1. Four datasets from the UCI machine learning data repository

Date Set	Training Records	Test Records	Numerical Fields	Categorical Fields	No. of Classes	Decision Clusters
Heart	189	81	7	6	2	36
Credit Card	440	213	6	9	2	74
Diabetes	537	230	8	0	2	108
Satellite Image	4435	2000	36	0	6	254

Table 2. Comparisons of DCC models with other classifiers

	Heart		Credit Card		Diabetes		Satellite Image	
	Train	Test	Train	Test	Train	Test	Train	Test
DCC	90.49	87.65	90.23	87.79	83.99	81.74	91.64	91.60
C5.0	96.30	87.65	90.00	84.98	80.26	76.09	98.84	85.90
Boosted C5.0	98.94	87.65	99.09	87.32	96.65	73.91	99.95	90.45
Discrim	68.50	60.70	85.10	85.90	78.00	77.50	85.10	82.90
Bayes	64.90	62.60	86.40	84.90	76.10	73.80	69.20	72.30
KNN	100.00	52.20	100.00	81.90	100.00	67.60	91.10	96.60

References

1. Agrawal, R., Gehrke, J, Gunopulos, D. and Raghavan, P., Automatic subspace clustering of high dimensional data for data mining applications. In Proceedings of SIGMOD Conference, (1998).
2. Anderberg, M.R., *Cluster Analysis for Applications*. Academic Press, (1973).
3. Bezdek, J.C, *Pattern Recognition with Fuzzy Objective Function*. Plenum Press (1981).
4. Bobrowski, L. and Bezdek, J.C., c-Means Clustering with the l_1 and l. Norms', *IEEE Transactions on Systems, Man and Cybernetics* **21**, 545-554 (1991).
5. Chen, Ning, Chen, An and Zhou, Long-xiang, Fuzzy k-prototypes algorithm for clustering mixed numeric and categorical valued data. *Journal of Software* **12**, 1107-1119 (2001).
6. Dubes, R. and Jian, A.K., Validity Studies in Clustering Methodologies. *Pattern Recognition* **11**, 235—254 (1979).
7. Ester, M., Kriegel, H.-P., Sander, J. and Xu, X., A density-based algorithm for discovering clusters in large spatial databases with noise. In Proceedings of the 2nd International Conference on Knowledge Discovery in Databases and Data Mining, Portland, Oregon, USA (1996).
8. Faloutsos, C. and Lin, K., Fastmap: a fast algorithm for indexing, data-mining and visualization of traditional and multimedia datasets. In Proceedings of ACM-SIGMOD, 163-174 (1995).
9. Gordon, A. D., Cluster validation. In Data Science, Classification, and Related Methods, ed. by C Hayashi, N Ohsumi, K Yajima, Y Tanaka, H-H Bock and Y Baba, Springer, Tokyo, 22-39 (1998).

10. Huang, Z., Extensions to the k-means algorithm for clustering large data sets with categorical values. *Data Mining and Knowledge Discovery* **2**, 283-304 (1998).

11. Huang, Z. and Lin, T., A visual method of cluster validation with Fastmap. PAKDD2000, Japan, Springer, (2000).

12. Huang, Z. and Ng, M. K., A fuzzy k-modes algorithm for clustering categorical data. *IEEE Transactions on Fuzzy Systems* **7** ,446-452 (1999).

13. Huang, Z. Ng, M. K., Lin, T. and Cheung, D., An interactive approach to building classification models by clustering and cluster validation. Proceedings of IDEAL2000, LNCS 1983, Springer, 23-28 (2000).

14. Huang, Z., Ng, M. and Cheung D., An Empirical Study on the Visual Cluster Validation with Fastmap, In Proceedings of DASFAA (2001).

15. Jain, A. K. and Dubes, R. C., *Algorithms for Clustering Data*. Prentice Hall, (1988).

16. MacQueen, J.B., Some Methods for Classification and Analysis of Multivariate Observations. Proceedings of the 5th Berkeley Symposium on Mathematical Statistics and Probability, 281-297 (1967).

17. Milligan, G.W., A Monte Carlo Study of Thirty Internal Criterion Measures for Cluster Analysis. *Psychometrika* **46** ,187—199 (1981).

18. Milligan, G. W., Clustering validation: results and implications for applied analysis. In Clustering and Classification, ed. by O. Arabie, L. J. Hubert and G. De Soete, World Scientific, 341-375 (1996).

19. Milligan, G.W. and Isaac, P.D., The Validation of Four Ultrametric Clustering Algorithms. *Pattern Recognition* **12** ,41-50 (1980).

20. Ng, R. and Han, J., Efficient and effective clustering methods for spatial data mining. In Proceedings of VLDB, (1994).

21. Ng, M. and Huang, J. Z., M-FastMap: A modified FastMap algorithm for visual cluster validation in data mining, Pacific Asia Conference on Knowledge Discovery and Data Mining (PAKDD2002), May 6-8, Teipei, Springer (2002).

22. Rousseeuw, P. J., Silhouettes: a graphical aid to the interpretation and validation of cluster analysis. *Journal of Computational and Applied Mathematics* **20**, 53-65 (1987).

23. Ruspini, E.R., A New Approach to Clustering. *Information Control* **19** ,22-32 (1969).

24. Selim, S.Z. and Ismail, M.A., k-Means-Type Algorithms: A Generalized Convergence Theorem and Characterization of Local Optimality. *IEEE Transactions on Pattern Analysis and Machine Intelligence* **6**,81-87 (1984).

25. Zhang, T. and Ramakrishnan, R.,BIRCH: A new Data Clustering Algorithm and Its Applications. *Data Mining and Knowledge Discovery* **1**,141-182 (1997).

CLUSTER ANALYSIS USING UNIDIMENSIONAL SCALING

PUI LAM LEUNG, CHI YIN LI

Department of Statistics, Faculty of Science
The Chinese University of Hong Kong
E-mail: plleung@cuhk.edu.hk

KIN-NAM LAU

Department of Marketing, Faculty of Business Administration
The Chinese University of Hong Kong

This paper presents a new method for cluster analysis based on unidimensional scaling (UDS). UDS is a technique to find the coordinates of n objects on a real line so that the interpoint distances can best approximate the observed dissimilarities between pairs of objects. First, we propose a simple and effective way to find the coordinates of the objects by minimizing the squared error fucntion. Then the coordinates of these n objects are used to detect the hidden clusters. Large jumps or gaps in the coordinate indicate possible boundaries of two clusters. Real and simulated examples are used to illustrate and to compare our method with the K-Means clustering.

1. Introduction

Cluster analysis is a procedure to find hidden groups in data. Many clustering algorithms are available and they are divided into hierarchical or nonhierarchical clustering methods. Among the nonhierarchical clustering methods, K-means clustering is most common and widely used method since it can classify large number of objects easily. However, there are some problems with this K-means clustering. For example, the number of clusters has to be specified in advance, the result depends on the initial seed.

In this paper, we present a new nonhierarchical clustering method based on unidimensional scaling(UDS). The main purpose of UDS is to find the coordinates of n objects on a real line, so that the interpoint distances best approximate the observed dissimilarities between pairs of objects. These coordinates in the UDS solution provide some useful information to uncover hidden clusters in the objects. Large jumps or gaps in the coordinate incdicate a possible boundary bewteen two clusters. Our method is consists of two stages. First, a UDS solution of the objescts is obtained. Then statistical test is used to detect if there are large jumps or gaps in the coordinates.

Our present paper is organized as follow. In Section 2, we briefly introduce two algorithms for UDS, namely the Guttman [3] updating algorithm and Pliner [6] smoothing algorithm. Futhermore, we proposed a new method for finding a better starting configuration for these algorithms. Our proposed method actually improves the final UDS solution obtained. Once the coordinates of these n objects are obtained, we can test whether there are large jumps or gaps in the coordinates. In Section 3, we introduce the Schwarz Information Criterion (SIC) given in Chen and Gupta [1] for detecting jumps or gaps in the coordinates. We illustrate our proposed method by the Fisher's famous Iris data as well as by a simulated data. We find that our method outperform the K-means clustering method. Conclusive remarks and further extensions are discussed in Section 4.

2. Unidimensional Scaling

UDS can be formulated as to minimize the following loss function:

$$\sigma(x) = \sum_{i<j}^{n}(d_{ij} - |x_i - x_j|)^2 \tag{1.1}$$

where d_{ij} is the observed dissimilarity between object i and j with $d_{ij} = d_{ji}$, x_i is the coordinate of object i and $x = (x_1, \ldots, x_n)$ is the vector of coordinates of the n objects we want to estimate. Note that the solution x corresponds to the minimum of (1.1) is not unique. For example, translation and reflection of x will gives the same minimum value of $\sigma(x)$. Usually, a centering constraint (i.e., $\sum_{i=1}^{n} x_i = 0$) is imposed. Guttman [3] derived the following algorithm for finding x:

$$x_i^{(t+1)} = \frac{1}{n}\sum_{j=1}^{n} d_{ij} \ sign(x_i^{(t)} - x_j^{(t)}), \quad \text{for all} \quad i = 1, \ldots, n \tag{1.2}$$

where $x_i^{(t)}$ is the coordinate of ith object at the tth iteration. de Leeuw and Heiser [2] showed that this updating algorithm converged to a stationary point in a finite number of steps. The solution obtained are also self-centered. However, loss function (1.1) has many local minima and the number of local minimum increase with n. The solution obtained from the Guttman's updating algorithm depends on the quality of the starting configuration $x^{(0)}$ and often gives a local minimum rather than a global minimum especially when n is large. To overcome this difficulty, Pliner [6] proposed the following smoothing algorithm:

$$x_i^{(t+1)} = \frac{1}{n} \sum_{j=1}^{n} d_{ij} u_\epsilon(x_i^{(t)} - x_j^{(t)}), \quad \text{for all} \quad i = 1, \ldots, n, \qquad (1.3)$$

where

$$u_\epsilon(t) = \begin{cases} (t/\epsilon)(2 - |t|/\epsilon), & \text{if } |t| < \epsilon; \\ sign(t), & \text{otherwise.} \end{cases}$$

This is a sequential minimization method. A decreasing sequence of $\epsilon_i = \epsilon_1(N - i + 1)/N$ for $i = 2, \ldots, N$ is first constructed. Taking $\epsilon = \epsilon_1$, a solution x is obtained by iterating the algorithm (1.3). This solution is used as the initial configuration for the second stage with $\epsilon = \epsilon_2$. The solution in the second stage is used as the initial configuration for the third stage and so on. This process continue up to the Nth stage. Pliner's smoothing algorithm provides a better solution than Guttman's updating algorithm but it also requires longer computational time as well. In both algorithms, the solution obtained depends on the quality of the initial configuration $x^{(0)}$. Therefore, a good starting configuration is very important to these algorithms. In practice, these algorithms are repeated many times with randomly chosen starting configuration and pick the best solution among them.

We propose a method for finding a good starting configuration for the Guttman's updating algorithm and Pliner's smoothing algorithm. Let $S_i = \sum_{j=1}^{n} d_{ij}$ be the sum of the total distances of object i to other objects. Suppose that object k has the maximum total distance from other objects, i.e., $S_k = \max\{S_i : 1 \leq i \leq n\}$, and let $(r_1, \ldots, r_n)$ be the rank of $(d_{k1}, \ldots, d_{kn})$. Then this rank $(r_1, \ldots, r_n)$ will be a good starting configuration for the Guttman's updating algorithm (denoted by GUm) as well as the Pliner's smoothing algorithm (denoted by PLm). The motivation of using this rank is as follows: if object k has the maximum total distance from other objects, object k should probably be the first or the last object in the UDS solution. The distances of other objects to object k, $(d_{k1}, \ldots, d_{kn})$, should reflect how similar of these objects to object k. Therefore, the rank $(r_1, \ldots, r_n)$ should be a good approximation to the true ordering in the UDS solution. We illustrate this method by two examples taken from Robinson [7]: the 8×8 dissimilarity matrix for the Mani collection of archaeological deposits, and a 17×17 matrix for the Kabah collection. These examples were also used as test cases by Hubert and Arabie [4], Pliner [6] and Lau, Leung and Tse [5].

Table 1. Dissimilarity matrix from Mani collection.

								Row Total
0.00	1.34	1.31	1.61	1.89	1.96	1.95	1.99	12.05
1.34	0.00	0.99	1.50	1.73	1.96	1.97	1.99	11.48
1.31	0.99	0.00	1.18	1.34	1.70	1.71	1.74	9.97
1.61	1.50	1.18	0.00	0.28	0.90	0.92	0.93	7.32
1.89	1.73	1.34	0.28	0.00	0.81	0.86	0.85	7.76
1.96	1.96	1.70	0.90	0.81	0.00	0.05	0.04	7.42
1.95	1.97	1.71	0.92	0.86	0.05	0.00	0.04	7.50
1.99	1.99	1.74	0.93	0.85	0.04	0.04	0.00	7.58

Table 1 gives the 8×8 dissimilarity matrix and their row total S_i. Note that the first row has the maximum total distance ($S_1 = 12.05$), therefore the rank of the first row (1,3,2,4,5,7,6,8) is used as a starting configuration for the Guttman's updating algorithm (1.2) and Pliner's smoothing algorithm (1.3). Both (1.2) and (1.3) gives the same solution as in Heiser and Arabie [4], Pliner [6] or Lau, Leung and Tse [5] with global minimum $\sigma(x) = 2.765$. Similarly for the 17×17 matrix for the Kabah collection, our method provides the optimal solution with global minimum $\sigma(x) = 5.472$. To compare our method with random starting configuration, 150 trials are performed with the Guttman's updating algorithm (denoted by GUr) and Pliner's smoothing algorithm (denoted by PLr). Table 2 gives the minimum, mean and maximum of $\sigma(x)$ of these 150 trials.

Table 2. 150 trials using random starting configuration.

	Mani		Kabah	
	GUr	PLr	GUr	PLr
minimum	2.765	2.765	5.818	5.472
mean	16.037	10.803	18.511	12.783
maximum	28.458	28.458	34.118	33.009

These results show that GUr and PLr often trapped in a local minimum. In fact, for mani's collection, only 4 out of these 150 trials give the global minimum for GUr and 19 out of 150 trials for PLr. For Kabah's collection, none of these 150 trials give the global minimum for GUr and only 2 out of 150 trials for PLr. Our proposed methods GUm and PLm are clearly much better than GUr or PLr. Thess results are also consistant with a large scale simulation with $n = 2000$. Another important optimal property of GUm is that if the interpoint distances d_{ij} is measured without error, (i.e., $d_{ij} = |x_i - x_j|$), then the true coordinates $(x_1, \ldots, x_n)$ can be obtained in one iteration of GUm.

3. Cluster analysis using UDS

In section 2, we proposed an easy and efficient method for choosing starting configuration for Guttman's updating algorithm (GUm) and Pliner's smoothing algorithm (PLm). These algorithms give a reasonably good UDS solution even when n is large. The coordinates in the UDS solution also provide some useful information to uncover hidden clusters in the objects. Large jumps or gaps in the coordinate indicate a possible boundary between two clusters. We first illustrate this method by Fisher's famous Iris data set. This data set contains $n = 150$ observations with 4 variables, sepal length and width, petal length and width (denoted by $y_{i1}, \ldots, y_{i4}$). There are 3 groups (Iris setosa, vericolor, and virginica) in the data set. The data are arranged so that the first 50 observations belong to a group followed by next 50 observations belong to the second group and the final 50 observations belong to the third group. The distance between object i and j are computed using Euclidean metric, i.e., $d_{ij} = \sqrt{\sum_{l=1}^{4}(y_{il} - y_{jl})^2}$. We apply PLm to the iris data, the coordinates $x_1, \ldots, x_{150}$ are obtained. The index plot of x_i against i is given in Figure 1. From Figure 1, there is a large gaps in the coordinates between the 100th and the 101th observation. The UDS solution successfully identifies the first group in the data set.

Since the objects are arranged in a linear order according to their similarity, there are more sophisticated statistical techniques for detecting boundary of clusters. This is called 'change point analysis' in the literature. We adopt the Schwarz Information Criterion (SIC) given in Chen and Gupta [1] to detect the clusters. The problem can be formulated as follows: let $y_1, \ldots, y_n$ be a sequence of independent p-dimensional normal random vectors with parameters $(\mu_1, \Sigma_1), \ldots, (\mu_n, \Sigma_n)$, respectively. We are interested in testing the hypothesis (one cluster)

$$H_0 : \mu_1 = \ldots = \mu_n \quad \text{and} \quad \Sigma_1 = \ldots = \Sigma_n$$

versus the alternative (change point at k)

$$H_1 : \mu_1 = \ldots = \mu_k \neq \mu_{k+1} = \ldots = \mu_n$$

$$\text{and } \Sigma_1 = \ldots = \Sigma_k \neq \Sigma_{k+1} = \ldots = \Sigma_n.$$

Define

$$SIC(n) = pn \log 2\pi + n \log |\widehat{\Sigma}| + \frac{n + p(p+3)}{2} \log n,$$

$$SIC(k) = pn \log 2\pi + k \log |\widehat{\Sigma}_{(1)}| + (n-k) \log |\widehat{\Sigma}_{(2)}| + n + p(p+3) \log n,$$

where $\widehat{\Sigma}$ is the sample covariance matrix of $(y_1, \ldots, y_n)$; $\widehat{\Sigma}_{(1)}$ and $\widehat{\Sigma}_{(2)}$ is the sample covariance matrix of $(y_1, \ldots, y_k)$ and $(y_{k+1}, \ldots, y_n)$ respectively.

We accept H_0 if $SIC(n) < \min\{SIC(k) : p < k < n-p\}$ and accept H_1 if $SIC(n) > SIC(k)$ for some k. Furthermore, we estimate the position of the change point by $\widehat{k}$ such that $SIC(\widehat{k}) = \min\{SIC(k) : p < k < n-p\}$. We apply this SIC to iris data and successfully find three clusters and compare our result to $K-means$ clustering method. Table 3 summarize the classification results.

Table 3.   Classification table for Fisher's Iris data.

	UDS			K-means			
	1	2	3	1	2	3	Total
Virginica	37	13	0	36	14	0	50
Versicolor	0	50	0	3	47	0	50
Setosa	0	0	50	0	0	50	50
Total	37	63	50	39	61	50	150

The numbers on the off-diagonal represent misclassification. Clearly, our clustering method based on UDS is better than the $K-means$ clustering. As a final example, we consider an interesting simulated 'ring' data set. 60 points are equally spaced on the circumference of a circle with radius 3 units and 100 points are generated independently from N(0,0.025) and the plot of these points is given in Figure 2 in the appendix. To human eyes, the points on the circle are considered as a cluster and the points inside the circle are considered as another cluster. We test our UDS clustering and the $K-means$ clustering methods using this data set. First, the UDS solution of these 160 points are obtained using PLm. The index plot of the UDS coordinates versus the order is given in Figure 3. There are two large gaps in the coordinates and hence the points are naturally divided into 3 clusters. We also perform the $K-means$ clustering with $K = 3$. The classification results are given in Table 4, Figures 4 and 5.

$K-means$ clustering fails to find the correct clusters but divide the points into two half (see Figure 4). Although our UDS clustering gives three clusters, it correctly identifies the points inside the circle (see Figure 5).

Table 4.   Classification table for the Ring example.

	UDS			K-means		Total
Inside	100	0	0	54	46	100
Circle	0	23	37	30	30	60
Total	100	23	37	84	76	160

4. Conclusion

With the growth of technology in hardware, large amount of data can be accumulated, typical examples are bank customer's database, supermarket's scanner database, credit cards transaction records ... etc. One basic operation in data mining is to find hidden clusters in these huge databases. GUm and PLm are useful and effective algorithms for arranging and placing large number of objects on a real line according to their interpoint distances. Based on large jumps or gaps in the coordinates, we can identify possible boundaries of clusters. In this paper, only the basic idea of UDS clustering is presented. There are several problems and extensions worth further investigation:

(1) In the iris data or the simulated ring example, we used the Euclidean metric to represent the interpoint distances. This is suitable only for continuous variables. When the variables are binary, categorical or of mixed type, other suitable metric should be used.

(2) In pratice, variables may have many missing values. Suitable formula is needed for computing interpoint distances when there is missing value.

(3) Other optimization criteria such as $tr(W)$, $det(W)$ or $tr(BW^{-1})$ can be used instead of SIC, where W and B is the within group covariance matrix and between group covariance matrix respectively.

(4) We can group variables in the data set as well. Suitable intervariable distances can be used to represent the dissimilarity between two variables. For example, $d_{ij} = 1 - |r_{ij}|$, where r_{ij} is correlation coefficient between variable i and j.

(5) In data mining, the number of objects is huge. GUm and PLm may not be appliable. Other modified algorithm is needed to arrange the objects. For example, divide the whole data set into several blocks and perform UDS on each block. Join these UDS solutions at the final stage.

(6) UDS clustering can be extented to other statistical models such as regression and time series.

There are many other possiblities and extensions of this UDS clustering exist. We leave them for future research.

References

1. J. Chen and A. K. Gupta, *Parametric Statistical Change Point Analysis*, Birkhauser (2000).
2. J. de Leeuw and W. J. Heiser, *Convergence of Correction-Matrix Algorithms for Multidimensional Scaling*, in Geometric Representations of Relational Data: Readings in Multidimensional Scaling, Ed., J.C. Lingoes, Ann Arbor, MI:Mathesis, 735-752.
3. L. Guttman, *A General Nonmetric Technique for Finging the Smallest Coordinate Space for a Configuration of Points*, Psychometrika, **33**, 469-506 (1968).
4. W. J. Heiser and P. Arabie, *Unidimensional Scaling and Combinatorial Optimization*, in Multidimensional Data Analysis, Ed., J. de Leeuw, W. Heiser, J. Meulman, and F. Critchley, Leiden, The Netherlands: DSWO Press, 181-196 (1986).
5. K. Lau, P. L. Leung and K. Tse, *A Nonlinear Programming Approach to Metric Unidimensional Scaling*, Journal of Classification, **15**, 3-14 (1998).
6. V. Pliner, *Metric Unidimensional Scaling and Global Optimization*, Journal of Classification, **13**, 3-18 (1996).
7. W. S. Robinson, *A Method for Chronologically Ordering Archaeological Deposits*, American Antiquity, **16**, 293-301 (1951).

AUTOMATIC STOCK TREND PREDICTION
BY REAL TIME NEWS

GABRIEL PUI CHEONG FUNG, JEFFREY XU YU AND WAI LAM

Department of Systems Engineering and Engineering Management
The Chinese University of Hong Kong
Shatin, New Territories, Hong Kong, China
E-mail: {pcfung, yu, wlam}@se.cuhk.edu.hk

Mining textual document and time series concurrently, such as predicting the movements of stock prices based on news articles, is definitely an emerging topic in data mining society nowadays. Previous research has already suggested that relationships between news articles and stock prices do exist. In this paper, we try to explore such an opportunity and propose a systematic framework for predicting the movement of stock trends by analyzing the influence of news articles. In particular, we investigate the immediate impacts of news articles onto the stock market based on the Efficient Markets Hypothesis (EMH). Several data mining and text mining techniques are used in a novel way. Extensive experiments using real-life data are conducted, and encouraging results are obtained.

1. INTRODUCTION

Without a doubt, human behaviors are always influenced by the environment. One of the most significant impacts that affect our behaviors certainly comes from the mass media, or to be more specific, from the news articles. Several research from different fields has already developed some well-defined theories to support it[2,3]. For the stock prices fluctuation, it is totally because of we, human beings, who perform the bidding and asking activities. As news will influence our decisions and our decisions will influence the stock market, news will, in turn, affect the stock market indirectly.

However, the frequency of news articles boardcast is so quick such that, take Reuters as an example, news articles will be announced for nearly every minute. It is definitely impossible for us to read through them one by one. Extracting information and knowledge from news articles automatically so as to help us analyze the stock market is thus a critical topic.

In fact, mining textual document and time series concurrently is now an emerging topic in the data mining society. An increasing number of researches are conducted in this direction. Fawcett and Provost[6] formulated a stock forecasting problem. However, a detailed procedure is lacking. Lavrenko et al.[13] proposed a language modeling approach for predicting the stock trend movement. In their approach, news articles that are announced five hours before the happening of a given trend type are aligned back to it, which is then used as the basis for generating the language model. However, this approach may lead to many conflicts[a], and also contradict against the Efficient Markets Hypothesis (EMH).

According to EMH, the current market is an efficient information processor which immediately reflects the assimilation of all of the information available[2,3,14]. In other words, a long time lag is normally impossible.

In this paper, we present a system, based on EMH, to predict the future behaviors of the stock market using real-time boardcasted news articles by news agents. Predictions are made soley according to the newly broadcasted news articles. Thus, our system is event-driven. The unique features of our system are: 1) a new t-test based piecewise segmentation algorithm for trend discovery is proposed; 2) interesting trends are grouped together by an agglomerative hierarchical clustering algorithm; 3) news articles are aligned to the interesting trends based on EMH; 4) a new differentiated weighting scheme is proposed for assigning weights to the features according to their importance.

The rest of the paper is organized as follows. Section 2 presents the system architecture in details. Section 3 evaluates the system performance. A summary and conclusion is given in Section 4.

2. A NEWS SENSITIVE STOCK TREND PREDICTION SYSTEM

The overview of our system is shown in Figure 1(a) and Figure 1(b) using the Unified Model Language (UML).

The system training phase includes six modules: 1) trend discovery for identifying trends within different periods; 2) trend labeling for grouping similar trends together; 3) feature extraction for extracting the key words in the news articles; 4) articles-trend alignment for associating related news articles to the trends; 5) feature weighting for assigning weights to the features according to their importance; and 6) model generation for generating the desire model.

The operational phase is used for predicting the future trends according to the content of the newly broadcasted article. The unique features and details of these procedures are presented in the following subsections.

---

[a]For example, the same article may align to more than one trend type.

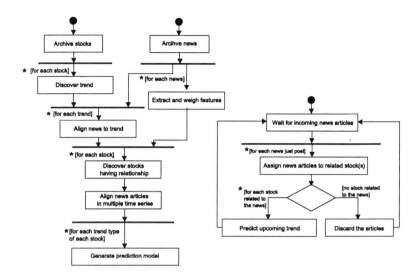

Figure 1. Overview of the system architecture

2.1. *Stock Trend Discovery*

From the stock trader point of view, the general trends within different time horizons on the time series is far more informative than the exact fluctuation, as our decision of bidding or asking is based on the recent trends rather than the exact stock prices. Thus, discovering trends on the time series is properly the first procedure.

Technical analysis is properly one of the easiest way to decomposite a time series into trends[1]. However, it has too many variations, in which, unfortunately, none of them has a very good supporting background. Thus, a data mining perspective is chosen here.

Fourier coefficients[5] and parametric spectral models[15] are some well-known segmentation algorithms. However, if a time series consists of transient behaviors, i.e. stock prices, they are not suitable to use, as they will have very weak spectral signatures[11].

Another popular technique for segmenting time series is piecewise linear segmentation. Boardly speaking, they have three different variations: 1) top-down; 2) bottom-up; and 3) sliding-window. In their paper, Keogh et al.[12] gave a comparison of the strengths and weaknesses of these approaches.

In our system, we implement a split-and-merge segmentation algorithm which includes both the top-down and bottom-up techniques. The splitting phase aims at discovering all of the interesting trends on the time series, whereas the merging phase aims at avoiding over-segmentation. The details of the algorithm are as follows.

Initially, the whole time series is regarded as a single segment. A regression line is formulated on top of it. In order to decide whether the regression line is adequate for representing the time series, a normal probability plot of the residuals is plotted. A one-tail t-test is formulated to test whether the residuals fall approximately along a straight line:

$$
\begin{aligned}
H_0 &: \mu = 0 \\
H_1 &: \mu > 0
\end{aligned}
\tag{1}
$$

where μ is the mean error norm of all residuals. The error norm of each residual is calculated by the distance between it and the straight line:

$$
E_i = |\sin\theta \cdot x_i + \cos\theta \cdot y_i - d|
\tag{2}
$$

where x_i and y_i are the coordinates of residual i; θ is the angle between the line and the x-axis; d is the perpendicular distance from the origin to the line. Finally, the mean error norm is compared with the t-statistics:

$$
t = \frac{\bar{E} - \mu}{s \sqrt{n}}
\tag{3}
$$

where s is the standard deviation of the error norms and $\bar{E}$ is the mean error norm.

The motivation of such formulation is that if the mean error norm of the residuals under a normal probability plot is nearly zero, then the residuals should fall approximately on a straight line, and thus the regression line should be adequate to represent the segment. If the t-statistics is rejected, splitting will occur at the point where the error norm of the residual is maximum, and the splitting phase continues on each segment recursively.

Since the splitting phase is carried out on each segment independently, over-segmentation may frequently occur. The merging phase aims at avoiding over-segmentation by merging adjacent segments, provided that the error norm after merging will not exceed the threshold which is determined by t-test automatically. The merging phase is exactly the same as the splitting phase, except that segments are merged rather than split. Figure 2 illustrate the idea.

2.2. Stock Trend Labeling

In reality, a stock trader will never be interested in the trends that are relatively steady, as they provide neither opportunities nor threats. In order

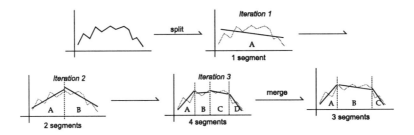

Figure 2. t-test based piecewise segmentation

to group the trends into some interesting categories, a two dimensional agglomerative hierarchical clustering algorithm is formulated. It is based on: 1) the slope of the segment (m) and 2) the coefficient of determination (R^2). m is chosen because it is one of the most concerning issues for the stock traders. R^2 is chosen because it is a measurement for the goodness of fit of the regression line. Details of clustering could refer to other literature[10]. R^2 is defined as:

$$R^2 = \frac{\sum_{i=1}^{n}(\widehat{y_i} - \overline{y})^2}{\sum_{i=1}^{n}(y_i - \overline{y})^2} \qquad (4)$$

where y_i is the original data; $\widehat{y_i}$ is the segmented data corresponding to y_i; $\overline{y}$ is the mean of the original data in that segment.

Thus, the numerator is the regression sum of squares and the denominator is the corrected sum of squares. All slopes are normalized within 1 and -1 in order to have consistent clustering results across different stocks. Note that R^2 is always between 0 and 1. Each segment is thus represented by (m, R^2), and is regarded as an individual cluster object. The segments are merged according to the minimum group average distance (GAD):

$$GAD(C_i, C_j) - \frac{\sum_{i \in C_i} \sum_{j \in C_j} d_{ij}(i,j)}{|C_i||C_j|} \qquad (5)$$

where $|C_i|$ and $|C_j|$ are the magnitudes of the cluster C_i and C_j respectively; $d(i,j)$ is the distance between the objects inside C_i and C_j:

$$d_{ij}(i,j) = \sqrt{(m_i - m_j)^2 + (R_i^2 - R_j^2)^2} \qquad (6)$$

The clustering procedure terminates when the number of clusters are equal to three as we are interested in grouping the trends into three classes (Rise/Drop/Steady). Based on the average slope in the three clusters, those segments in the cluster having the maximum (minimum) value are labeled as `Rise` (`Drop`). Segments in the remained cluster are labeled as `Steady`. Note that although simple threshold strategy on the slope could be used for grouping the trends, we claim that it is not scientific and difficult to define such a threshold among all stocks.

2.3. *Article and Trend Alignment*

Article alignment is the process of associating news articles to the stock trends such that the aligned news articles are believed to account for the happening of these trends.

Extreme cares have to be paid in this process, otherwise biasing or even meaningless results would be obtained. Different scholars in financial engineering may have different interpretations on how the alignment process should be done. It is difficult, if not impossible, to find a completely consensus among them. Some may favor to have a time lag between the article boardcast and the trend begins[13], so as to denote the time that the market has to be consumed for absorbing the information.

In our model formulation, we claim that a long time lag is normally impossible. This is actually according to the Efficient Market Hypothesis (EMH). EMH states that the current market is an efficient information processor which would reflect the assimilation of all of the information available immediately. Thus, the alignment process goes in the way such that all of the news articles announced under a particular trend are aligned back to that trend immediately. Figure 3 illustrates such an idea. The motivation of such formulation is based on the strong form of EMH in the sense that all of the information arise will be absorbed by the market with only a negligible time lag.

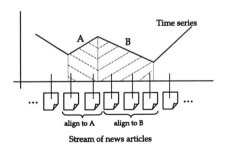

Figure 3. An example to illustrate the basic idea of alignment process

2.4. Differentiated Feature Weighting

After the alignment process, a set of news articles are aligned to the trends. Feature weighting is aimed at distinguish the importance of each feature in each cluster.

For most of the existing weighting schemes, the basic idea is: features which rarely occur over a collection are valuable. However, note that we are interested in figuring out the features which frequently occur in one of the cluster (rise/drop) but rarely occur in the other one. Thus, none of the existing weighting schemes fully fits into our requirementsj.

A new weighting scheme is proposed here. In our formulation, word independence is assumed, which is a common practice in text classification research. Furthermore, preserving the word dependence may not necessarily help to improve the accuracy of the model, or to some extents may even make it worse[16,4].

In order to differentiate the feature appearing in one of the cluster but not the other, two coefficients are used: inter-cluster discrimination coefficient (CDC) and intra-cluster similarity coefficient (CSC):

$$CDC = (\frac{n_{i,t}}{N_t})^2 \tag{7}$$

$$CSC = \sqrt{\frac{n_{i,t}}{n_i}} \tag{8}$$

where $n_{i,t}$ is the number of articles in cluster i containing term t; N_t is the total number of articles containing term t; n_i is the total number of different terms appearing within cluster i.

The intuition of CDC and CSC is, in fact, according to the distribution of words across news articles. As noted by Holt et al.[8], the occurrence of any keyword across news articles is extremely rare. Thus, instead of assuming a linear relationship, a quadratic relationship should be expected. Note that both CDC and CSC are always between 0 and 1. For CDC, the higher the value of it, the more powerful for it to discriminate the feature across clusters. For CSC, the higher the value of it, the more of the articles in the cluster contains the specific feature.

The weight of each feature in each document is finally calculated as follows:

$$w(t,d) = tf_{t,d} \times CDC \times CSC \tag{9}$$

where $tf_{t,d}$ is the frequency of term t in the article d. Term frequency is used for improving the recall of the model[4]. Finally, each news article is represented by a vector-space model in which it is normalized into unit length, so as to account for the documents with different lengths.

2.5. *Learning and Prediction*

Support Vectors Machine (SVM) is used for generating the relationships between features and trends. SVM is a learning algorithm proposed by Vapnik to solve two-class pattern recognition problem by using the structural risk minimization principle[17]. Recent research shows that it could obtain very accurate results in text classification and outperform many other techniques[9,18].

For the system training, two classifiers are built for each trend type. One is responsible for predicting the rise event, and the other is responsible for the drop event.

For the system operation, we pass the newly collected news article to the pair of related classifiers and decide which of the signal the article will fire. For instance, an article is believed to signal a rise (drop) event if the output value of the rise (drop) classifier is positive. If both classifiers are of the same sign, we simply ignore this article and conclude that this article is ambiguous.

3. EVALUATION

A prototype system is developed for evaluation. Stock data and news articles are archived through Reuters Market 3000 Extra[b]. All features are stemmed and converted to lower case, in which punctuation marks are removed, numbers, web page addresses and stop-words are ignored. Training and operation are done by SVM^{light}[c].

Stock prices and news articles from 1st October 2001 to 1st April 2002 are used. 614 companies are selected from the Hong Kong Exchange Market. The number of stock data varies from stock to stock, and is around 2,000 ticks for each stock. The total number of news articles archived are around 350,000. Data from the first six months are used for training, while the last month is used for evaluation.

3.1. *Trends Discovery and Labeling*

A typical result after the time series segmentation is shown in Figure 4. The shape of the time series after segmentation is preserved, while the number of data points reduced up to one-tenth.

One of the biggest concerns about trend discovery process is its quality and reliability. In our trend discovery algorithm, each trend is the regression

---

[b]http://www.reuters.com
[c]http://svmlight.joachims.org

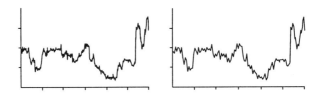

Figure 4. A time series before and after segmentation. On the top: original time series. On the bottom: t-test based piecewise segmented time series

line of the original data points in that segment. A common practice in statistics for measuring the adequacy of a regression line is using coefficient of determination (R^2). A high value of R^2 could imply that the regression line formulated is likely to fit the original data points. Figure 5 shows a typical result of such a plot.

Each symbol in the graph corresponds to a distinct segment. Note the special "T" shape of the graph. Those segments with steep slopes will have high values of R^2. The "T" shape shows that the quality of our stock trend labeling is high. Misclassification is unlikely to happen as we are interested in those steep slopes only. It is very important because it could maintain sufficient high quality training examples.

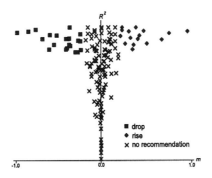

Figure 5. A plot of m Vs R^2 for the same time series in Figure 4

3.2. Overall System Performance

In our market simulation, the following two strategies are used:

- If the prediction of the upcoming trend is positive, then shares of that stock are purchased immediately. Shares would be sold after holding for 24 hours. If it is a holiday, then shares would be sold immediately at the beginning of the next active trading day.

- If the prediction of the upcoming trend is negative, then shares of that stock are sold for short. The shorted shares are purchased back immediately after 24 hours. If it is a holiday, then shares would be purchased immediately at the beginning of the next active trading day.

In order to calculate the overall profit (loss) accumulated, rate or return[d] is being used[7]. Since we are only concerned with the rate of return, how much shares are bought in each transaction is ignored. The assumption of zero transaction cost is taken which is the usual practice for stock market simulation.

Since all of the predictions made are based on the news articles, the frequency of the news articles broadcast must be a critical factor for affecting the prediction performance. Figure 6 shows a plot of our system with the frequency of news announced versus resulting profits. All of the stocks are ranked based on the total number of news articles that are associated with in the training period. They are further divided into different categories in which every category contains the same number of stocks.

In the figure, the smaller the number the x-axis is, the fewer number of news articles are aligned to that stock. In general, our approach is highly profitable, except for a stock receives too many or too few news articles. This is properly because if a stock receives too few articles, the model would not have enough examples to train. Similarly, if a stock receives too many articles, the probability of having noise would be higher.

4. Conclusions

In this paper, we have proposed a systematic framework for mining time series and textual documents concurrently. As news articles will influence our behaviors and the stock prices fluctuation is due to our decisions of bidding and asking, it is reasonable and logical to say that news articles will influence the stock market indirectly. In fact, such associations do exist according to many other researches, and some theories have already developed. We could see that an increasing number of researches will be conducting in this direction.

The major difference between our system and the existing forecasting

---

[d]Some relaxation about the stock exchange restriction is assumed under the buy-and-hold test, such as the acceptance of shorting the stock.

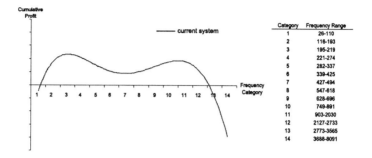

Figure 6. The relationship between the frequency of news announced and the resulting profit

techniques is that we take non-quantifiable information into account for prediction. News articles are served as the major source of such information.

Our approach does not need the assumption of requiring a fixed period for aligning news articles to a trend. Several data and text mining techniques are incorporated in the system architecture. A t-test based piecewise segmentation algorithm and an agglomerative hierarchical clustering algorithm are used for discovering and labeling trends respectively. A new weighting scheme is formulated to identify the important features within the collection. Finally, a market simulation based on a very simple Buy-and-Hold test is conducted. The encouraging results indicated that our approach is highly feasible.

References

1. S. B. Achelis. *Technical Analysis from A to Z*. Irwin Professional Publishing, second edition (1995).
2. P. A. Adler and P. Adler. *The Social Dynamics of Financial Markets*. Jai Press Inc. (1984).
3. W. J. Eiteman, C. A. Dice, and D. K. Eiteman. *The Stock Market*. McDGraw-Hill Book Company, forth edition, (1966).
4. S. Fabrizio. Machine learning in automated text categorization. *ACM Computing Surveys*, **34**, 1-47 (2002).
5. C. Faloutsos, M. Rangantathan, and Y. Manalopoulos. Fast subsequence matching in time-series database. In *Proceedings of the 1994 ACM SIGMOD International Conference on Management of Data*, 419-429 (1994).
6. T. Fawcett and F. Provost. Activity monitoring: Noticing interesting changes in behavior. In *Proceedings of the 5th ACM SIGKDD International Conference on Knowledge Discovery and Data Mining*, 53–62 (1999).
7. T. Hellstrom and K. Holmstrom. Predicting the stock market. Technical Re-

port IMa-TOM-1997-07, Malardalen University (1998).

8. J. D. Holt and S. M. Chung. Efficient mining of association rules in text databases. In *Proceedings of the 8th International Conference on Information Knowledge Management*, 234–242 (1999).

9. T. Joachims. Text categorization with support vector machines: Learning with many relevant features. In *Proceedings of the 10th European Conference on Machine Learning*, 137–142 (1998).

10. L. Kaufman and P. J. Rousseeuw. *Finding Groups in Data - An Introduction to Cluster Analysis*. John Wiley & Sons Inc. (1990).

11. E. Keogh and P. Smyth. A probabilistic approach to fast pattern matching in time series databases. In *Proceedings of the 3rd International Conference on Knowledge Discovery and Data Mining*, 24-40 (1997).

12. E. J. Keogh, S. Chu, D. Hart, and M. J. Pazzani. An online algorithm for segmenting time series. In *Proceedings of the 2001 IEEE International Conference on Data Mining*, 289-296 (2001).

13. V. Lavrenko, M. Schmill, D. Lawire, P. Ogilvie, D. Jensen, and J. Allan. Mining of concurrent text and time series. In *Workshop of the 6th ACM International Conference on Knowledge Discovery and Data Mining* (2000).

14. C. Pratten. *The Stock Market*. Cambridge University Press (1993).

15. P. Smyth. Hidden markov models for fault detection in dynamic systems. *Pattern Recognition* **27**, 149-164 (1994).

16. C. J. van Rijsbergen. A theoretical basis for the use of co-occurance data in information retrieval. *Journal of Documentation* **33**, 106-119 (1997).

17. V. N. Vapnik. *The Nature of Statistical Learning Theory*. Springer (1995).

18. Y. Yang and X. Liu. A re-examination of text categorization methods. In *Proceedings of the 22nd Annual International ACM SIGIR Conference on Research and Development in Information Retrieval*, 42-49 (1999).

FROM ASSOCIATED IMPLICATION NETWORKS
TO INTERMARKET ANALYSIS

PHIL C. TSE [2] AND JIMING LIU [1] [*]

[1] *Department of Computer Science, Hong Kong Baptist University*

Kowloon Tong, Hong Kong jiming@comp.hkbu.edu.hk

[2] *TuitionKing.Com, Hong Kong philtse@tuitionking.com*

Abstract

Current attempts to analyze international financial markets include the use of financial technical analysis and data mining techniques. These efforts, however, do not make a clear distinction between the local and global perspectives of intermarket actions. In this paper, we propose a new approach that incorporates implication networks, i.e., a variation of probabilistic network, and association rules to form an associated network structure. The proposed approach explicitly addresses the issue of local vs. global influences in knowledge domains. It is found from our validation experiments that this approach can adequately model different international markets based on the discovered associated network structure when some real-world market data is given. The associated network structure can be used for financial analysis purposes, yielding satisfactory and stable analysis results.

1. Introduction

Conventional wisdom has it that financial markets around the globe are interrelated. They are in some ways interrelated that they do not move separately without interfering each other. To cite an example, commodity prices and the U.S. dollar move in an opposite direction. This is conceivable because the rise of commodity prices often implies the surge of inflation, and often there are cases in which the U.S. Federal Reserve would raise the interest rate to suppress inflation. This, however, inevitably puts the U.S. dollar into a bear market. Another example is that the price of gold and some of the currencies such as the

---

[*] Corresponding author.

Australian dollar are having a positive relationship. This is because the Australian economy relies much on the export of gold and other metals, and the rise of gold and other metals' prices will be beneficial to the Australian economy, which in turn fuels the price of Australian dollars.

Actually this kind of intermarket actions can be further divided into two perspectives. In a local perspective, various markets in a certain country, such as stock, currency and bond markets, interact with each other. While in a global perspective, the same kind of markets tends to be highly correlated. As many can still remember, the tumble of the U.S. stock market in 1987 slashed several other important stock markets in the world severely. These market relationships, as many economists have claimed, were driven by the flow of capital. Not surprisingly, investors are profit-driven and always want to put their "smart money" into the most promising markets. Their leaving and entering of different markets account for the prescribed intermarket actions.

Researchers have tried to analyze the fore mentioned market relationships. De facto attempts include the application of financial technical analysis on different international markets. Other recent innovations bring state-of-the-art data mining techniques into play, in which pattern and association rule mining dominate. These data mining efforts, however, paid little attention on the formulation and distinction of the aforementioned local and global perspectives of intermarket actions. As supported by most of the economists, local markets are much more correlated than the oversea markets do. The lack of the awareness of this distinction, therefore, can be problematic. We argue that unless the distinction can be well considered and formulated, we cannot capture the whole picture of the intermarket actions.

In this light, we propose a new paradigm to analyze these intermarket actions by mining probabilistic networks and association rules. The discovered networks and rules form an associated network structure in which the distinction of the local and global perspectives becomes possible. As we will show later, probabilistic networks, or often referred to as Bayesian networks, can represent the markets in a global perspective, while the association rules can formulate the relatively weaker relationships of related markets around the globe. Our approach will be validated using real-world financial data.

1.1. Related Work

As we have mentioned, financial analysts inclined to apply financial technical analysis to deal with intermarket actions. Murphy [12], to our best knowledge, is the first who formulated the problem in this area. Thereafter many data mining efforts have been paid which use pattern and association rule mining.

In our approach, we employ probabilistic networks to formulate interactions in a global perspective. Some traditional examples of inferring schemes over probabilistic networks are presented in Charniak's [4] work, with other more recent approaches such as VanLehn et al. [18], which prior and posterior probabilities are compared to update the beliefs of nodes in a network.

A number of algorithms were proposed to derive probabilistic networks (e.g. [5][8][9][14][15]). More modern works in this field include Liu and Desmarais [11], which proposed a method of learning implication networks, being a variation of probabilistic networks, from empirical data. Myers et al. [13] proposed a method of learning Bayesian networks from incomplete data using evolutionary algorithms.

1.2. Contributions

The main contributions of this paper can be summarized as follows:

(1) Provides a new paradigm that incorporates probabilistic networks and association rules for analyzing financial intermarket actions. With multiple networks connected by association rules, international markets can be better modeled. We will describe later that each of the probabilistic networks is able to have its own set of parameters to show the uniqueness of different financial markets.

(2) Extends and improves existing algorithms of mining probabilistic networks and association rules to form an associated network structure in an automatic way.

(3) Provides an efficient algorithm for analyzing intermarket actions with the discovered **network structure**.

(4) Assesses the proposed approach by a validation process using real-world market data. As will be shown later, the proposed approach yields stable and satisfactory results.

1.3. Organization of the Paper

This paper is organized as follows: Section 2 provides details on the proposed approach including its components and algorithms with several formal definitions. The inference algorithm which is used for analyzing financial markets will be described in Section 3. Section 4 is concerned with the validation of our proposed approach. Section 5 concludes the paper by highlighting the key results of this work.

2. Associated Network Structure and its Discovery

In this section, we will describe the components and algorithms of an associated network structure as used for analyzing financial intermarket actions. Section 2.1 provides the key definitions, and Section 2.2 describes the algorithm used to discover an associated network structure.

2.1. Problem Statement

As mentioned before, the proposed approach uses multiple probabilistic networks and some connecting association rules for financial intermarket analysis. We use the term *associated network structure* to refer to the aggregate of these networks and rules.

Definition. *An associated network structure is a duple* <ℵ, ℜ> *where* ℵ *is a finite set of probabilistic networks and* ℜ *is a finite set of association rules connecting the networks.*

Probabilistic network, often referred to as Bayesian network, causal network or knowledge map, is a data structure used to represent knowledge in an uncertain domain. A probabilistic network comprises a set of random variables making up the nodes of the network and a set of directed links or arrows connecting the pairs of nodes. Associated with each directed link or arrow is the probability that the consequent node happens if the antecedent node happens. The probability can be in form of conditional probability or in form of weighting. Each node has its own belief, and the beliefs can be updated through evidence propagation in the network once new evidence is observed. A typical probabilistic network is depicted in Figure 1.

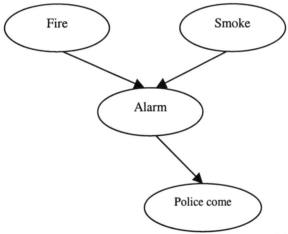

Figure 1. A typical probabilistic network. Random variables are shown as ovals with directed links showing the relationships between the random variables.

As mentioned already in Section 1, there exist several approaches to build and infer inside a probabilistic network. Among those approach, Liu and Desmarais [11] proposed an approach to learning probabilistic networks, or what they referred to as implication networks, from a small number of empirical data samples. This approach outperforms others in terms of computational efficiency and complexity, as it emphasizes on inference accuracy rather than the actual topology corresponding to a knowledge structure. Specifically, the method requires only one-hundredth of the CPU time that is required by Pearl's stochastic simulation method. This method, therefore, will be incorporated to discover implication networks in our study.

The method formally defined an implication network:

$$Net \in \aleph, Net = <N, I, p_{min}, \alpha_c> \quad (1)$$

where "N is a finite set of nodes and I is a finite set of arcs connecting the nodes. p_{min} is the minimal conditional probability to be estimated in the arcs and α_c is the network induction error allowed" [11].

Association rules are used in our proposed approach to connect the implication networks discovered through the nodes in set N in (1). Mining association rules is the process of discovering rules and relationships from a massive amount of data, such as those in relational databases. An association rules has the form of $X \rightarrow Y$, where X and Y are set of attributes. A rule implies that the set of attributes Y tends to have true values when another set of attributes X are true. Usually each rule is associated with support and confidence, where support is the ratio of the records having true values for the attributes of $(X \cup Y)$ to the number of all records. Confidence is the ratio of the number of records having true values for the attributes $(X \cup Y)$ to the number of records having true values for attributes of X. An introduction to the mining of association rules and the variations of mining algorithms are given by Cengiz in [3].

Association rules are suitable for the proposed approach to connect the networks. As pointed out by Bowes et al. [2], causal inference algorithms extract relationships that are always stronger than association rules, because the elicitation of these relationships is based on rigid statistical testing. The tests, however, are sometimes too rigid, and some subtle but novel rules would be rejected during the testing process. Association rules, on the other hand, often represent more novel (e.g. support can be as low as 0.1, depends on the nature of the domain) but useful relationships, which always exist between two variables in two different knowledge domains.

For the sake of convenience in the later discussion, a formal representation of association rules is defined as follows:

$$Rule \in \mathfrak{R}, Rule = <X, Y, p_c, s> \quad (2)$$

where X and Y are sets of attributes, or referred to as itemsets in data mining terminology. As mentioned, p_c and s are confidence and support of the rule, respectively.

In summary, the components of an associated network structure are illustrated in Figure 2.

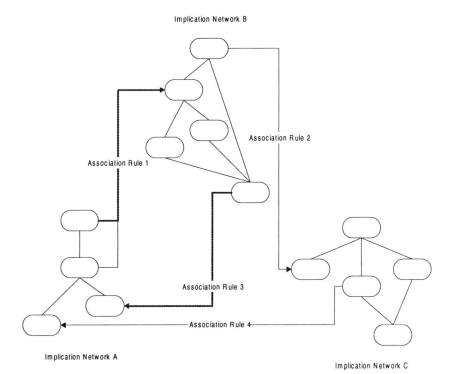

Figure 2. An example of an associated network structure consisting of three implication networks. The implication networks are further connected with each other by association rules. Within each implication network are some implication relationships.

2.2. Discovery of an Associated Network Structure

The first phase in discovering an associated network structure is the elicitation of implication relationships. From Figure 2, it can be noted that implication relationships connect the nodes within an implication network. As pointed out by Liu and Desmarais [11], six types of implication relationship exist between any pair of nodes, namely the positive implication (A $\Rightarrow$ B), forward-negative implication (A $\Rightarrow$ ~B), inverse negative implication (~A $\Rightarrow$ B), negative implication (~A $\Rightarrow$ ~B), positive equivalence (A $\Leftrightarrow$ B) and negative equivalence (A $\Leftrightarrow$ ~B). The elicitations of these implication relationships are based on statistical examinations, which are referred to as hypothesis tests on empirical data [6].

The hypothesis testing works as follows: For any implication relation A $\Rightarrow$ B, the following two conditions must be satisfied:

$$P(B \mid A) = 1 \qquad (3)$$

$$P(\sim A \mid \sim B) = 1 \qquad (4)$$

The hypothesis testing examines Conditions (3) and (4) by computing the lower bound of a $(1-\alpha_c)$ confidence interval around the measured conditional probabilities. This would allow the elicitation of implication relationship become possible under sampling errors.

The implication induction algorithm of Liu and Desmarais [11] is stated as follows:

Algorithm 1: Liu's and Desmarais' Implication Induction Algorithm
Begin
    set a significance level α_c and a minimum conditional probability p_{min} for a network.
    for node$_i$, $i \in [0, n_{max}-1]$ and node$_j$, $j \in [i+1, n_{max}]$
    Begin
    for all empirical case samples
        compute a contingency table

$T_{ij} =$
N_{11}
N_{12}

N_{21}
N_{22}

        Where $N_{11}, N_{12}, N_{21}, N_{22}$ are the numbers of occurrences with respect to the following combinations:

        N_{11}: node$_i$ = TRUE $\wedge$ node$_j$ = TRUE
        N_{12}: node$_i$ = TRUE $\wedge$ node$_j$ = FALSE
        N_{21}: node$_i$ = FALSE $\wedge$ node$_j$ = TRUE
        N_{22}: node$_i$ = FALSE $\wedge$ node$_j$ = FALSE

    for each implication type k out of the six possible cases
    Begin
        test the following inequality:

$$P(x \leq N_{error\_cell}) < \alpha_c$$

        based on the lower tails of binomial distributions $Bin(N, p_{min})$ and $Bin(\overline{N}, p_{min})$, where N and $\overline{N}$ denote the occurrences of antecedent satisfactions in the two inferences using a type k implication relation, i.e., in *modus ponens* and *modus tollens*, respectively.
        if the test succeeds, **then**
            return a type k implication relation.
    End
    End
End

Associated with each established relationship are weights representing the certainty of the relation. In order to facilitate the later inferences, the weights are estimated during the network structure discovery phase. Theoretically, two weights are associated with each type of implication relationship, as an inference can be made either in forward or backward direction. For instance, a forward implication would mean $A \Rightarrow B$ and $\sim B \Rightarrow \sim A$, which are logically equivalent, and one weight should be associated with $A \Rightarrow B$ and one for $\sim B \Rightarrow \sim A$.

The weights are estimated from the empirical data samples as well. Specifically, the estimated conditional probability of the relation is used as the weight. The general formula for the estimation of positive implication and negative implication can be stated as follows:

$$w = P_{est} = \frac{k+1}{n+2} \qquad (5)$$

where

$$N = \begin{cases} N_{A \cap B} + N_{A \cap \bar{B}} & \text{for P(B | A)} \\ & \text{for P(} \sim A \text{ | } \sim B\text{)} \\ N_{\bar{A} \cap \bar{B}} + N_{A \cap \bar{B}} & \text{for P(A | B)} \\ N_{A \cap B} + N_{\bar{A} \cap B} & \text{for P(} \sim B \text{ | } \sim A \text{)} \\ N_{\bar{A} \cap B} + N_{\bar{A} \cap \bar{B}} \end{cases}$$

and,

$$K = \begin{cases} N_{A \cap B} & \text{for P(B | A)} \\ N_{\bar{A} \cap \bar{B}} & \text{for P(} \sim A \text{ | } \sim B\text{)} \\ N_{A \cap B} & \text{for P(A | B)} \\ N_{\bar{A} \cap \bar{B}} & \text{for P(} \sim B \text{ | } \sim A \text{)} \end{cases}$$

For other types of implication relationships, please refer to the original works where a more detailed theory is presented.

The second phase of the network discovery process is to mine the association rules $R \in \Re$, linking up the empirically discovered implication networks.

As can be noted from (2), each rule is associated with a confidence value p_c and a support value s. Therefore, the first step of mining association rules is to determine the minimum confidence p_c and support s of the rules that would be selected during the mining process.

In our proposed approach, the Apriori algorithm [1][17] is used to mine the association rules. The nodes in set N in each implication network $Net \in \aleph$ are regarded as the items for the algorithm to generate itemsets which are required by the rules. After the itemsets are generated, rules with minimum confidence p_c and support s are discovered. These generated rules form the initial set of association rules $\Re_{init}$.

Note that the role of association rules in our proposed approach is to connect the empirically discovered implication networks in order to enable inferences between them. Therefore, it is only desirable to have association rules which connect different implication networks but do not connect the nodes in the same network. In other words, not all the rules in $\Re_{init}$ are accepted, as some of the rules in $\Re_{init}$ may violate this requirement. Figure 3 shows some examples of this kind of unaccepted association rules. These rules do not bridge the various networks in an associated network structure and have to be rejected in a filtering process. After the filtering process, the remaining rules form the final set of association rules $\Re$.

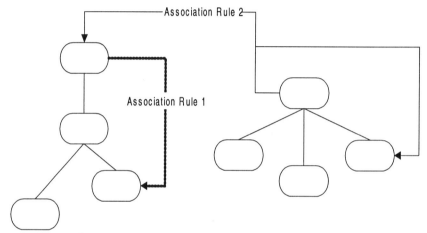

Figure 3. Association rule 1 connects the nodes in the same network
and therefore should be rejected.

A summary of the association rule mining process is presented as follows:

Algorithm 2: Association Rule Mining Algorithm
Begin
    set a minimum confidence p_c and a minimum support s for the rules.
    mine association rules with Apriori algorithm and form an initial set of association rules
        $\Re_{init}$.
    for each rule *Rule* in $\Re_{init}$ *// filtering process*
    Begin
        for each node in the antecedent itemset
            put the corresponding implication network in a linked list $link_{ante}$
        for each node in the consequent itemset
            put the corresponding implication network in another linked list $link_{cons}$
        if $link_{ante} \cap link_{cons} = \varnothing$ (null set)
            accept *Rule* and put it in set $\Re$.
        else reject *Rule*.
    End

return $\mathfrak{R}$.
End

After the induction of implication networks and the mining of association rules, an associated network structure is ready for uncertainty reasoning. In the next section an inference scheme over an associated network structure will be discussed.

3. The Inference Scheme

Our proposed inference scheme is divided into two parts, namely the inference with implication networks and inference with association rules. The processes of inference with implication networks and inference with association rules iterate, until all the observed evidences are considered and all the necessary belief revisions have taken place. The inference with implication networks precedes the inference with association rules, but once the inference with association rules updated some beliefs in another network, a new cycle of inference with implication networks in that network will be triggered, if the changes of the beliefs in the second network are significant.

A brief idea of the inference scheme can be stated in the following pseudocode:

The Inference Scheme
Begin
    Repeat
        perform Inference with Implication Networks (Algorithm 3)
        perform Inference with Association Rules (Algorithm 4)
    Until all the observed nodes are considered **and** all the necessary belief revisions have taken
        place.
End

In the following sections, more details on inference with implication networks and inference with association rules will be discussed.

3.1. Algorithm for Inference with Implication Networks

The basic idea of the inference with implication networks is as follows: Once a piece of evidence is obtained as a node is observed, the node's belief is first reviewed and the updated belief can be propagated to other nodes through the implication relationships as their new evidences. The new evidences for the nodes are further combined with the current beliefs of the corresponding nodes. After traversing all the nodes, the new beliefs in the nodes reflect the new certainties.

In our proposed approach, we deploy a belief revision algorithm based on Liu and Desmarais' [11] work to revise the beliefs of nodes when evidences are observed. In the algorithm, a belief updating function update_belief() is defined and it employs the Dempster's Rule of Combination and Dempster-Shafer method of evidential reasoning [10]. For the readers' convenience, the whole algorithm is given as follows:

Algorithm 3: Inference with Implication Networks
Begin
    Store all the observed node in a linked list, $link_{observ}$
    For each observed node, q_i, in link $link_{observ}$, do
    Begin
        insert(q_i, queue);
        while queue is not empty, do
            node ← get_next_node(queue);
            if node = TRUE, then
                for each rule: node $\Rightarrow q_j$, node $\Rightarrow \sim q_j$, $q_j \Rightarrow \sim$node, and $\sim q_j \Rightarrow \sim$node do
                    $Bel(q_j)$ ← update_belief(node, q_j),
                    If $\Delta Bel(q_j)$>a threshold, • , **then**
                        Insert(q_j, queue);
        Else
            For each rule: $q_k \Rightarrow$ node, $\sim q_k \Rightarrow$ node, $\sim$node $\Rightarrow q_k$, and $\sim$node $\Rightarrow \sim q_k$ do
                $Bel(q_k)$ ← update_belief(node, q_k),
                If $\Delta Bel(q_k)$>a threshold, • , **then**
                    Insert(q_k, queue);
    End
End

After all the necessary revisions in each of the implication networks have taken place, the updated nodes are recorded in a list $link_{updated}$. It will be used by inference with association rules, which is described in the next section.

3.2. Algorithm for Inference with Association Rules

Association rules are playing the role of bridging the implication networks in the proposed approach. After the inference with implication network is finished, a list $link_{updated}$ storing all the updated nodes is prepared. Every node in the list will be compared to see if it can be fit into any of the rules in the association rules set $\Re$. Those rules, which each of the items in the antecedent itemset is matched with a node, will be stored in a list $link_{rule}$ used to propagate beliefs from one network to another.

A belief updating function update_belief($X,Rule,q_i$)is used here. It adds all the beliefs of the items in the antecedent itemset X and multiplies the result with the confidence p_c of the corresponding association rule. The result will be combined with the current beliefs of each of the items in the consequent itemset Y with the Dempster's Rule of Combination as their new beliefs.

The algorithm of inference with association rules can be stated as follows:

Algorithm 4: Inference with Association Rules
Begin
    For each $Rule \in \Re$
        if for every item i in antecedent itemset X there match a node in $link_{updated}$,
            Insert($Rule$, $link_{rule}$);

For each *Rule* in link$_{rule}$
    For each item q_i in consequent itemset Y
    Begin
      $Bel(q_i) \leftarrow$ update_belief(X,*Rule*,q_i)
      If $\Delta Bel(q_k)>$ a threshold, • , **then**
         Insert(the corresponding implication network of q_k, queue$_{net}$);
    End
End

After the inference with association rules, a queue of implication network, queue$_{net}$, is ready for storing those networks having significantly changed nodes. If the queue is not empty, another cycle of inference with implication network will start, and the whole process iterates until no more significant update can be made.

In summary, the inference scheme that we have proposed can be stated as follows:

The Inference Scheme
Begin
    Store all the implication networks with observed nodes in queue$_{net}$
    Repeat
      For each implication network in *Net* in queue$_{net}$
         perform Inference with Implication Networks with *Net* (Algorithm 3)
         perform Inference with Association Rules (Algorithm 4)
    Until queue$_{net}$ is empty.
End

4. Empirical Validation on Financial Market Analysis

In order to validate our proposed approach, we analyze several markets with an associated network structure discovered from empirical market data. Specifically, the validation aims at finding out the relationships between various financial markets around the world, such as stock, bond, commodity and currency markets. These relationships form an associated network structure which allows further analysis of market trends.

Murphy [12] points out the existing key relationships between the financial markets around the globe. Among others, there are four principal interrelated market sectors, namely currencies, commodities, bonds and stocks. Besides, interest rates also play a significant role in affecting the markets. Although it is difficult to conclude which market action precedes, a rough model can be drawn as in Figure 5.

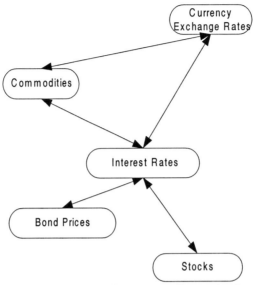

Figure 5. An economic model drawn according to the description of
market actions by Murphy [12].

The idea of the validation process is inspired by the fore mentioned
relationships. If these relationships hold, some empirical data samples of the
above markets can be used to discover a proposed network structure which
reflects the relationships. The empirically derived network structure can further
be used to analyze the trends of the involved markets. The goal of the validation
process is twofold:

1. It shows the ability of the proposed approach to discover an associated
   network structure from some empirical data samples if the samples are
   extracted from some interrelated financial markets.
2. It demonstrates the analysis capability of the proposed approach by using
   the inference scheme.

4.1. The Validation Procedure

In order to achieve the above goal, we will carry out two validation experiments
based on the following procedure:

1. **Selection of Financial Markets to be Analyzed.** According to the
   relationships pointed out by Murphy [12], select a set of interrelated
   financial markets and other related economic indicators for our analysis.
2. **Preparation of Empirical Data Samples.** Prepare empirical data
   samples from the selected set of financial markets in Step 1. This process

includes the gathering, preprocessing and storing of empirical data samples. Besides, these empirical data samples will further be divided into a training set and testing set of empirical data to discover and validate an associated network structure, respectively.

3. **Discovering an Associated Network Structure**. In this step, the training set prepared in Step 2 will be used to discover an associated network structure by using the induction and mining algorithms as described above.

4. **Analysis using the Discovered Network Structure**. The future trends of the selected financial markets in Step 1 are analyzed with some given evidences. Here, the empirical data samples in the testing set are used. For each of the samples, the computer randomly picks two nodes and uses their values as evidences. The updated beliefs of other nodes reflect the trends of the corresponding markets.

5. **Analysis Evaluation.** The inferred nodes are compared with those in the empirical data samples in the testing set to validate the analysis results of the proposed approach.

The validation procedure can be summarized in a flowchart as in Figure 4.

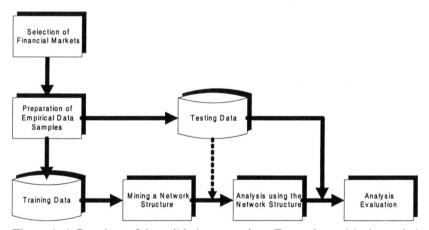

Figure 4. A flowchart of the validation procedure. For each empirical sample in the testing data, two nodes will be randomly picked (dotted line) to analyze other nodes. The actual data of the other nodes (solid line) will be compared with the inferred results.

4.2. Settings for the Validation Experiments

The actual settings in our validation experiments are as follows:

1. **Financial Market Selection.** With reference to the key intermarket relationships defined by Murphy [12], markets from the four principal

market sectors from the United States and Japan are selected. The discovered network structure is expected to be similar to the economic model described above in Figure 5. In our study, some economic indicators will also be added as random variables to examine their effect to the markets. Specifically, the following financial indices and indicators will be used to represent the aforementioned markets. The following represents the financial markets in the United States:

   a) **USD Index**. It is an index created based on the exchange rate of the U.S. dollars to a bracket of other foreign currencies. This index can reflect the value of U.S. dollars.

   b) **CRB Index**. The Commodity Research Bureau in the United States created this index to reflect the value of a basket of 21 commodities. This index can reflect the value of the most frequently trades commodities in different commodity markets.

   c) **10-Year Treasury Bond Yield**. Treasury Bonds refers to the bonds issued by the government of the United States. 10-year treasury bond yield is used in the case study to reflect the direction of the bond market. Bond prices and yields move in opposite direction. Readers may refer to Faerber [7] for a explanation for this phenomenon.

   d) **Dow Jones Industrial Average**. It is a weighted average of the 30 most actively traded blue chip stocks listed on the New York Stock Exchange. It is used in the case study as a barometer of the U.S. stock market.

   e) **Federal Reserve Fund Rate**. It is an indicator of the direction of the interest rate in the United States. Economists point out that the interest rate of a country affects a lot the financial markets, so the interest rate is also considered in our case study.

and the following five indices and indicators reflect the market directions in Japan:

   f) **Nikkei 225 Stock Average**. It is a Japanese equivalent of the U.S.'s Dow Jones Industrial Average. It is a price-weighted average of 225 stocks listed on the Tokyo Stock Exchange.

   g) **Japanese Yen Effective Exchange Rate**. It is a Japanese equivalent of the USD Index. It is calculated based on the exchange rate of the Japanese Yen to a bracket of other currencies. This indicator reflects the strength of the Japanese Yen.

   h) **Japanese 10-Year Benchmark Bond Yield**. It is the yield of the Japanese government issued bond. Again, this yield goes in opposite direction with the bond price. It reflects the direction of the bond market in Japan.

i) **Japanese Discount Rate**. A Japanese equivalent of the U.S. Federal Reserve Fund Rate. It reflects the direction of the interest rate in Japan.

j) **Composite Index of Business Indicators**. It is a composite index calculated based on various leading indices in Japan. It reflects the current economic situation in Japan. The higher the index the better the economy, and as the economy blooms, other markets would follow the direction of the index.

A summary of the selected markets is presented in Table 1.

	Japanese Market	U.S. Market
Currencies	Japanese Yen Effective Exchange Rate	USD Index
Commodities		CRB Index
Stocks	Nikkei 225 Stock Average	Dow Jones Industrial Average
Bonds	10-Year Benchmark Bond Yield	10-Year Treasury Bond Yield
Interest Rates	Discount Rate	Federal Reserve Fund Rate
Other Indicators	Composite Index of Business Indicators	

Table 1. Selected financial markets and its corresponding indices or indicators as in the case study.

. **Preparation of Empirical Data Samples**. In this case study, data is gathered from the Internet and a financial service institute. Since the case study aims at investigating the long-term relationships of the selected financial markets, monthly data is chosen for the experiments. The data collected is within the period of December 1982 to December 2001, inclusively.

The data gathered, however, is only in a form of numerical values. In the current study, we are interested in the relationships between the markets, e.g., if the greenback goes down, the commodities go up. Therefore, it is necessary to define what is 'up' (increase) and what is 'down' (decrease) before any actual experiments can be carried out. Therefore, data has to be preprocessed to show the up and down trends of the markets.

Various methods can be used for this purpose, including the use of single moving average, double moving average and comparison of volatility [16]. Among others, the use of a single moving average line yields the best result in the experiments. A moving average, as explained by Murphy [12], works as follows:

"...Moving averages smooth out price action but operate with a time lag. A simple 10-day moving average of a stock, for example, adds up the last 10 days' closing price and divides the total by 10. This procedure is repeated each day. Any number of moving averages can be employed, with different time spans..."

Mathematically, a moving average consists of average values of closing prices of *n* recent days. In the current case study, the time span of the moving averages is 12 months, i.e., $n = 12$.

With a moving average, 'increase' and 'decrease' can be defined. Specifically, if the value of day k on the moving average is larger than that of day $k-1$, there is an upward trend in the market (increase), and vice versa.

The monthly uptrends and downtrends are obtained by comparing the values on the moving averages. Some example samples are given in Table 2.

	USD Index	Dow Jones	Nikkei 225	Discount Rate
Jan 1990	0	1	0	0
Feb 1990	1	0	1	1
Mar 1990	0	0	0	1
Apr 1990	0	1	0	0
May 1990	0	0	1	1

0 = downtrend 1 = uptrend

Table 2. Some examples of preprocessed empirical data samples with defined downtrend and uptrend.

For the sake of computational efficiency and convenience for the upcoming experimental steps, we further preprocess the data by initially defining the anticipated relationships between the markets according to the economic model illustrated by Murphy [12]. In other words, we associate an initially defined 'uptrend' or 'downtrend' with each random variable. This would allow the later induction to take care about only the positive implications (A $\Rightarrow$ B and ~B $\Rightarrow$ ~A) and negative implications (B $\Rightarrow$ A and ~A $\Rightarrow$ ~B) between the selected random variables. This act would not affect the final experimental result, as eventually other impossible implication relationships such as forward-negative implications and inverse negative implications will simply be rejected during the hypothesis tests in the implication network induction stage.

The initially defined directions for the random variables are as follows:

U.S. Market
  a) USD Index *Decreases*;
  b) CRB Index *Increases*;
  c) Federal Reserve Fund Rate *Increases*;
  d) 10-Year Treasury Bond Yield *Increases*;
  e) Dow Jones Industrial Moving Average *Decreases*;

Japanese Market
  f) Japanese Discount Rate *Increases*;
  g) Nikkei 225 Stock Average *Decreases*;
  h) Japanese Yen Real Effective Exchange Rate *Decreases*;
  i) 10-Year Benchmark Bond Yield *Increases*;
  j) Composite Index of Business Indicators *Decreases*.

Some examples of data samples after this preprocessing step are illustrated in Table 3.

	USD Index Down	Dow Jones Down	Nikkei 225 Down	Discount Rate Up
Jan 1989	0	0	0	1
Feb 1989	1	0	1	1
Mar 1989	1	0	0	1
Apr 1989	0	1	0	1
May 1989	1	0	1	1

0 = false 1 = true

Table 3. Some examples of preprocessed empirical data samples after the second preprocessing step.

The empirical data samples are further divided into a training set for the discovery of an associated network structure and a testing set for analysis and validation. In the case study, the training set includes empirical data samples from November 1983 to November 1992, inclusively. The testing set includes those from December 1992 to December 2001, inclusively. Note that the empirical data samples from December 1982 to November 1983, inclusively, are used for calculating the moving average values of December 1983 to November 1984, inclusively. That explains why they are not included in any of the sets.

3. **Discovery of an Associated Network Structure.** As pointed out by Murphy [12], the local financial markets influence each other more than the international markets do. In this connection, two implication networks will be generated: one for the U.S. market and one for the Japanese market. The implication relationships within implication networks show the strong influences between the markets in a local perspective, and the

association rules linking up the two implication networks show the weaker relations between the international markets.

The significance level α_c and a minimum conditional probability p_{min} for the implication networks are 0.2 and 0.5, respectively. These parameters yield reasonable networks showing the implication relations of the financial markets. The minimum confidence p_c and minimum support s for the association rule mining are 0.6 and 0.1, respectively.

4.3. Experimental Results

This section presents the discovered network structure, and the analysis and validation results obtained from two experiments conducted with the discovered network structure.

4.3.1. The Discovered Network Structure

With the empirical data samples from the training set, the following implication networks can be discovered with the induction algorithm as stated in Section 2 (Figures 6 and 7).

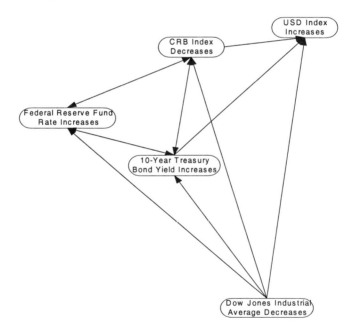

Figure 6. An implication network for the U.S. financial markets
$(p_{min}= 0.5, \alpha_c= 0.2)$.

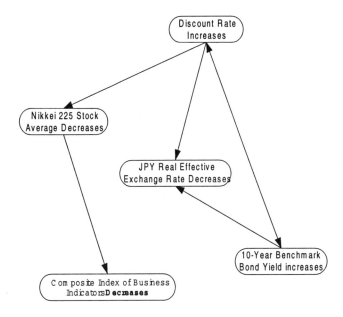

Figure 7. An implication network for the Japanese financial markets
(p_{min}= 0.5, α_c= 0.2).

4.3.2. Association Rules Connecting the Networks

After the induction of the two implication networks, the selected financial markets are used to generate itemsets for mining association rules. The following association rules can be mined with the empirical data samples from the training set with the mining algorithm as stated in Section 2.

Rule 1: {Japanese 10-Year Benchmark Bond Yield Increases/Decreases} →
{10-Year Treasury Bond Yield Increases/Decreases}
Rule 2: {Japanese 10-Year Benchmark Bond Yield Increases/Decreases} →
{CRB Index Increases/Decrease}
Rule 3. {Composit Index of Business Indicators Decreases/Increases} →
{USD Index Decreases/Increases}
Rule 4. {Nikkei 225 Stock Average Decreases/Increases} →
{USD Index Decreases/Increases}
Rule 5. {Nikkei 225 Stock Average Decreases/Increases, Composit Index of Business Indicators Decreases/Increases} →
{USD Index Decreases/Increases}
Rule 6. {USD Index Decreases/Increases, Dow Jones Industrial Average Decreases/Increases} →

{10-Year Benchmark Bond Yield Increases/Increases}
Rule 7. {USD Index Decreases/Increases, 10-Year Treasury Bond Yield Increases/Decreases, Dow Jones Industrial Average Decreases/Increases} → {10-Year Benchmark Bond Yield Increases/Decreases}

The above association rules, along with the two implication networks, constitute an associated network structure as defined in Section 2.

4.3.3. Experiment to Evaluate the Overall Analysis Performance

In this experiment, two nodes from the U.S. markets are randomly picked from each monthly empirical data sample as observed evidence. When the observed value is TRUE, a belief value of 1 is given to the node. On the other hand, if the observed value is FALSE, a belief value of 0 is given. The beliefs of the other nodes in the two implication networks are revised accordingly with the implication relationships and association rules. When the updated belief value of a node is larger than 0.5, a TRUE value is assigned to the node, or vice versa. The estimated values of the updated nodes are further compared to the actual values in the same empirical data samples in the same month. Meanwhile, the total number of correct guesses is recorded. In the experiment, the above process is repeated five times and each of them will be referred to as a "cycle" in the following discussions.

For each cycle, all the 109 monthly empirical data samples in the testing set are used. We record the total number of correct and incorrect guesses within the implication network corresponding to the U.S. financial markets, and also the total number of correct and incorrect guesses by the association rules and the implication network corresponding to the Japanese financial markets.

The experimental data is summarized in Table 4.

Cycle	Analysis using the U.S. Implication Network			Analysis using the Association Rules and the Japanese Implication Network		
	Correct Guesses	Incorrect Guesses	Accuracy (%)	Correct Guesses	Incorrect Guesses	Accuracy (%)
1	118	84	58.4158	52	35	59.7701
2	122	81	60.0985	49	29	62.8205
3	122	80	60.3960	84	40	67.7419
4	108	80	57.4468	74	32	69.8113
5	103	81	55.9783	63	23	73.2558

Table 4. Analysis results using (1) the U.S. implication network and (2) association rules and the Japanese implication network.

The mean of the analysis accuracies using the U.S. market implication network is 58.4671 percent, with a standard deviation of 1.8453 percent. For the other nodes in the Japanese market implication network, the mean of the analysis accuracies is 66.6799 percent, with a standard deviation of 5.4041 percent. The overall analysis performances of the discovered network structure are shown in Table 5.

In general, the accuracies of analysis using the discovered network structure remain stable at around 60 percent. Specifically, the mean of the accuracies is 61.2508 percent, with a small standard deviation of 1.604 percent.

Cycle	Overall Performance		
	Correct Guesses	Incorrect Guesses	Accuracy (%)
1	170	119	58.8235
2	171	110	60.8541
3	206	120	63.1902
4	182	112	61.9048
5	166	104	61.4815

Table 5. Overall analysis performances using the discovered network structure.

4.3.4. Experiment to Investigate the Effect of the Number of Observed Nodes on Analysis Performance

In this experiment, the number of nodes observed as evidences is controlled to see its effect on analysis performances. The experimental procedure is similar to that in the preceding experiments, except the number of observed nodes which will be different. The mean and standard deviation of the analysis accuracies with the U.S. markets implication network are provided in Table 6.

Number of Nodes Observed	Mean Accuracy (%)	Standard Deviation (%)
1	59.91	2.40
2	58.47	1.85
3	55.74	2.32

Table 6. Overall analysis performances using the discovered network structure with different number of nodes observed.

4.4. Discussion

The experiments show that the proposed analysis approach is able to model international financial markets with an automatic means of discovering an associated network structure. Given some correlated financial markets with empirical data samples, the proposed approach can derive two implication networks, one represents the U.S. financial markets while the other represents the Japanese financial markets (Section 4.3.1). The association rules discovered can also connect the two implication networks (Section 4.3.2).

Despite the relatively low analysis accuracy of approximately sixty percent, the experiments demonstrate the analysis ability of our proposed approach (Section 4.3.3). It is believed that the innate weakly correlated nature of the financial markets is accountable for the low accuracy. The stability of the proposed approach, however, is remarkably high. This is reflected by the small standard deviation of the analysis accuracy (1.604 percent). Undoubtedly, the stability of a analysis approach is of fundamental importance, as its performance can be predicted, audited and controlled when it is actually implemented in real-world applications. The experiments show that the proposed approach can effectively demonstrate this inevitable characteristic.

One surprising result, as mentioned before, is that the analysis accuracy decreased slightly as the number of observed nodes increased (Section 4.4.4). The reason, subject to further examination, is that multiple-path traversal is allowed in the multiply connected implication networks in this study. This would allow the recent observed node to have enormous influences on the neighboring nodes through multiple paths. This would be destructive enough to override the effects of the previously observed node, thus affecting the analysis result.

Two of the important components in *Net* are the minimal conditional probability p_{min} and the induction error tolerance α_c. These parameters vary from networks to networks according to the nature of the financial market. For those implication networks representing weakly correlated markets, the value of p_{min} may be smaller and that of α_c is higher, or vice versa. In our experiments, the two networks have the same p_{min} and α_c of 0.5 and 0.2, respectively. However, in other applications which use an associated network structure consisted of both strongly and weakly correlated financial markets, the implication networks may have different p_{min} and α_c to reflect the unique nature of the markets. Because of the uniqueness of the implication networks, it is necessary to find a way to bridge them in an associated network structure, and association rules provide a good means to do so.

5. Conclusion

This paper has presented a novel approach to analyzing financial intermarket actions with a combination of implication networks and association rules. The proposed approach contains an automatic means for discovering an associated network structure which consists of implication networks and association rules. The potential of the proposed approach was studied with empirical validation experiments. Specifically, the overall analysis performance of analyzing various future market trends and the effect of the number of observed nodes on the analysis performance were studied. It was found that the associated network structure discovered from empirical data samples yielded satisfactory and stable results.

As can be noted from the experiments, one factor seriously affecting analysis results is the way of traversing the implication networks. An interesting extension of the present work, therefore, would be to investigate the optimal traversing method for the implication networks. Although Charniak [4] points out there may not exists any single belief network evaluation method for all the applications, an automatic means for finding the most suitable evaluation scheme for a network should be found out. This could make the whole network structure discovery and inference process fully automatic.

References

[1]   Agrawal, R., and Shafer, J. C., Fast Algorithm for Mining Association Rules, In *Proceedings of the 20th International Conference on Very Large Databases*, Santiago, Chile, 1994.

[2]   Bowes, J., Neufeld, E., Greer, J. E., and Cooke, J. A, Comparison of Association Rule Discovery and Bayesian Network Causal Inference Algorithms to Discover Relationships in Discrete Data. In *Proceedings of Canadian Conference on AI*, pages 326-336, 2000.

[3]   Cengiz, • ., *Mining Association Rules*, Department of Computer Engineering and Information Science, Bilkent University, Turkey, 1998.

[4]   Charniak, E., Bayesian Networks without Tears. *AI Magazine,* pages 53-61, 1991.

[5]   Cooper, G. F., and Herskovits, E., A Bayesian Method for the Induction of Probabilistic Networks from Data, *Machine Learning,* 9, pages 309-347, 1992.

[6]   Desmarais, M. C., Maluf, A., and Liu, J., User-expertise modeling with empirically derived probabilistic implication networks. *User Modeling and User Adaptive Interactions*, 5(3-4), pages 283-315, 1996.

[7]   Faerber, E., *Fundamentals of the Bond Market*. McGraw-Hill, 2001.

[8]   Geiger, D., An Entropy-Based Learning Algorithm of Bayesian Conditional Trees, *Uncertainty in Artificial Intelligence,* pages 92-97, San Mateo, California, 1992.

[9]   Geiger, D., Paz, A., and Pearl, J., Learning Simple Causal Structures, *International Journal of Intelligent Systems*, 8, pages 231-247, 1993.

[10]   Giarratano, J., Riley, G., *Expert Systems: Principles and Programming*, pages 275-290. Boston, PWS-KENT, 1989.

[11]   Liu, J., Desmarais, M. C., A Method of Learning Implication Networks from Empirical Data: Algorithm and Monte-Carlo Simulation-Based Validation. *IEEE Transactions on Knowledge and Data Engineering,* 9(6), pages 990-1004, 1997.

[12]   Murphy, J. J., *Intermarket Technical Analysis: Trading Strategies for the Global Stock, Bond, Commodity, and Currency Markets.* John Wiley, 1991.

[13]   Myers, J. W., Laskey, K. B., and DeJong, K. A., Learning Bayesian Networks from Incomplete Data using Evolutionary Algorithms. In *Proceedings of the Genetic and Evolutionary Computation Conference.* Orlando, FL, Morgan Kaufmann, 1999.

[14]   Olesen, K.G., Lauritzen, S. L., and Jensen, F. V., aHUGiN: A System Creating Adaptive Causal Probabilistic Networks, *Uncertainty in Artificial Intelligence,* pages 223-229, San Mateo, California.

[15]   Pitas, I., Milios, E., and Venetsanopoulos, A. N., A Minimum Entropy Approach to Rule Learning from Examples. *IEEE Transactions on Systems, Man and Cybernetics,* 22(4), pages 621-635.

[16]   Schwager, J. D., *Schwager on Futures: Technical Analysis.* John Wiley, 1996.

[17]   Srikant, R., Fast Algorithms for Mining Association Rules and Sequential Patterns, *Ph. D. Thesis,* University of Wisconsin-Madison, 1996.

[18]   VanLehn, K., Niu, Z., Siler, S., and Gertner, A., Student Modeling from Conventional Test Data: A Bayesian Approach without Priors. In *Proceedings of the 4th Intelligent Tutoring Systems ITS98 Conference,* pages 434-443. Berlin Heidelberg, Springer-Verlag, 1998.

AUTOMATING TECHNICAL ANALYSIS

PHILIP L.H. YU

Department of Statistics and Actuarial Science
The University of Hong Kong
Pokfulam Road, Hong Kong
E-mail: plhyu@hku.hk

K. LAM

Department of Finance and Decision Science
Hong Kong Baptist University
Waterloo Road, Kowloon, Hong Kong
E-mail: lamkin@hkbu.edu.hk

S. H. NG

Department of Statistics and Actuarial Science
The University of Hong Kong
Pokfulam Road, Hong Kong
E-mail: sshng@graduate.hku.hk

Technical analysis aims at identifying trading signals via the detection of patterns by visual inspection of price charts. However, the effectiveness of the inspection depends on technical analysts' subjective judgement. This paper proposes a systematic approach of detecting chart patterns and their trading signals. We suggest using the filter rule to identify the local extrema. We apply the proposed method to the daily stock price data of Hong Kong in the period from 1980 to 1999.

1. Introduction

Despite the academicians' strong belief in the efficient market hypothesis of the semi-strong form, which claims that on a risk-adjusted basis, no additional benefit will be gained by using public information related to the stock market, market practitioners still practise fundamental and technical analysis in order to time the market. Among the technical analysts, some rely on quantitative measures like moving averages and momentum indicators, others rely on chart patterns like resistance and support lines, head-and-shoulders etc. From an empirical point of view, it is easier to judge whether the technical indicators of the first kind work or not, because the buy/sell signals can be constructed on a rigorous basis and hence their effectiveness can be tested. Empirical tests of this kind are abundant in the literature, see for example, Bessembinder and Chan (1995), Bollerslev and Hodrick (1999), Brook, Lakonishok and LeBaron (1992), Corrado and Lee (1992), Hudson, Dempsey and Keasey (1996), Lukac, Brorsen and Irwin (1988), Chang and Osler (1999), Sweeney (1988) and Taylor (1992), just to name a few. On the other hand, empirical tests on the effectiveness of chart patterns are difficult because technical analysts rely on their own subjective judgement to detect a pattern, and one analyst may differ from another on the formation of a particular chart pattern. Recently Lo, Mamayski and Wang (2000) proposed to bridge this gulf between technical analysis and quantitative finance by developing a systematic approach to identify chart patterns by modern techniques in pattern recognition. Basically, they first smooth the daily prices by kernel regression where a suitable bandwidth has to be determined using cross-validation methods. Using data over a 31-year sample period, they showed that certain technical patterns do provide incremental information and may have some practical values.

While it is fruitful to reproduce a chart pattern by automated means, such an automation process is not entirely problem-free. For example, in Lo et al. (2000) they have to modify the cross-validated bandwidth in order that the patterns obtained match well with those observed by the technical analysts. They admitted that the approach is ad hoc and "it remains an important challenge for future research to develop a more rigorous pattern." They further suggested that kernel estimators suffer from a number of well-known deficiencies and alternatives have to be considered for further improvements in the pattern-recognition algorithm.

This paper attempts to offer an alternative algorithm to automatically identify chart patterns. Instead of using sophisticated techniques unfamiliar to technical analysts, we use methods popular among technical analysts to identify peaks and troughs in a time series of stock prices. The details will be given in Section two of the paper. Other than using a new algorithm to automatically identify chart patterns, this paper also contributes in testing whether the chart patterns can help in improving trading performances. One problem in trading signals arising from charting patterns is that they signify a trend but they do not specify when the trend will reverse. This paper deals with this problem by using the event study methodology proposed by Brown and Warner (1985). In this paper, we treat the onset of a trading signal as an event and cumulative returns on following days will be computed and analysed by standard event study techniques as in Fung, Mok and Lam (2000).

Section 2 of this paper will report the methods in identifying peaks and troughs in a price chart. Section 3 will describe the data and the event methodology for later analysis. Section 4 contains the empirical findings and its interpretation. Section 5 concludes the paper.

2. Identifying Peaks and Troughs in a Price Chart

Mathematically speaking, it is easy to identify a local minimum price and a local maximum price in a chart of stock prices. If a price p_t satisfies the condition that p_t is larger than p_{t+1} and p_{t-1}, then p_t is identified as a local maximum. Similarly if p_t is smaller than p_{t+1} and p_{t-1} then p_t is identified as a local minimum. However, some of these local extrema are not important in the eyes of a chartist because there are not enough price movements around the extrema. For a price to be at a peak, prices must have rose sufficiently from some low before, and it must fall sufficiently after the formation of a peak. Similarly for a price to be at a trough, prices must have fallen sufficiently before from some peak, and it must rebound sufficiently after the formation of a trough. This idea of having sufficient price movement as a pre-condition for peaks and troughs is actually not new in the finance literature. In Alexander (1961, 1964), a trading rule is introduced which generates a sell signal when prices fall from a high by more than $100c\%$, and generates a buy signal when prices rise from a low by more than $100c\%$. Here c is referred to as a filter size and the trading rule is called a filter rule in the finance literature. It is one of the most studied trading rules for the purpose of testing the efficient market hypothesis. Chang and Osler (1999) also mentioned the identification of peaks and troughs using similar methods, but they did not point out the relevance to the filter trading rule. By linking it to the filter trading rule, one advantage is that the filter size can have economic meaning which will be explained later.

While the emphasis of a filter rule is on the buy/sell signals it generates, an implicit step in a filter rule is the concept of peaks and troughs. Since a sell signal is generated when prices have dropped sufficiently from a high, the high before the sell signal is then a peak. Similarly, since a sell signal is generated when prices have rose sufficiently from a low, the relevant low can then be treated as at a trough. We will explain this idea using stock prices as shown in Figure 1.

Initially the stock price is $50. Consider a 3% filter rule for this particular stock. Once the price rises above $51.5 (3% above $50), we buy the stock and hold it until its price drops below $58.2 (3% below the subsequent high of $60). Then we sell the stock and wait for the next buy signal that appears when its price rises above $41.2 (3% above the subsequent low $40). The high of $60 and the low of $40 referred to in the filter rule are naturally taken as a peak and a trough of the time series of prices. Note that there exist other local minima between the drop from $60 to $40 (point A in Figure 1 for example) but they should be ignored because the local movement there are not large enough to guarantee the formation of a trough.

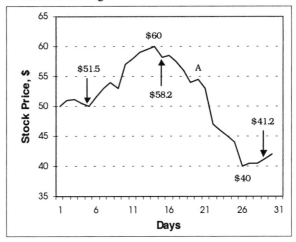

Figure 1. A 3% filter trading rule.

Notice that here peaks and troughs are defined once a filter size is specified. Since chartists may be using different filter sizes to discern local extrema, it is understandable that they may identify different peaks and troughs and hence different chart patterns. In this paper, we choose a filter size so that the chance of emergence of a particular pattern agrees with that of the chartists. In other words, we are estimating the average filter sizes of the chartists by choosing its value so that the number of patterns identified equals to the average number of patterns identified by a group of chartists. It is interesting to note that the filter size so chosen agrees well with the economical interpretation of a filter size. In Lam and Lam (2000), it is proved that to obtain the best peaks and troughs that can identify perfect buy/sell timing, one has to use a filter rule with filter size equal to the 1-way transaction cost. It turns out that the analysts have automatically taken transaction costs into their judgment and come up with a filter size comparable to a cost of transaction.

Once we have automated the identification of peaks and troughs, charting patterns such as head-and shoulders, inverted head-and shoulders, broadening tops and bottoms, triangle tops and bottoms, rectangle tops and bottoms, double tops and bottoms can then be identified using the same techniques as in Lo et al. (2000). In the following section we will describe the data and describe the method of analysis once the charting patterns are identified.

3. Data and Methodology

Daily data for the stocks traded in the main board of the Hong Kong Exchange and Clearing Limited in the period from January 1980 to December 1999 are used in the present study. We split the data into four five-year periods: 1980-1984, 1985-1989, 1990-1994 and 1995-1999. To obtain a broad cross section of stocks, in each period, we randomly select 5 stocks from each of five market-capitalization quintiles. Altogether there are 129904 stock trading days in the sample data. Various filter sizes are used to detect local extrema as described in Section 2. As the filter size increases, the number of extrema decreases. Once we have identified the extrema, we can use the rules described in Lo et al. (2000) to identify the various chart patterns. For example, for the formation of a head-and-shoulders top, we need a sequence of five extrema E1, E2, E3, E4 and E5 satisfying the following conditions:

(1) E1 is a maximum,
(2) E1>E2 and E3>E5,
(3) E1 and E5 are within 1.5% of their average,
(4) E2 and E4 are within 1.5% of their average,
(5) A subsequent price (S) drops below the line joining E2 and E4 (see Figure 2) where S signifies a sell signal,
(6) The number of trading days between E5 and S is five days or less,
(7) The number of trading days between E1 and S is 30 days or less.

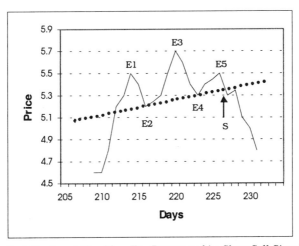

Figure 2. A Head-and-Shoulders Top Pattern and its Short Sell Signal.

Criteria (1)-(4) are to detect the possible formation of a head-and-shoulders pattern and criteria (5)-(7) are to detect if there is any suitable selling opportunity subsequent to the formation of the pattern.

As in Lo et al. (2000), the following chart patterns are studied. They are head-and- shoulders tops (HST), head-and-shoulders bottoms (HSB), broadening tops (BROADT) and bottoms (BROADB), triangle tops (TRIT) and bottoms (TRIB), rectangle tops (RECT) and bottoms (RECB), and double tops (DOUBLET) and bottoms (DOUBLEB). The number of extrema together with the number of chart patterns detected for each filter size is presented in Table 1.

Table 1. Number of Extrema and Chart Patterns Detected.

Chart Patterns	Filter Size					
	0.6%	0.8%	1.0%	1.2%	1.4%	1.6%
HST	1290	1163	1039	929	818	715
HSB	1215	1041	898	782	722	623
BROADT	223	209	209	200	200	194
BROADB	244	238	218	209	208	212
TRIT	524	477	447	423	396	360
TRIB	523	480	459	448	426	408
RECT	875	727	627	534	466	402
RECB	966	813	681	586	515	438
DOUBLET	599	561	549	518	489	457
DOUBLEB	620	582	555	516	496	463
Number of Extrema	38555	35777	33351	31221	29375	27261

To evaluate the trading effectiveness of the chart patterns, we first have to fix a filter size. As is mentioned in Section 2, we choose a filter size so that the incidence rate of a chart pattern per stock is roughly equal to that identified by technical analysts. Take the head-and-shoulders top for example. If we use a filter size of 1.6%, the total number of patterns per stock is about 1.4 per year and if we use a filter size of 1.0%, the total number of patterns per stock is about 2.1 per year. These incidence rates sound close to those detected by technical analysts. Hence the appropriate filter size is 1.0%-1.6%. In the following, we only report the results using these two filter sizes.

Subsequent to the formation of a chart pattern, the stock's price will have a break-through and that gives the on-set of a buy or sell signal, which is now treated as an event and is subjected to the standard treatment of an event study. For example, in the head-and-shoulders top pattern, the point S in Figure 2 signifies the on-set of a sell signal. The day when the signal is triggered is designated as day 0 in the event study. The stock's returns as well as the trading profits in the following days are recorded. We also record the cumulative returns of the stock and cumulative trading profits in subsequent days. Notice here that for a sell signal, the trading profit is equal to the negative of the stock's return. The performance of the trading strategy will then be compared to that of a buy-and-hold strategy the profit of which will be estimated by the long-term performance of the particular stock concerned.

4. Empirical Results

Table 2 tabulates the cumulative profit of the ten trading strategies and the cumulative profit for the buy-and-hold strategy. The filter rule used here is 1.0%. For each trading rule, we report the cumulative average trading profits for one up to ten days. The standard error of each average profit is also provided and so is the t-statistic, a test statistic for the alternative hypothesis that the average head-and-shoulder trading profit is larger than the average profit of the buy-and-hold strategy. Table 3 tabulates similar results when the filter size used is 1.6% instead of 1.0%.

Figure 3 plots the cumulative profits of the trading rules when the filter size used is 1.6%. The corresponding plot when the filter size is 1.0% is quite similar and will be omitted here.

It can be seen that not all ten trading rules are reliable. Among ten trading rules, only head-and-shoulders bottom, triangle tops and triangle bottoms can beat the buy-and-hold strategy for some holding periods. In particular, triangle bottoms can achieve a significant larger cumulative profit than the buy-and-hold strategy for holding periods of various lengths. It is interesting to see that the rectangle tops always perform significantly poorer than the buy-and-hold strategy. This indicates that the sell signals generated by the rectangle tops might worthy be treated as buy signals. Further study in this aspect is needed.

Table 2. Cumulative Profit of Trading Strategies for Filter Size of 1.0%.

Trading Patterns	Profit (%)	Trading Days									
		1	2	3	4	5	6	7	8	9	10
HST	Mean	-0.02	0.09	-0.10	0.10	0.12	-0.10	0.01	-0.29	-0.34	-0.18
	SD	2.86	3.58	4.85	5.31	6.19	6.66	7.81	8.20	8.74	9.46
	t-stat.	-0.20	0.60	-0.63	0.38	0.38	-0.53	-0.10	-1.08	-1.18	-0.65
HSB	Mean	0.12	0.33	0.55	0.72	0.61	0.51	0.46	0.69	0.61	0.86
	SD	3.59	4.54	5.84	6.72	7.46	8.48	8.45	8.97	9.52	10.14
	t-stat.	0.77	1.64	2.18	2.48	1.87	1.32	1.18	1.70	1.38	1.89
BROADT	Mean	0.41	-2.85	-2.21	-2.69	-3.20	-3.17	-2.70	-1.99	-0.79	0.19
	SD	3.27	8.19	9.96	11.17	15.96	18.55	19.06	19.73	20.19	21.08
	t-stat.	0.46	-1.31	-0.84	-0.91	-0.76	-0.65	-0.54	-0.39	-0.16	0.02
BROADB	Mean	0.01	0.53	2.33	3.70	2.89	2.53	2.16	2.34	2.97	0.63
	SD	2.82	5.52	6.05	7.00	6.81	8.35	7.90	9.55	10.05	9.93
	t-stat.	0.00	0.30	1.21	1.66	1.33	0.95	0.85	0.76	0.92	0.18
TRIT	Mean	0.29	0.39	0.71	0.36	0.43	0.22	0.01	-0.28	-0.51	-0.64
	SD	4.29	5.44	6.16	6.86	8.06	9.11	10.07	11.22	12.46	13.34
	t-stat.	1.32	1.39	2.24	0.96	0.98	0.40	-0.07	-0.57	-0.88	-1.04
TRIB	Mean	0.76	1.00	1.28	1.24	0.89	0.81	0.90	1.04	1.07	0.91
	SD	3.93	5.38	6.58	8.08	10.02	11.01	11.46	12.58	12.21	14.28
	t-stat.	3.88	3.71	3.88	3.05	1.74	1.43	1.51	1.59	1.68	1.20
RECT	Mean	-0.48	-0.65	-0.73	-0.62	-0.71	-0.82	-0.79	-0.92	-1.08	-1.19
	SD	2.63	3.30	4.17	4.86	5.82	5.94	7.07	6.79	7.51	8.07
	t-stat.	-3.59	-3.86	-3.47	-2.54	-2.43	-2.77	-2.27	-2.74	-2.90	-2.98
RECB	Mean	-0.66	-0.34	-0.30	-0.12	0.06	0.03	0.04	0.42	0.46	0.72
	SD	4.63	5.01	5.62	5.93	6.66	7.40	7.92	8.31	8.44	8.58
	t-stat.	-2.98	-1.46	-1.17	-0.50	0.10	-0.01	0.00	0.94	1.01	1.59
DOUBLET	Mean	0.22	0.12	0.17	-0.32	-0.54	-0.55	-0.88	-1.06	-1.07	-1.72
	SD	2.55	3.28	4.47	5.06	5.43	5.70	6.15	7.10	6.91	7.61
	t-stat.	0.44	0.18	0.18	-0.36	-0.55	-0.54	-0.79	-0.82	-0.85	-1.23
DOUBLEB	Mean	1.09	0.58	-0.12	-0.10	-0.36	-0.10	0.07	-0.10	-0.15	0.17
	SD	6.41	4.87	4.93	5.67	5.39	5.98	6.74	8.36	8.35	9.41
	t-stat.	1.25	0.87	-0.21	-0.15	-0.54	-0.17	0.04	-0.13	-0.18	0.09
Buy-and-Hold	Mean	0.006	0.011	0.017	0.022	0.028	0.034	0.040	0.045	0.051	0.056

Table 3. Cumulative Profit of Trading Strategies for Filter Size of 1.6%.

Trading Patterns	Profit (%)	Trading Days									
		1	2	3	4	5	6	7	8	9	10
HST	Mean	-0.08	-0.08	0.07	0.39	0.32	0.02	0.01	-0.19	0.00	0.18
	SD	3.06	3.55	4.63	5.31	6.19	6.70	7.95	8.49	9.00	9.74
	t-stat.	-0.57	-0.53	0.23	1.40	0.96	-0.04	-0.07	-0.57	-0.11	0.27
HSB	Mean	-0.02	0.27	0.60	0.79	0.83	0.64	0.62	0.90	1.02	1.33
	SD	4.00	5.00	6.57	7.62	8.31	9.50	9.43	9.95	10.73	11.27
	t-stat.	-0.12	1.00	1.69	1.91	1.83	1.21	1.17	1.64	1.72	2.15
BROADT	Mean	1.35	-2.83	-2.79	-2.81	-1.80	-2.17	-1.75	-0.63	0.22	0.86
	SD	2.44	9.41	11.37	12.78	18.85	21.63	22.63	23.30	23.85	24.74
	t-stat.	1.83	-1.00	-0.82	-0.73	-0.32	-0.34	-0.26	-0.10	0.02	0.11
BROADB	Mean	-0.04	0.23	1.67	2.75	1.50	0.76	1.02	0.40	1.11	-1.24
	SD	3.02	6.05	5.87	4.96	5.42	7.43	7.38	7.56	8.08	9.44
	t-stat.	-0.04	0.10	0.75	1.46	0.72	0.26	0.35	0.12	0.35	-0.36
TRIT	Mean	0.42	0.54	0.93	0.62	0.90	0.90	0.57	0.41	0.20	-0.07
	SD	5.07	6.27	6.86	7.31	7.94	9.05	10.25	11.64	12.87	14.01
	t-stat.	1.35	1.38	2.18	1.33	1.81	1.57	0.85	0.51	0.19	-0.15
TRIB	Mean	0.64	0.85	1.14	1.28	1.21	1.20	1.34	1.53	1.68	1.42
	SD	4.05	5.27	6.50	8.03	9.64	10.82	11.46	12.76	12.22	14.45
	t-stat.	2.84	2.89	3.12	2.84	2.23	1.96	2.05	2.09	2.41	1.70
RECT	Mean	-0.58	-0.92	-0.94	-0.80	-0.83	-1.01	-1.08	-1.30	-1.69	-1.62
	SD	3.14	3.42	4.68	5.35	6.43	5.93	7.56	7.24	8.17	8.95
	t-stat.	-2.63	-3.86	-2.88	-2.17	-1.89	-2.48	-2.08	-2.62	-3.00	-2.64
RECB	Mean	-1.02	-0.61	-0.47	-0.32	-0.12	-0.13	-0.16	0.33	0.40	0.64
	SD	5.44	5.44	6.15	6.36	7.15	7.98	8.64	9.14	9.22	9.28
	t-stat.	-3.01	-1.83	-1.25	-0.86	-0.33	-0.33	-0.38	0.49	0.60	1.01
DOUBLET	Mean	0.35	0.08	0.77	0.28	0.13	0.17	-0.52	-0.82	-1.02	-1.42
	SD	2.74	3.32	5.19	5.91	6.36	7.09	7.31	8.64	8.82	9.32
	t-stat.	0.63	0.10	0.73	0.22	0.08	0.10	-0.38	-0.50	-0.61	-0.79
DOUBLEB	Mean	1.51	1.03	0.49	0.63	0.05	0.42	0.48	0.31	0.38	0.44
	SD	6.60	4.74	4.47	5.32	5.02	5.55	6.35	8.11	8.02	8.97
	t-stat.	1.59	1.50	0.74	0.80	0.03	0.48	0.49	0.23	0.29	0.30
Buy-and-Hold	Mean	0.006	0.011	0.017	0.022	0.028	0.034	0.040	0.045	0.051	0.056

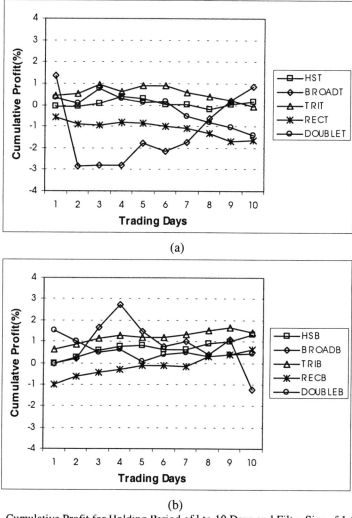

(a)

(b)

Figure 3. Cumulative Profit for Holding Period of 1 to 10 Days and Filter Size of 1.6%.

5. Conclusion

Although human judgment is still superior to most computational algorithms in the field of pattern recognition and signal detection, our attempt to automate the generation of technical trading signals seems to have worked well. It provides a mean of testing whether the trading signals generated are effective or not. It may happen that the signals generated are still different from those visualized by the chartists, but our attempt is to make the art of chart pattern detection more like a science. The idea of using the filter rule to identify the local extrema seems to have worked well here. Since many chart patterns are built upon the identified local extrema, the same techniques can be used to detect other chart patterns not studied in this paper. Currently we are applying the techniques to identify support and resistance lines which are very popular tools for technical analysts. Further findings will be reported in the future.

References

1. S. Alexander, Price movements in speculative markets: trends or random walks. *Industrial Management Review* **II**, 7-26 (1961).
2. S. Alexander, Price movements in speculative markets: trends or random walks, No. 2. *Industrial Management Review* **V**, 25-46 (1964).
3. H. Bessembinder and K. Chan, The profitability of technical trading rules in the Asian stock markets, *Pacific-Basin Finance Journal* **3**, 257-284 (1995).
4. T. Bollerslev and R. J. Hodrick, Financial Market Efficiency Test, In *Handbook of Applied Econometrics, Volume 1: Macroeconomics*, M. H. Pesaran and M. R. Wickens, (eds.), Blackwell Publishers, 415-458 (1999).
5. W. Brook, J. Lakonishok and B. LeBaron, Simple technical trading rules and the stochastic properties of stock returns", *Journal of Finance* **47**, 1731-1764 (1992).
6. S. J. Brown and J. B. Warner, Using daily stock returns: the case of event studies, *Journal of Financial Economics* **14**, 3-32 (1985).
7. P. H. K. Chang and C. L. Osler, Methodical madness: technical analysis and the irrationality of exchange-rate forecasts, *Economic Journal* **109**, 636-661 (1999).
8. C. J. Corrado and S. H. Lee, Filter rule tests of economic significance of serial dependencies in daily stock returns, *Journal of Financial Research* **15**, 369-387 (1992).
9. A. K. W. Fung, D. M. Y. Mok and K. Lam, Intraday price reversals for index futures in the US and Hong Kong, *Journal of Banking and Finance* **24**, 1179-1201 (2000).
10. R. Hudson, M. Dempsey and K. Keasey, A note on the week form efficiency of capital market: The application of simple technical rules to UK stock price—1935 to 1994, *Journal of Banking and Finance* **20**, 1121-1132 (1996).
11. Lam, K. and Lam, K.C., Forecasting for the generation of trading signals in financial markets, *Journal of Forecasting* **19**, 39-52 (2000).
12. A. W. Lo, H. Mamaysky and J. Wang, Foundations of technical analysis: computational algorithms, statistical inference, and empirical implementation, *Journal of Finance*, 1705-1765 (2000).

13. L. P. Lukac, B.W. Brorsen and S. H. Irwin, Similarity of computer guided technical systems, *Journal of Futures Markets* **8**, 1-13 (1988).
14. R. J. Sweeney, Some new filter rule test: methods and results, *Journal of Financial and Quantitative Analysis*, **23 (Sep)**, 258-300 (1988).
15. S. J. Taylor, Rewards available to currency futures speculators: Compensation for risk or evidence of inefficient pricing? *Economic Record* **68**,105-116 (1992).

A DIVIDE-AND-CONQUER FAST IMPLEMENTATION OF RADIAL BASIS FUNCTION NETWORKS WITH APPLICATION TO TIME SERIES FORECASTING*

RONG-BO HUNAG

Department of Mathematics
Zhong Shan University
Guangzhou, PRC
E-mail: hrongbo@163.net

YIU-MING CHEUNG AND LAP-TAK LAW

Department of Computer Science
Hong Kong Baptist University
Hong Kong, PRC
E-mail: ymc@comp.hkbu.edu.hk, ltlaw@comp.hkbu.edu.hk

From the dual structural radial basis function network (DSRBF) (Cheung and Xu 2001), this paper presents a new divide-and-conquer learning approach to radial basis function networks (DCRBF). The DCRBF network is a hybrid system consisting of several sub-RBF networks, each of which takes a sub-input space as its input. Since this system divides a high-dimensional modeling problem into serveral low-dimensional ones, it can considerably reduce the structural complexity of a RBF network, whereby the net's learning is much faster. We have experimentally shown its outstanding learning performance on forecasting two real time series as well as synthetic data in comparison with a conventional RBF one.

1. Introduction

Radial basis function (RBF) networks are one of the most popular models in neural network, In the literature, RBF nets have been intensively studied with a lot of applications, e.g. in data mining [8], pattern recognition [11], and time series forecasting [4,9]. In general, the structural complexity of a RBF network depends on the number of the hidden nodes which is further related to the input dimension. Often, the node number increases along with the increase of the net's input dimension. Hence, effective dimension reduction

---

*The work described in this paper was fully supported by a Faculty Research Grant of Hong Kong Baptist University with Project Number: FRG/02-03/I-06.

of the net's input space can considerably decrease the network structural complexity, whereby the network's learning converges faster. Traditionally, principle component analysis (PCA) is a prevalent statistical tools for input dimension reduction. The basic rule is to select first several principal components of the observations as the RBF inputs. Since the PCA technique only uses second-order statistics information, it renders the principal components de-correlated but not really independent. That is, some useful information in the non-principal components may be discarded as well during the dimension reduction process. Consequently, the performance of the RBF network may become worse after PCA preprocess [5].

In the past decade, independent component analysis (ICA) has been widely studied in the fields of neural networks and signal processing. It uses high-order statistics to map the multivariate observations into new representations with their redundancy as reduced as possible. In the literature, it has been shown that ICA outperforms PCA in extracting the hidden feature information and structures from the observations [1,2,6,14]. Actually, our recent paper [5] has successfully applied ICA to reduce the input dimension of a RBF network without deteriorating the net's generalization ability. However, ICA generally does not assign a specific principle order to the extracted components. To our best knowledge, selecting first several principle independent components is still an open problem.

Recently, Kai Tokkola [10] applied a nonlinear dimension-reducing transformation to map high dimensional space to low dimensional one, i.e., $T : \Re^D \to \Re^d, d < D$. In his work, he coupled a nonparametric density estimator with a mutual information criterion based on Renyi's entropy to learn discriminative dimension-reducing transforms. However, this technique has at least two drawbacks to reduce the RBF input dimension. One is that the nonlinear dimension-reducing transforms lies in computational difficulties since it involves density estimation, resulting in a large amount of computing cost. The other drawback is that it makes the RBF performance degraded as the output dimension increases.

In our recent paper [3], a dual structural radial basis function network has been proposed to accomplish a recursive RBF by two sub-networks. In this dual system, the input is divided into two parts with each modelled by a sub-network. The preliminary studies have shown its success on recursive function estimation. In this paper, we further extend its concept and give out a divide-and-conquer approach to radial basis function (DCRBF) network. This DCRBF is a hybrid system consisting of several sub-RBF networks, each of which takes a sub-input as its input. That is, such a system has decomposed the original large input space into a direct sum of sub-input spaces with the output being a linear combination of these sub-RBF networks' ones. We give out an algorithm to learn the combination coefficients as well as the parameters in each sub-network. We have experimentally shown its outstanding learning performance on forecasting two real time series as well as synthetic data in comparison with a conventional RBF network.

2. DCRBF Network

2.1. *Architecture*

The architecture of the DCRBF network is shown in Figure 1. We decompose a RBF network into q sub-networks denoted as $RBF_1, RBF_2, \ldots, RBF_q$, respectively. Let k_r represent the number of radial basis functions in the rth sub-network, denoted as RBF_r, where $r = 1, 2, \ldots, q$. In the DCRBF, the input separator divides the input space into q sub-ones by direct sum decompositions. That is, the input of the RBF_r is

$$\mathbf{x}_t(r) = [x_t^{(i_1)}, x_t^{(i_2)}, \ldots, x_t^{(i_{d_r})}] \in \mathbf{V}_r \tag{1}$$

where $\{i_1, i_2, \ldots, i_{d_r}\} \subset \{1, 2, \ldots, d\}$. $\mathbf{V}_r$ is the rth direct sum subspace of $\mathbf{V}$ such that

$$\mathbf{V}_1 \oplus \mathbf{V}_2 \oplus \ldots \oplus \mathbf{V}_q = \mathbf{V} \tag{2}$$

where $\oplus$ means for any $\mathbf{v} \in \mathbf{V}$, there exists a unique $\mathbf{v}_i \in \mathbf{V}_i$ such that $\mathbf{v} = [\mathbf{v}_1^T, \mathbf{v}_2^T, \ldots, \mathbf{v}_q^T]^T$, and d_r is the dimension of subspace $\mathbf{V}_r$ with

$$\sum_{r=1}^{q} d_r = d. \tag{3}$$

We let $\hat{\mathbf{y}}_t$ be the actual output of the DCRBF network with

$$\hat{\mathbf{y}}_t = \sum_{r=1}^{q} c_r \mathbf{z}_t(r), \tag{4}$$

where $\mathbf{z}_t(r)$ is the RBF_r's output, and c_r is the linear combination coefficient.

2.2. *Learning Algorithm*

Given the desired output $\mathbf{y}_t$ at time step t, we calculate the output residual

$$\hat{\mathbf{e}}_t = \mathbf{y}_t - \hat{\mathbf{y}}_t. \tag{5}$$

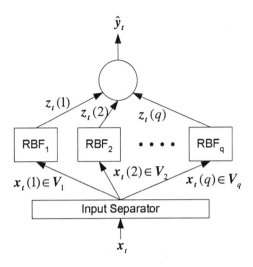

Figure 1. The DCRBF network model.

Consequently, we can learn the combination coefficients c_r in Eq. (4) as well as the parameters of each RBF_r's by minimizing the cost function

$$J(\Theta) = \frac{1}{N} \sum (\mathbf{y}_t - \hat{\mathbf{y}}_t)^T (\mathbf{y}_t - \hat{\mathbf{y}}_t) \tag{6}$$

where N is the number of inputs, $\Theta = \mathbf{C} \bigcup \Theta_1 \bigcup \Theta_2 \bigcup \ldots \bigcup \Theta_q$ with $\mathbf{C} = \{c_1, c_2, \ldots, c_q\}$, and Θ_r being the parameters of the RBF_r. In implementation, at each step time t, we adaptively tune Θ with a little small step along the descent direction of minimizing $(\mathbf{y}_t - \hat{\mathbf{y}}_t)^T (\mathbf{y}_t - \hat{\mathbf{y}}_t)$. That is, we adjust Θ by

$$c_r^{new} = c_r^{old} + \eta \hat{\mathbf{e}}_t^T \mathbf{z}_t(r), r = 1, 2, \ldots, q \tag{7}$$

$$\Theta_r^{new} = \Theta_r^{old} - \eta \frac{\partial J(\Theta)}{\partial \Theta_r} |_{\Theta_r^{old}} \tag{8}$$

where η is the learning rate.

The detailed steps in Eq. (8) depend on the implementation of each RBF_r, $r = 1, 2, \ldots, q$. In general, each sub-RBF networks can be realized by a variety of RBF network models. In this paper, we adopt the Extended Normalized RBF (ENRBF) network proposed in [12]. The general architecture of an ENRBF network is shown in Figure 2, which consists of a k-units hidden layer and an n-units output layer. The net's output is

$$\mathbf{z}_t = \sum_{j=1}^{k} (\mathbf{W}_j \mathbf{x}_t + \beta_j) O_j(\mathbf{x}_t) \tag{9}$$

where $\mathbf{z}_t = [z_t^{(1)}, z_t^{(2)}, \ldots, z_t^{(n)}]^T$, $\mathbf{x}_t = [x_t^{(1)}, x_t^{(2)}, \ldots, x_t^{(d)}]^T$ is an input, $\mathbf{W}_j$ is an $n \times d$ matrix and β_j is an $n \times 1$ vector. $O_j(\mathbf{x}_t)$ is the output of unit j in the hidden layer with

$$O_j(\mathbf{x}_t) = \frac{\phi[(\mathbf{x}_t - \mathbf{m}_j)^T \mathbf{\Sigma}_j^{-1} (\mathbf{x}_t - \mathbf{m}_j)]}{\sum_{i=1}^{k} \phi[(\mathbf{x}_t - \mathbf{m}_i)^T \mathbf{\Sigma}_i^{-1} (\mathbf{x}_t - \mathbf{m}_i)]} \tag{10}$$

where $\mathbf{m}_j$ is the center vector, and $\mathbf{\Sigma}_j$ is the receptive field of the basis function $\phi(.)$. In common, the Gaussian function $\phi(s) = exp(-0.5s^2)$ is chosen. Consequently, Eq. (9) becomes

$$\mathbf{z}_t = \sum_{j=1}^{k} (\mathbf{W}_j \mathbf{x}_t + \beta_j) \frac{exp[-0.5(\mathbf{x}_t - \mathbf{m}_j)^T \mathbf{\Sigma}_j^{-1} (\mathbf{x}_t - \mathbf{m}_j)]}{\sum_{i=1}^{k} exp[-0.5(\mathbf{x}_t - \mathbf{m}_i)^T \mathbf{\Sigma}_i^{-1} (\mathbf{x}_t - \mathbf{m}_i)]}. \tag{11}$$

In the above equation, two parameter sets should be learned. One is $\{\mathbf{m}_j, \mathbf{\Sigma}_j | j = 1, 2, \ldots, k\}$ in the hidden layer, and the other is $\{\mathbf{W}_j, \beta_j | j = 1, 2, \ldots, k\}$ in the output layer. In the paper [12], these parameters learning has been connected with the mixture-of-experts model, whereby an expectation-maximization (EM) based single-step learning algorithm is proposed. Here, for simplicity, we prefer to learn the two parameter sets in the same way as the traditional approaches with the two separate steps:

Step 1: Learn $\{\mathbf{m}_j, \mathbf{\Sigma}_j | j = 1, 2, \ldots, k\}$ in the hidden layer via a clustering algorithm such as k-means [7] or RPCL [13];

Step 2: Learn $\{\mathbf{W}_j, \beta_j | j = 1, 2, \ldots, k\}$ in the output layer under the least mean square criteria. That is, we learn them as well as $\mathbf{C}$ by minimizing Eq. (6). Consequently, the detailed implementations of Step 2 (i.e., Eq. (8)) are given as follows:

Step 2.1: Given $\mathbf{x}_t$ and $\mathbf{y}_t$, we calculate $\hat{\mathbf{y}}_t$ by Eq. (4).

Step 2.2: We update

$$\mathbf{W}_j^{new}(r) = \mathbf{W}_j^{old}(r) + \eta \triangle \mathbf{W}_j(r) \tag{12}$$

$$\beta_j^{new}(r) = \beta_j^{old}(r) + \eta \triangle \beta_j(r) \tag{13}$$

with

$$\triangle \mathbf{W}_j(r) = c_r^{old} O_j(\mathbf{x}_t(r)) \hat{\mathbf{e}}_t \mathbf{x}_t(r)^T \tag{14}$$

$$\triangle \beta_j(r) = c_r^{old} O_j(\mathbf{x}_t(r)) \hat{\mathbf{e}}_t \tag{15}$$

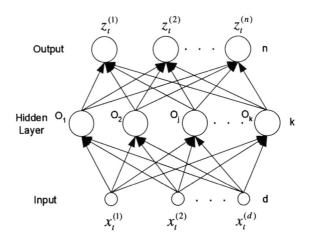

Figure 2.   ENRBF network model.

where $\{\mathbf{W}_j(r), \beta_j(r) | j = 1, 2, \ldots, k_r, \ r = 1, 2, \ldots, q\}$ is the parameter set of the RBF_r.

The iterations of Step 2.1 and 2.2 do not stop until the parameters converge.

3. Experimental Results

3.1. *Experiment 1*

We investigated the performance of the DCRBF network in time series forecasting. We generated 5,100 data points of a time series data with order 9 as follows:

$$u(t) = 0.08u^2(t-1) - 0.33u(t-2) + \sin(u(t-3)) + 0.08u(t-4)$$
$$+ 0.2u(t-5) + 0.064u^2(t-6)u(t-7) - 0.6u(t-8)u(t-9) \quad (16)$$

Let,

$$x_t = [x_t^{(1)}, x_t^{(2)}, \ldots, x_t^{(9)}]$$
$$= [u(t-1), u(t-2), \ldots, u(t-9)]$$

be the input of the RBF network and $y_t = u(t)$ be the output. We let the first 5,000 data points be the training set, and the remaining 100 data points be the testing set. The input space of RBF network is decomposed into three subspaces with the input dimension $d_1 = 2, d_2 = 3, d_3 = 4$ respectively. Meanwhile, the RBF network is decomposed into three subnetworks. Let the size of hidden units in the conventional ENRBF network be $k = 6$ while each of the sub-network in the DCRBF network to be $k_1 = 2, k_2 = 2, k_3 = 2$ respectively. In the experiment, we fixed the learning rate $\eta = 0.0001$ and measured the net's performance under the MSE criterion. After repeatedly scanning the training data set 300 times, the performance of ENRBF and DCRBF under the MSE criterion is shown in Figure 3. We found that the DCRBF network converges much faster than the ENRBF network.

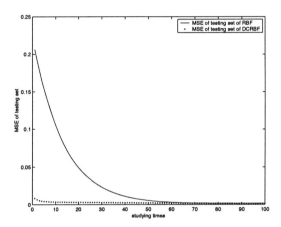

Figure 3. The comparison between the performance of ENRBF network and DCRBF network on the synthetic time-series data.

3.2. Experiment 2

We performed an experiment on the benchmark data getting from the famous Rob Hyndman's Time Series Data Library. We used the FOREX daily foreign exchange rates of 9 countries from 31st December, 1979 to 31st December, 1998 with size 4,774 data in this experiment. We let the first 4,674 data be the training set, and the remaining 100 data be the testing set. Also, we set the dimension of input space of ENRBF network at $d = 9$, which was further decomposed into three subspaces with the input dimension $d_1 = 2, d_2 = 3, d_3 = 4$ respectively. We let the number of hidden units in the ENRBF network be $k = 8$, while the number of hidden units in the three sub-networks of the DCRBF be $k_1 = 2, k_2 = 3, k_3 = 3$ respectively. The experimental result is shown in Figure 4. It can be seen again that the DCRBF network converges much faster than the ENRBF with a slight improvement of net's generalization ability.

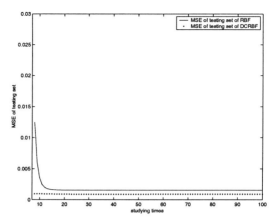

Figure 4. The comparison between the performance of RBF network and DCRBF network on FOREX daily foreign exchange data.

3.3. *Experiment 3*

We applied the DCRBF in the famous time series of annual average number of the sunspot from year 1700 to 1979 observed by Rudolph Wolf. We used the first 250 data to be the training set, and the remaining 30 to be the testing set. The number of hidden units of the ENRBF network was $k = 8$, while the hidden units of the three sub-networks in the DCRBF were $k_1 = 2, k_2 = 3, k_3 = 3$. We let the input dimension of the ENRBF be $d = 9$, and the input dimension of three decomposed sub-network in DCRBF be $d_1 = 3, d_2 = 3, d_3 = 3$. The experimental results are shown in Figure 5. Once again, we found that the DCRBF converges much faster than the ENRBF with a slight better generalization ability.

4. Concluding Remarks

We have presented a divide-and-conquer learning approach for RBF network (DCRBF), which is a hybrid system consisting of several sub-RBF networks. Each sub-RBF network takes a sub-input spaces as its own input. The whole DCRBF network output is a combination of sub-RBF networks' outputs. Since this system divides a high-dimensional modelling problem into several low-dimensional ones, its structural complexity is generally simpler than a conventional RBF network. The experiments have shown that the proposed approach gives a slight better generalization ability with a much faster learning speed. In this paper, we just decompose the input space into sub-input spaces heuristically rather than having a general rule to follow. It is therefore expected that a more appropriate

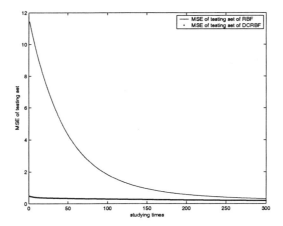

Figure 5. The comparison between the performance of the ENRBF and the DCRBF networks on sunspot data.

decomposition method exists to give a better net's performance.

References

1. A. D. Back, A. S. Weigend, "A First Application of Independent Component Analysis to Extracting Structure from Stock Returns," *International Journal of Neural System*, Vol. 8(4), pp. 473–484, 1997.
2. M. S. Bartlett, H. M. Lades, T. J. Sejnowski, "Independent Component Representations for Face Recognition," *Proceedings of the SPIE Symposium on Electronic Imaging: Science and Technology; Conference on Human Vision and Electronic Imaging III*, pp. 528–539, 1998.
3. Y. M. Cheung, L. Xu, "A Dual Structure Radial Basis Function Network for Recursive Function Estimation," *Proceedings of International Conference on Neural Information Processing (ICONIP'2001)*, Vol. 2, pp. 1903–1097, 2001.
4. N. Davey, S. P. Hunt, R. J. Frank, "Time Series Prediction and Neural Networks," *Journal of Intelligent and Robotic Systems*, Vol. 31, pp. 91–103, 2001.
5. R. B. Huang, L. T. Law, Y. M. Cheung, "An Experimental Study: On Reducing RBF Input Dimension by ICA and PCA," to be appeared in *Proceedings of 1st International Conference on Machine Learning and Cybernetics 2002 (ICMLC'02)*, Beijing, Novermber 4-5, 2002.
6. G. J. Jang, T. W. Lee, Y. H. Oh, "Learning Statistically Efficient Features for Speaker Recognition," *Proceedings of IEEE International Conference on Acoustics, Speech and Signal Processing*, Salt Lake City, Utah, May, 2001.
7. J. MacQueen, "Some Methods for Classification and Analysis of Multivariate Observations," *Proceedings of the Fifth Berkeley Symposium on Mathematical statistics and probability, Berkeley, University of California Press*, Vol. 1, pp. 281–297, 1967.
8. K. J. McGarry, S. Wermter, J. MacIntyre, "Knowledge Extraction from Radial

Basis Function Networks and Multilayer Perceptrons," *Proceeding of International Joint Conference on Neural Networks*, Vol. 4, pp. 2494–2497, 1999.

9. A. Saranli, B. Baykal, "Chaotic time-series prediction and the relocating LMS (RLMS) algorithm for radial basis function networks," *European Signal Processing Conference (EUSIPCO)*, Vol. 2, pp. 1247–1250, September 1996.

10. K. Torkkola, W. M. Campbell, "Mutual Information in Learning Feature Transformations," *Proceedings of International Conference on Machine Learning (ICML)*, Stanford, CA, June 29–July 2, 2000.

11. B. Verma, "Handwritten Hindi Character Recognition using RBF and MLP Neural Networks," *IEEE International Conference on Neural Networks (ICNN)*, Perth, pp. 86–92, 1995.

12. L. Xu, "RBF Nets, Mixture Experts, and Bayesian Ying-Yang Learning," *Neurocomputing*, Vol. 19, No. 1-3, pp. 223–257, 1998.

13. L. Xu, "Rival Penalized Competitive Learning, Finite Mixture, and Multisets Clustering," *Proceedings International Joint Conference on Neural Networks*, May 5-9, 1998, Anchorage, Alaska, Vol. II, pp. 2525–2530, 1998.

14. A. Ziehe, G. Nolte, T. Sander, K. R. Muller, G. Curio, "A Comparison of ICA-based Artifact Redction Methods for MEG," 12th *International Conference on Biomagnetism*, Helsinki University of Technology, Finland, 2000.

LEARNING SUNSPOT SERIES DYNAMICS BY RECURRENT NEURAL NETWORKS

LEONG KWAN LI

Department of Applied Mathematics
The Hong Kong Polytechnic University
Hong Kong, China
Email: malblkli@polyu.edu.hk

Sunspot series is a record of the activities of the surface of the sun. It is chaotic and is a well-known challenging task for time series analysis. In this paper, we show that we can approximate the transformed sequence with a discrete-time recurrent neural networks. We apply a new smoothing technique by integrating the original sequence twice with mean correction and also normalize the smoothened sequence to [-1,1]. The smoothened sequence is divided into a few segments and each segment is approximated by a neuron of a discrete-time fully connected neural network. Our approach is based on the universal approximation property of discrete-time recurrent neural network. The relation between the least square error and the network size are discussed. The results are compared with the linear time series models.

1. Introduction

In our solar system, the sun undergoes a periodic activity called the 'solar maximum' for almost every 11.3 years and then follows by a period of quiet called the 'solar minimum'. Sunspots are relatively cool areas that appear as dark blemishes on the surface of the sun. They are formed when magnetic field lines just below the sun's surface are twisted and poked through the solar photosphere. During the solar maximum there are many sunspots, solar flares, and coronal mass ejections, that affect telecommunications on the earth. The atmospheric weather is also deeply influenced by the changes of the activities of the surface of the sun. Besides this, advance knowledge of solar activity is extremely important to space missions and planning of satellite orbits. One way we track solar activity is by measuring sunspots. Sunspot series is chaotic and a well-known challenging task for time series analysis.

Weigend, Huberman and Rumehart [6] approximated the sunspot series using feedforward neural networks as artificial neural networks are sometimes considered as a non-linear regression model. After Hornik, Stinch-combe and White [1] demonstrated the capability of feedforward neural net-works, thousands of researches applied feedforward nets for modelling un-known input output relations. On the other hand, recurrent neural net-works(RNN) consist of feedback connections forming complicated dynam-ics. There are two major applications for RNN: one is to construct as-sociative memory and another important application is to approximate a desired trajectory in R^n. For a given neural network and we adjust the neu-ral parameters so that the output comes close to the sunspot series. This process of modifying parameters is called 'learning'. Williams and Zipser [7] derived the learning algorithms for trajectories of a discrete-time RNN but the question of the capability of the recurrent network is still unknown. Here, we show that we can approximate the transformed sunspot series with a discrete-time RNN.

In this paper, we shall define the mathematical model of the RNN. In section 3, we describe our method on approximation of a given sequence by normalization and segmentation. Then, we show a new learning algorithm for discrete-time RNN and show the relations between least square errors and the network sizes. We also compare our results with linear time series models.

2. Mathematical Models of Recurrent Neural Networks

For a continuous-time model, the dynamics of an analog n RNN are of-ten represented by the Leaky Integrator model defined as a system of n nonlinear differential equations:

$$\frac{dy}{dt} = -Ay + W\sigma(y) + J, \tag{1}$$

where $y(t) \in R^n$ denotes the state of the neurons. A is a diagonal matrix with positive diagonal elements. W is the synaptic connection weight ma-trix. J is the external input to the system. If J is a constant vector, the system is autonomous. If J is identically equal to zero, it is a closed system. σ is an activation function which is a bounded and differentiable monotonic function. Here σ or σ^{-1} of a matrix means the function σ or σ^{-1} operates on each element of the matrix respectively, e.g. $(\sigma'(W))_{ij} = \sigma'(W_{ij})$. In this paper, we let $\sigma(a) = tanh(a)$.

Sometimes, the Leaky Integrator model may be considered as another system of n nonlinear differential equations:

$$\frac{dx}{dt} = -Ax + \sigma(Wx + \theta), \tag{2}$$

where θ is called the threshold or bias vector of the system. In fact, both systems are mathematically equivalent. For a discrete-time model and fixed neural parameters W, the states of a RNN are given by a system of recursive equations $x^{i+1} = f_w(x^i)$. For simplicity, we take A to be the identity matrix and a widely used model is

$$x^{i+1} = f_w(x^i) = x^i + h_i[-x^i + \sigma(Wx^i + \theta)], \qquad (3)$$

which is an approximation of the differential system (2) by Euler's method. In particular, many researchers use this model with a uniform time step with all $h_i = 1$, i.e. $x^{i+1} = W\sigma(x^i)$. Note that Euler's method is good for small h, but not every difference equation comes from a differential equation, there may not be a close relation between these two models. Hence, the dynamics of the systems (1) and (2) need not be the same though they share same set of fixed points. Wang and Blum [5] discussed these dynamics between the discrete-time and continuous time models and we do not repeat their results here.

3. Methodology

Consider the task of approximating a given sequence $s(t)$ of length m by a fully connected RNN of network size n, i.e. n neurons, with dynamics as given in (3). We define that a dynamical system is *exactly capable* if there exists some neural parameters W, θ, J and h such that the error between the system output $x(t)$ and $s(t)$ is zero. If the least square error between the output of the system and the smoothed sequence is less than some prescribed tolerance, then the network is considered to be *capable*.

Recall that equation (3) is the discretization of (2) by Euler's method, we constraint ourself to approximate smooth sequence only. Thus, before applying the dynamical RNN process of equation (3), we need three stages preprocessing $s(t)$ as described below.

In the first stage, the original signal sequence $s(t)$ is processed by mean correction to $s_0(t)$, i.e.

$$s_0(t) = s(t) - \bar{s} \qquad \text{where } \bar{s} = \text{mean } (s(t)). \qquad (4)$$

Suppose our objective is to approximate the sunspot series $s(t) \in R$ from Jan. 1900 to Jun 2002. For simplicity, we preprocess the sunspot series $s(t)$ so that we can put A to be the identity matrix and $\theta = 0$. Thus, the range of the sunspot series is changed from $[0, 253.8]$ to $[-61.829, 191.97]$. Then, $s(t)$ is rescaled by 5×10^{-3} to $[-0.309145, 0.95985]$ that is within the range of σ.

Usually, moving average, exponential smoothing or other techniques are used to smoothen the given sequence especially when it has noise or it is chaotic. The smoothened sequence is usually shorter than the original sequence. In the second stage, we apply a newly developed smoothing technique by considering the given sequence $s_0(t)$ as the discrete derivative of another sequence $s_1(t)$ defined iteratively as

$$s_1(t+1) \; = \; s_1(t) \; + \; s_0(t) \tag{5}$$

$s_1(1)$ is chosen such that the mean $\bar{s}_1$ is also zero. In fact, we may consider s_1 as the discrete integral of s_0. Similarly, we repeat the same process as (5) and we obtain the sequence $s_2(t)$ with mean $\bar{s}_2 = 0$.

$$s_2(t+1) \; = \; s_2(t) \; + \; s_1(t) \tag{6}$$

Note that $s_2(t)$ is of length $m + 2$.

After normalizing, rescaling and discrete integration, $s_2(t)$ is a one dimensional sequence of length $m + 2$. Without loss of generality, let $(m + 2) = np$. In the third stage, we partition $s_2(t)$ into n equal subsequences, or n segments with each having length p. In this case, the first neuron $x_1(t)$ with $t = 1, ..p$ is utilized to approximate the first subsequence. Let the initial state equals to the first term of the subsequence, i.e. $x_1(1) = s_2(1)$. Similarly, we have $x_2(1) = s_2(p+1)$, $x_3(1) = s_2(2p+1)$, and $x_n(1) = s_2((n-1)p+1)$. Then, for fixed h and W, the discrete-time RNN of equation (3) generates a system output $X(W) = \{x^i\}_{1 \le i \le p}$ after $(p-1)$ iterations that we may use it to approximate $\{s_2(t)\}$.

For simplicity, we denote S to be the n by p matrix of the rows of the subsequences, i.e.

$$S \; = \; \begin{pmatrix} s_2(1) & s_2(2) & \cdots\cdots & s_2(p) \\ s_2(p+1) & s_2(p+2) & \cdots\cdots & s_2(2p) \\ \cdots & \cdots & \cdots\cdots & \cdots \\ \cdots & \cdots & \cdots\cdots & \cdots \\ s_2((n-1)p+1) & s_2((n-1)p+2) & \cdots\cdots & s_2(np) \end{pmatrix}$$

Finally, we come to an optimization, that is we aim at adjusting the neural parameters so as to minimize the difference between the system output $X(W)$ and the embedded trajectory S.

The neural parameters used are h and W, so that we have $1+n^2$ parameters to be determined. For example, if we use a RNN of 10 neurons, we need to store 101 parameters. Similarly, if all the neural parameters W, θ, J and h are included, the total number of variables used is $(n^2 + 2n + 1)$.

Once the network size n is fixed, the values of RNN parameters W and h are optimized so as to minimize the least square error. Many researchers applied the learning algorithm developed by Williams and Zipser [7]. Note that under the above construction, we use no hidden neuron. Thus, the parameters can be obtained by learning algorithms similar to that for finding the fixed points of equation (3) as described in reference Li [2]. These learning algorithms are based on gradient method. Recently, there are a lot of learning algorithms proposed for neural network researchers. Yet, there is no guarantee to obtain the minimum error easily.

4. Learning Algorithm of Discrete-time Recurrent Networks

For given h and W, let $X_h(W) = (x^1, x^2, ..., x^p)$ be the n by p matrix of the collection of system outputs as define by Eq(2). For each fixed h, define the error function E_h,

$$E_h = \|S - X_h(W)\|^2$$

which measures the difference between the system output and the desired output. We use L_2 or l_2 norms in this paper. Now we come to a standard nonlinear least square problem

$$\min_W \|S - X_h(W)\|^2.$$

In neural networks, learning is a process of changing the parameters so that the system output will approach to the desired output. Pearlmutter [4] derived a learning algorithm for continuous time RNN while Williams and Zipser [7] demonstrate their recurrent back propagation algorithm for discrete time RNN. In the above, minimizing $E_h(W)$ defines an nonlinear optimization problem, so, gradient, conjugate gradient, Newton or other numerical optimization techniques can be applied as learning algorithms for this problem. Since any change in just one neural parameter W_{ij} will affect the whole trajectory, learning algorithms based on gradient descent methods are complicated and time consuming for RNN, because we need to compute the partial derivatives along the trajectory. Nevertheless, learning process stops if we get a solution that the error is less than a prescribed tolerance rather than the true optimal solution W^*.

In the following, we present a new algorithm that takes no derivative. In fact, for each fixed network, finding the optimal neural parameters to fit the given sequence defines an optimization problem.

For fixed step size $h_i = h$, the least square error is

$$\|S - X_h(W)\|^2 = \|\textstyle\sum_{i=1}^{p-1} S^{i+1} - x^{i+1}(W)\|^2$$

$$= \|\textstyle\sum_{i=1}^{p-1} S^{i+1} - (x^i + h[-x^i + \sigma(Wx^i)])\|^2.$$

The optimal W^* cannot be to obtain easily for nonlinear optimization problem. But we can get a feasible W^+ for (3) by setting x^i as S^i in the above expression and solve the least square problem

$$\sum_{i=1}^{p-1} \left[\sigma^{-1}(\frac{S^{i+1} - S^i}{h} - S^i) - W S^i \right]^2 \tag{7}$$

The optimal solution W^+ for (7) can be obtained easily. Of course, if the network is exactly capable, i.e. $E_h = 0$, then

$$W^* = W^+.$$

In many researches, people use this W^+ or perturb W^+ with some random numbers as the initial guess for some gradient descent algorithm. Note that if $E_h \neq 0$, that implies this problem will have no exact solution. One simple optimization strategy is to vary h and repeatedly solve W^+ by equation (7) if we assume that the network will have exactly capable solution. Otherwise, we proceed some other nonlinear optimization techniques.

In this paper, we propose that after we get W^+, we shall use (3) to generate the sequence $X(W^+)$. In next iteration, instead of approximating S we find a W to approximate the new trajectory S^+ formed by a convex combination

$$S^+ = \alpha_i S + (1 - \alpha_i)X(W^+) \qquad \alpha_i \in (0,1). \tag{8}$$

This new learning algorithm will converge if α_i converges to zero. Actually, we store the best solution for each α_i. The change of how α_i from 1 to 0 is not discussed here. In each iteration, instead of moving in the parameter space W, we search around a neighborhood of S in the state space. If the E_h is not zero, that is to say that S is not reachable for this h and we assume that S is not attainable in some neighborhood of S as well. As $X(W^+)$ is attainable, by continuity of W, there is some α such that $S^+ = \alpha S + (1 - \alpha)X(W^+)$ is attainable in the state space. We just approximate the attainable state S^+.

5. Results and Discussions

Li, Chau and Leung [3] use discrete-time RNN to compress some UV-spectra and the methods are similar. Their work aimed at using minimum neural parameters needed and the compression ratio with respect to network sizes was discussed. The UV-spectra tested are smooth sequences. After preprocessing, the sequence $s_2(t)$ is rather smooth. We choose some fully connected recurrent neural networks with vary network sizes, α_i decreases from 1 to 0 uniformly with step size 10^{-3}. For convenience, 1200 data of s_2 was used except for $n = 11$. The best result is kept as the optimal solution. The least square errors are summaries in Table 1.

$NetworkSize$	Dynamical System	step size h	Parameters used
5	2.1216e-1	3.1700e-2	26
6	6.0210e-2	5.4100e-2	37
8	1.1044e-2	1.4590e-1	65
10	2.3551e-3	2.0950e-1	101
11	1.4348e-3	2.3200e-2	122
12	1.1081e-3	2.1652e-2	145
15	5.9204e-4	3.3970e-2	226

Not surprisingly, the errors decrease as the network sizes increase which means that the errors decrease as the number of of parameters used increases. The magnitude of h seemed to have no special indication. The result obtained in these experiments are satisfactory but may not be the optimal ones because the capability of RNN is not fully known. Hence, various learning strategies were attempted to derive the parameters that leads to an acceptable error level.

Recall that S is collection of rows of $s_2(t)$. If multi-linear time series models are used, the information are updated and let $Y(t)$ be the model output, i.e. for a cubic linear model, we have

$$Y(t+1) = AS(t) + BS(t-1) + CS(t-2)$$

where A, B and C are n by n the matrices. The least square errors are given in Table 2.

Matrix Dimension n	Linear	Quaratic	Cubic
5	6.5626e-3	3.0492e-4	2.6944e-4
6	4.3166e-3	2.5738e-4	2.3072e-4
8	1.5665e-3	2.3072e-4	2.0555e-4
10	8.5042e-4	1.9004e-4	2.8540e-4
11	4.8761e-4	1.8560e-4	2.6974e-4
12	4.0457e-4	1.4254e-4	7.2709e-4
15	2.6596e-4	2.4870e-4	4.7892e-4

If multi-linear dynamical system are considered, for example a cubic model we have

$$Y(t+1) = AY(t) + BY(t-1) + CY(t-2).$$

With the same initial states, and regression matrices founded in above results, the least square errors are in Table 3.

Matrix Dimension	Linear	Quaratic	Cubic	RNN
5	4.0203e-1	2.3071e-1	2.9127e-1	2.1216e-1
6	1.1755e-1	1.1491e-2	1.0067e-1	6.0210e-2
8	1.6101e-2	5.6789e-3	5.1472e-2	1.1044e-2
10	8.1827e-3	1.2085e-2	8.4574e-2	2.3551e-3
11	8.3373e-3	6.9371e-3	4.6263e-2	1.4348e-3
12	2.0474e-3	1.4482e-2	3.2408e-2	1.1081e-3
15	1.2440e-3	4.8648e-2	2.6983e-2	5.9204e-4

It is clear that errors from discrete-time RNN dynamics are less than the multi-linear dynamical systems for the corresponding dimensions. Note that in these results, the initial states used for higher order multi-linear models are more and the propagation is a few steps less but the results are not significantly better than linear model.

6. Concluding Remarks

From the above experiment, we can see that we can use a fully connected discrete-time RNN with no hidden neuron to approximate the sunspot series closely since discrete-time RNN can be universal approximators of trajectories.

The learning algorithm with no hidden neuron for a discrete-time RNN will be an interesting topic for further research.

Acknowledgments:

This research is supported by research grant of The Hong Kong Polytechnic University (Grant No. G-YD38)

References

1. K. Hornik, M. Stinchcombe and H. White, *Multilayer Feedforward Networks are Universal Approximators*, Neural Networks, **2**, 359-366 (1989).

2. L. K. Li, *Capacity of Recurrent Networks*, Proceedings of IJCNN, Singapore, **3**, 1330–1335 (1991).
3. L. K. Li, F. T. Chau and K. M. Leung, *Compression of Ultraviolet-visible Spectrum with Recurrent Neural Network*, Chemoetrics and Intelligent Laboratory Systems, **52**, 135-143 (2000).
4. B. A. Pearlmutter, *Learning State Space Trajectories in Recurrent Networks*, Neural Computation, **1**, 263-269 (1989).
5. X. Wang and E. Blum, *Discrete-time Versus Continuous-time Models of Neural Networks*, Journal of Computer and System Sciences, **45**, 1-19 (1992).
6. A. Weigend, B. Huberman and D. Rumehart, *Predicting the Future: a Connectionist Approach*, International Journal of Neural Systems, **1**, 193-209 (1990).
7. R. Williams and D. Zipser, *A Learning Algorithm for Continually Running Fully Recurrent Neural Networks*, Neural Computation, **1**, 270-280 (1989).

INDEPENDENT COMPONENT ANALYSIS: THE ONE-BIT-MATCHING CONJECTURE AND A SIMPLIFIED LPM-ICA ALGORITHM *

ZHI-YONG LIU, KAI-CHUN CHIU AND LEI XU

Department of Computer Science and Engineering
The Chinese University of Hong Kong,
Shatin, N.T., Hong Kong, P.R. China
E-mail: {zyliu,kcchiu,lxu}@cse.cuhk.edu.hk

The one-bit-matching conjecture in independent component analysis (ICA) is usually stated as "all the sources can be separated as long as there is a one-to-one same-sign-correspondence between the kurtosis signs of all source probability density functions (pdf's) and the kurtosis signs of all model pdf's". Although this conjecture have been supported by many ICA studies, such as LPM-ICA and Extended Infomax, we have no theoretical evidence for it yet. Here we prove it under the assumption of zero skewness for source and model pdf's. Based on the theorem, a simplified LPM-ICA algorithm with only one free parameter is suggested with experimental demonstrations.

1. Introduction

Independent component analysis (ICA) aims at blindly separating the independent sources **s** from their linear mixture **x = As** via:

$$\mathbf{y} = \mathbf{W}\mathbf{x}, \mathbf{x} \in \mathbb{R}^m, \mathbf{y} \in \mathbb{R}^n, \mathbf{W} \in \mathbb{R}^{m \times n} \qquad (1)$$

The recovered **y** is required to be as component-wise independent as possible where independence is defined as

$$q(\mathbf{y}) = \prod_{j=1}^{n} q(y^{(j)}). \qquad (2)$$

This effort is supported by the result of Tong, Inouye, & Liu in 1993 [1]. They showed that **y** recovers **s** up to constant scales and a permutation of components when the components of **y** become component-wise independent and at most one of them is Gaussian. The problem is further

---

*The work described in this paper was fully supported by a grant from the research grant council of the hong kong sar (project no: cuhk 4383/99e)

formularized by Comon in 1994 [2] under the name independent component analysis (ICA).

Also, the above ICA acts as a useful tool for data mining. A function $\mathbf{f}(\mathbf{x}|\theta)$ that maps $\mathbf{x}$ to a uniform density on $[0,1]^n$ represents a parametric cumulated distribution function (CDF) of $\mathbf{x}$, i.e., $\mathbf{p}(\mathbf{x}) = |\frac{d\mathbf{f}(\mathbf{x}|\theta)}{d\mathbf{x}}|$. That is, the density $\mathbf{p}(\mathbf{x})$ is completely described by the dependence structure of $\mathbf{f}(\mathbf{x}|\theta)$. Relaxing requiring the uniform density to a larger family of independent densities by (2) and considering a linear mapping $\mathbf{y} = \mathbf{W}\mathbf{x}$ that the dependence structure still catches main features of $\mathbf{p}(\mathbf{x})$, though it is no longer able to completely describe $\mathbf{p}(\mathbf{x})$.

Although ICA has been studied from different perspectives [3,4], in the case that $\mathbf{W}$ is invertible, all such approaches are equivalent to minimizing the following cost function:

$$D = -H(\mathbf{y}) - \sum_{i=1}^{n} \int p_{y_i}(y_i) \log p_i(y_i) dy_i \qquad (3)$$

where $H(\mathbf{y}) = -\int p(\mathbf{y}) \log p(\mathbf{y}) d\mathbf{y}$ is the entropy of $\mathbf{y}$, and $p_i(y_i)$ is the pre-fixed model pdf.

Conventionally, the model probability density function (pdf) $p_i(y_i)$ is either pre-fixed as sub-gaussian [4] or super-gaussian [3] according to the source property. However, this approach may not work in case the number of sub-gaussian and super-gaussian sources is not known a priori.

To solve the problem, a learnable mixture of sigmoid functions was adopted to model the model cumulative distribution function (cdf) [5]. Furthermore, $p_i(y_i)$ was suggested to be a flexibly adjustable density that was learned together with $\mathbf{W}$, in help of a parametric model (e.g., a mixture of parametric pdf's). As an example, the idea has been further implemented by the learned parametric mixture based ICA (LPM-ICA) algorithm [6], with successful results on the sources that can be either sub-gaussian or super-gaussian as well as any combination of both types.

Interestingly, it was also found that the model density $p_i(y_i)$, or cdf, only needs to be learned loosely instead of accurately. For instance, a simple sigmoid function such as $tanh(x)$ seems to work well on the super-gaussian sources [3], and a mixture of only two or three gaussians may be enough already [6,7] for the mixed sub- and super-gaussian sources. It led to the so-called one-bit-matching conjecture [7], which is usually stated as "all the sources can be separated as long as there is a one-to-one same-sign-correspondence between the kurtosis signs of all source pdf's and the kurtosis signs of all model pdf's". This conjecture has also been implied by some subsequent ICA studies [8,9].

However, although this conjecture is practically accepted by the ICA community, there exists no theoretical proof for this conjecture. In literature, although a proof [10] was given for the case of only two sub-gaussian sources, the result cannot be extended to a model either with more than two sources, or with mixed sub- and super-gaussian sources. The conditions for certain nonlinear function $\varphi_i(y_i) = -\frac{d}{dy_i} \log p_i(y_i)$ with stable and correct solutions were also theoretically studied [11]. However, it did not touch on the circumstances under which the algorithm would converge to a successful solution.

In this paper, we theoretically prove the one-bit-matching conjecture under the assumption of zero skewness for source and model pdf's. The entire proof proceeds in three stages. First, the observed mixture and recovered source signals are pre-whitened with zero mean and identity covariance matrix. Next, an equivalence is established between minimization of the cost function 3 and maximization of a sum of inner products. Finally, the proof is completed by observing the two basic properties of any orthonormal matrix.

The rest of the paper is organized it the following way. Section 2 is devoted to proof details of the conjecture. Section 3 introduces a simplified LPM-ICA algorithm with only one free parameter, with experimental illustrations given in section 4. Section 5 concludes the paper.

2. A Theorem on the One-Bit-Matching Conjecture

In this section, we prove the theorem on the one-bit-matching conjecture according to the three stages described in Section 1.

Assume the independent sources s is normalized with unit variance and the observed samples x with the zero mean are pre-whitened into y with the zero mean and identity covariance matrix, which can be made via $y = [E(xx^T)]^{-0.5}x$. As a result, we have $y = Rs$ with

$$E(yy^T) = RE(ss^T)R^T$$
$$\Rightarrow RR^T = I$$

That is, R is a orthonormal matrix. It further follows that the entropy $H(y) = H(s)$ in (3) is a Constant. Thus, minimizing (3) is equivalent to minimizing

$$\hat{D} = -\sum_{i=1}^{n} \int p_{y_i}(y_i) \log p_i(y_i) dy_i \tag{4}$$

where $p_{y_i}(y_i)$ can be observed via the orthonormal relationship between

$\mathbf{y} = \mathbf{Rs}$, with a orthonormal matrix $\mathbf{R} = [r_{ij}] \in \mathbb{R}^{n \times n}$ that implies

$$\sum_{r=1}^{n} r_{ir} r_{jr} = \sum_{r=1}^{n} r_{ri} r_{rj} = \begin{cases} 1 & \text{if } i = j \\ 0 & \text{otherwise} \end{cases} \tag{5}$$

Since $\mathbf{s} = [s_1, s_2, ...s_n]^T$ are component-wise independent and $E(s_i^3) = 0$, it follows that

$$E(y_i^3) = 0 \tag{6}$$

$$k_{y_i} = E(y_i^4) - 3 = E((r_{i1}s_1 + r_{i2}s_2 + \cdots + r_{in}s_n)^4) - 3$$

$$= \sum_{j=1}^{n} r_{ij}^4 E(s_j^4) + 6 \sum_{j=1}^{n} \sum_{r=1}^{n} r_{ij}^2 r_{ir}^2 - 3$$

$$= \sum_{j=1}^{n} r_{ij}^4 (E(s_j^4) - 3) = \sum_{j=1}^{n} r_{ij}^4 k_{s_j} \tag{7}$$

where k_{y_i} denotes the kurtosis of y_i, and similarly for k_{s_j}.

Based on the truncated Gram-Charlier expansion [12] up to kurtosis, we consider that then approximated as follows:

$$p_{y_i}(y_i) \approx g(y_i)(1 + \frac{k_{y_i}}{24}(y_i^4 - 6y_i^2 + 3)) \tag{8}$$

where $g(y_i)$ denotes the standard gaussian distribution density as $g(y_i) = \frac{1}{\sqrt{2\pi}} e^{-\frac{y_i^2}{2}}$.

Lemma 2.1. *When the skewness of source and model pdf's are zero, minimizing (4) is approximately equivalent to minimizing the sum of inner products* $\sum_{i=1}^{n} \varrho_i^T c_i$, *where* $\varrho_i = [r_{i1}^4, r_{i2}^4, \cdots, r_{in}^4]^T, c_i = [k'_{m_i} k_{s_1}, k'_{m_i} k_{s_2}, \cdots, k'_{m_i} k_{s_n}]^T, k'_{m_i} = \int g(y_i) \frac{y_i^4 - 6y_i^2 + 3}{24} \log(1 + \frac{k_{m_i}}{24}(y_i^4 - 6y_i^2 + 3)) dy_i$ *and* k_{m_i} *denotes the kurtosis of* $p_i(y_i)$.

Proof. By assuming zero skewness, the pre-fixed model pdf $p_i(y_i)$ in (4) can be approximated by the following truncated Gram-Charlier expansion:

$$p_i(y_i) \approx g(y_i)(1 + \frac{k_{m_i}}{24}(y_i^4 - 6y_i^2 + 3)) \tag{9}$$

where k_{m_i} denotes the kurtosis of $p_i(y_i)$.

Putting (9) and (8) into (3), it becomes to maximize the following cost function:

$$J(\mathbf{R}) = \sum_{i=1}^{n} \int g(y_i)(1 + \frac{k_{y_i}}{24}(y_i^4 - 6y_i^2 + 3))$$

$$\times \log(g(y_i)(1 + \frac{k_{m_i}}{24}(y_i^4 - 6y_i^2 + 3))) dy_i$$

$$= \sum_{i=1}^{n} \int g(y_i)(1 + \frac{k_{y_i}}{24}(y_i^4 - 6y_i^2 + 3)) \log(1 + \frac{k_{m_i}}{24}(y_i^4 - 6y_i^2 + 3))dy_i$$

$$- \frac{n}{2}(1 + \log 2\pi)$$

$$= \sum_{i=1}^{n} \int g(y_i)\frac{k_{y_i}}{24}(y_i^4 - 6y_i^2 + 3) \log(1 + \frac{k_{m_i}}{24}(y_i^4 - 6y_i^2 + 3))dy_i$$

$$+ \sum_{i=1}^{n} \int g(y_i) \log(1 + \frac{k_{m_i}}{24}(y_i^4 - 6y_i^2 + 3))dy_i - \frac{n}{2}(1 + \log 2\pi)$$

$$= \sum_{i=1}^{n} k_{y_i} \int g(y_i)\frac{y_i^4 - 6y_i^2 + 3}{24} \log(1 + \frac{k_{m_i}}{24}(y_i^4 - 6y_i^2 + 3))dy_i$$

$$+ C_2 - \frac{n}{2}(1 + \log 2\pi) \tag{10}$$

Because the parameter under consideration is $k_{y_i} = \sum_{j=1}^{n} r_{ij}^4 k_{s_j}$, the term $\sum_{i=1}^{n} \int g(y_i) \log(1 + \frac{k_{m_i}}{24}(y_i^4 - 6y_i^2 + 3))dy_i$ is taken as a constant C_2. Thus, the problem can be further simplified into maximizing the following cost function $\hat{J}(\mathbf{R})$:

$$\hat{J}(\mathbf{R}) = \sum_{i=1}^{n} k_{y_i} \int g(y_i)\frac{y_i^4 - 6y_i^2 + 3}{24} \log(1 + \frac{k_{m_i}}{24}(y_i^4 - 6y_i^2 + 3))dy_i$$

$$= \sum_{i=1}^{n} \varrho_i^T \mathbf{c}_i \tag{11}$$

where $\varrho_i = [r_{i1}^4, r_{i2}^4, \cdots, r_{in}^4]^T$, $\mathbf{c}_i = [k'_{m_i}k_{s_1}, k'_{m_i}k_{s_2}, \cdots, k'_{m_i}k_{s_n}]^T$, and

$$k'_{m_i} \triangleq \int g(y_i)\frac{y_i^4 - 6y_i^2 + 3}{24} \log(1 + \frac{k_{m_i}}{24}(y_i^4 - 6y_i^2 + 3))dy_i \tag{12}$$

□

Note the three terms $g(y_i)$, $\frac{y_i^4 - 6y_i^2 + 3}{24}$ and $\log(1 + \frac{k_{m_i}}{24}(y_i^4 - 6y_i^2 + 3))$ involved in the integration in (12). The first standard gaussian $g(y_i) > 0$. For the last two terms, their product has the same sign as that of k_{m_i} whenever $(y_i^4 - 6y_i^2 + 3) > 0$ or < 0. Thus, the sign of the product of the three terms is always the same as k_{m_i} (except for the four points of y_i that cause the product zero), and this then makes k'_{m_i} possess the same sign as k_{m_i}. Consequently, the one-bit-matching conjecture can be equivalently re-stated as "*as long as the signs of k'_{m_i} match those of k_{s_i}, maximizing (11) will ensure all sources being separated*".

Lemma 2.2. *For any orthonormal matrix $\mathbf{R}$, maximization of (11) would make $\mathbf{R}$ an identity matrix up to permutation and sign indeterminacy.*

Proof. Let $\mathbf{r}_i = [r_{i1}, r_{i2}, \cdots, r_{in}]^T$ and $\alpha_i = [r_{i1}^2, r_{i2}^2, \cdots, r_{in}^2]^T$. Since $\mathbf{R}$ is orthonormal, $\mathbf{r}_i^T \mathbf{r}_i = 1$. Maximization of $\alpha_i^T \mathbf{c}_i$ would make α_i take the form $d = [\cdots, 1, \cdots]$ with $\cdots$ denoting $r_{ij}^2 = 0$. The position $\hat{j}$ such that $r_{i\hat{j}}^2 = 1$ corresponds to the position of the maximum element of $\mathbf{c}_i$. Since $\varrho_i^T \mathbf{c}_i \leq \alpha_i^T \mathbf{c}_i$ and the equality sign holds when $\varrho_i = d$, which guarantees maximization of $\varrho_i^T \mathbf{c}_i$ in (11). At the same time, the orthogonal constraint $\mathbf{r}_i^T \mathbf{r}_j = 0$ if $i \neq j$ implies that $\alpha_i^T \alpha_j = 0$ if $i \neq j$. Consequently, for $i \neq j$, α_i and α_j could not have 1 in the same column. This also implies $\mathbf{R}$ being an identity matrix up to permutation and sign indeterminacy. $\square$

By the results of Lemma 2.1 and 2.2, it directly follows the following theorem:

Theorem 2.1. *Provided that the skewness of source and model pdf's are both zero and that (10) is approximately satisfied. All the sources can be separated as long as there is a one-to-one same-sign-correspondence between the kurtosis signs of all source pdf's and the kurtosis signs of all model pdf's.*

3. A Simplified LPM-ICA Algorithm with Only One Free Parameter

In this section, by adopting the theorem as a necessary condition, we design a simplified LPM-ICA algorithm in help of gaussian mixture with only one parameter that can smoothly switch between sub- and super-gaussian.

3.1. *Brief Review on LPM-ICA Algorithm*

The LPM-ICA approach models each model pdf $p_i(y_i)$ via a mixture density, such as the Gaussian mixture:

$$p_i(y_i | \xi_i) = \sum_{j=1}^{k} G(y_i | m_{ij}, \sigma_{ij}^2) \alpha_{ij} \tag{13}$$

where $\alpha_{ij} > 0$, $\sum_{j=1}^{k} \alpha_{ij} = 1$, $G(y_i | m_{ij}, \sigma_{ij}^2)$ denotes a Gaussian pdf with mean m_{ij} and variance σ_{ij}^2. The set of free parameters to be learned is $\Xi = \{\xi_1, ..., \xi_m\}$ with $\xi_i = \{m_{ij}, \sigma_{ij}, \alpha_{ij}\}_{j=1}^{k}$. The algorithm framework is as follows [6]:

(1) fix Ξ, update $\mathbf{W}$ along the natural gradient [4]:

$$\mathbf{W}^{new} = \mathbf{W}^{old} + \eta(\mathbf{I} + \phi(\mathbf{y})\mathbf{y}^T)\mathbf{W} \tag{14}$$

where $\phi(\mathbf{y}) = [\phi_1(y_1), ..., \phi_k(y_k)]^T$, $\phi_i(y_i) = \frac{d \ln p_i(y_i|\theta)}{dy_i}$, η is learning rate.

(2) fix $\mathbf{W}$, update Ξ:

$$\xi_{\mathbf{i}}^{new} = \xi_{\mathbf{i}}^{old} + \zeta\Delta\xi_{\mathbf{i}} \tag{15}$$

where $\Delta\xi_{\mathbf{i}}$ denotes the derivative of $\ln \sum_{j=1}^{k} G(y_i|m_{ij}, \sigma_{ij}^2)\alpha_{ij}$ with respective to $\xi_{\mathbf{i}}$ and ζ is learning rate.

3.2. A Simplified LPM-ICA Algorithm

The gaussian mixture based LPM-ICA involves estimating three free parameters for each model pdf. However, according to the one-bit-matching conjecture, there is only one bit of information needed to be specified for the pdf. Below we discuss how we can take advantage of the one-bit-matching conjecture to simplify the original LPM-ICA algorithm.

According to the assumptions accompanied with the one-bit-matching conjecture, the absolute skewness of the designed density function should be as small as possible. To fulfill such design, we first obtain the higher-order statistics of the gaussian mixture, whose moment generating function (mgf) [12] can be obtained via

$$\varphi(\tau) = \int_{-\infty}^{+\infty} e^{i\tau y}p(y)dy = \sum_{j=1}^{k} \alpha_j \exp\left\{\tau m_j i - \frac{\tau^2 \sigma_j^2}{2}\right\}; i \triangleq \sqrt{-1}. \tag{16}$$

Based on the cumulant generating function (cgf) $\phi(\tau) = \ln(\varphi(\tau))$, the cumulant c_n can be obtained by

$$c_n = (-i)^n \frac{d^n\phi(\tau)}{d\tau^n} \tag{17}$$

Specifically, we have

$$c_3 = m_3 = \mu_{30} + 3\mu_{12} + 2\mu_{10}^3 - 3\mu_{10}\mu_{02} - 3\mu_{10}\mu_{20}$$
$$c_4 = m_4 - 3m_2^2$$
$$= \mu_{40} + 6\mu_{22} + 3\mu_{04} + 12\mu_{10}^2\mu_{02} + 12\mu_{10}^2\mu_{20}$$
$$-12\mu_{10}\mu_{12} - 4\mu_{10}\mu_{30} - 3\mu_{02}^2 - 3\mu_{20}^2 - 6\mu_{02}\mu_{20} - 6\mu_{10}^4$$

where m_n refer to the nth-order moment and $\mu_{pq} \triangleq \sum_{j=1}^{k} \alpha_j m_j^p \sigma_j^q$. Actually, c_3, c_4 respectively represent the skewness and kurtosis of the gaussian mixture.

Based on the higher-order statistics of gaussian mixture we design the following pdf with only one parameter:

$$p(y|\theta) = \frac{1}{3}G(y|-\theta,1) + \frac{1}{3}G(y|0,4) + \frac{1}{3}G(y|\theta,1); 0 \leq \theta \leq 2 \qquad (18)$$

The changes of c_3 and c_4 as θ varies are shown in Fig. 1. Note with a zero skewness how the density changes smoothly from super-gaussian to sub-gaussian as θ varies from 0 to 2. Fig. 2 gives a pictorial view of the density $p(y)$ versus θ.

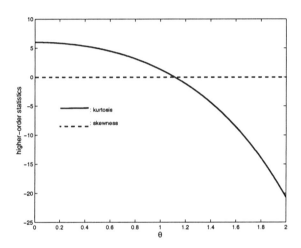

Figure 1.   skewness and kurtosis vs θ

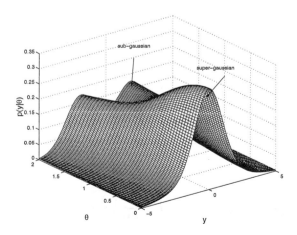

Figure 2.   Density variation with θ

According to the two steps for LPM-ICA, the algorithm for the simplified LPM-ICA is as follows:

(1) Fix $\Theta = [\theta_1, \theta_2, ..., \theta_m]^T$, update $\mathbf{W}$ according to (14), with

$$\phi_i(y_i) = -r_{i1}(y_i + \theta_i) - \frac{r_{i2}y_i}{4} - r_{i3}(y_i - \theta_i) \qquad (19)$$

where $r_{i1} = \frac{G(y_i|-\theta_i,1)}{3p(y_i|\theta_i)}, r_{i2} = \frac{G(y_i|0,4)}{3p(y_i|\theta_i)}, r_{i3} = \frac{G(y_i|\theta_i,1)}{3p(y_i|\theta_i)}$.

(2) Fix $\mathbf{W}$, update Θ:

$$\Theta^{new} = \Theta^{old} + \zeta\Delta\Theta \qquad (20)$$

where $\Delta\Theta = [\Delta\theta_1, \Delta\theta_2, ..., \Delta\theta_m]^T$, with

$$\Delta\theta_i = -r_{i1}(y_i + \theta_i) + r_{i3}(y_i - \theta_i) \qquad (21)$$

$\theta_i = \frac{2}{1+\exp(\varsigma_i)}$ is introduced to constrain $0 \leq \theta \leq 2$.

In fact, the idea of adopting only one free parameter such that the model can smoothly switch between sub- and super-gaussian is not new in the ICA studies. A typical example is referred to as the soft switching algorithm [13]. However, the new story here is that the one-bit-matching conjecture we have theoretically proved guides the design of pdf with negligible absolute skewness.

4. Experimental Illustration

In the section, we provide two experiments to illustrate the simplified LPM-ICA algorithm on synthetic and real data respectively.

4.1. On Synthetical Data

The 200 data samples used in this experiment are mixed from four sources: two sub-gaussian sources from uniform distribution and two super-gaussian sources from $sinh(x)$ with x from standard gaussian distribution. The algorithm accuracy performance is measured by the following error metric [4]:

$$E = \sum_{i=1}^{d}\left(\sum_{j=1}^{d}\frac{|p_{ij}|}{\max_k |p_{ik}|} - 1\right) + \sum_{j=1}^{d}\left(\sum_{i=1}^{d}\frac{|p_{ij}|}{\max_k |p_{kj}|} - 1\right) \qquad (22)$$

where $\mathbf{P} \triangleq \mathbf{WA}$.

The learning processes for the four pdf's are shown in Fig. 3 and the corresponding error metric is shown in Fig. 4. When the algorithms converged, the matrix $\mathbf{P} = \mathbf{WA}$ are

$$\mathbf{P} = \begin{pmatrix} -0.0054 & -0.0280 & 0.0220 & \mathbf{1.5889} \\ 0.0026 & \mathbf{2.0626} & -0.0078 & 0.0110 \\ \mathbf{2.0752} & 0.0202 & 0.0521 & -0.0675 \\ -0.0168 & 0.0197 & \mathbf{1.5422} & -0.0830 \end{pmatrix}$$

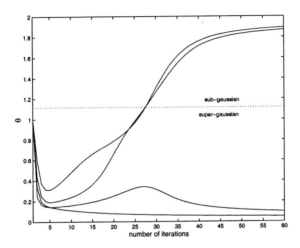

Figure 3.   Learning curve of the θ for the simplified LPM-ICA algorithm

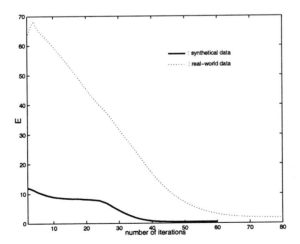

Figure 4.   Learning curve of the error metric

From Fig. 3 we can notice that the algorithm automatically detect the source properties via the learned θ, and thus results in the successful recovery as witnessed by Fig. 4 and matrix $\mathbf{P}$.

4.2. *On Real Data*

The purpose of this experiment is to test the simplified LPM-ICA algorithm on real data. The 50,000 10-dimensional samples are linearly mixed from 10 source signals, of which 7 are super-gaussian speech tracks and 3 are synthetic sub-gaussian signals[a].

The variances of θ and error metric E along with the number iterations are shown in Fig. 5 and Fig. 4 respectively, and the matrix $\mathbf{P} = \mathbf{WA}$ after convergence is shown in Fig. 6.

Fig. 5 illustrates how the algorithm automatically learns the source properties, and it is evident by direct inspection of $\mathbf{P}$ and Fig. 4 that the algorithm succeeds in recovering the original sources.

5. Conclusion

In summary, we theoretically proved the so-called one-bit-matching conjecture for ICA under the assumption of zero skewness for source and model pdf's. Based on the established theorem, a simplified LPM-ICA algorithm with only one free parameter is suggested with experimental demonstrations.

References

1. L.Tong, Y. Inouye, & R. Liu "Waveform-preserving blind estimation of multiple independent sources", *IEEE Trans. on Signal Processing 41*, 2461-2470, 1993.
2. P. Comon, "Independent component analysis: a new concept? " *Signal Processing, 36*, 287-314, 1994.
3. A. J. Bell and T. J. Sejnowski, "An information-maximization approach to blind separation and blind deconvolution", *Neural Computation*, 7, 1129-1159 (1995).
4. S. I. Amari, A. Cichocki and H. Yang, "A new learning algorithm for blind separation of sources", *Advances in Neural Infomation Processing*, 8, 757-763 (1996).
5. L. Xu, and H. H. Yang and S. I. Amari, "Signal source separation by mixtures accumulative distribution functions or mixutre of bell-shape density distribution functions", *Reseach Proposal*, RIKEN, Japan, April 10 1996.

---

[a]Data can be downloaded from http://sweat.cs.unm.edu/~bap/domos.html

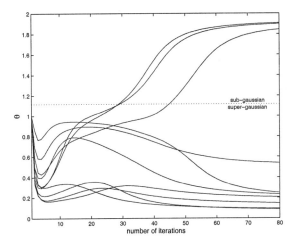

Figure 5. Learning curve of the θ for the simplified LPM-ICA algorithm

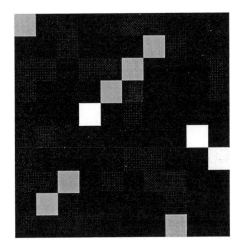

Figure 6. the resulted $P = WA$ matrix for the real-world data

6. L. Xu, C. C. Cheung and S. I. Amari, "Learned parametric mixture based ICA algorithm", *Neurocomputing*, **22**, 69-80 (1998).

7. L. Xu, and C. C. Cheung and S. I. Amari, "Furthere Results on Nonlinearity and Separtion Capability of a Liner Mixture ICA Method and learned LPM", *Proc. I&ANN'98*, 39-45 (1998).

8. R. Everson and S. Roberts, "Independent Component Analysis: A Flexible Nonlinearity and Decorrelating Manifold Approach", *Neural Computation*, **11**, 1957-1983 (1999).

9. T. W. Lee, M. Girolami and T. J. Sejnowski, "Independent Component Analysis Using an Extended Infomax Algorithm for Mixed Subgaussian and Su-

128

pergaussian Sources", *Neural Computation*, **11**, 417-441 (1999).
10. L. Xu, C. C. Cheung, J. Ruan and S. I. Amari, "Nonlinearity and Separation Capability: Futher Justification for the ICA Algorithm with A Learned Mixture of Parametric Densities", *Proc. ESANN97*, 291-296 (1997).
11. S. I. Amari, T. P. Chen and A. Cichocki, "Stability analysis of adaptive blind source separation", *Neural Networks Letter*, **10**, 1345-1351 (1997).
12. A. Stuart and J. K. Ord, *Kendall's Advanced Theory of Statistics, Volume 1: Distribution Theory*, Edward Arnold (1994)
13. M. Welling and M. Weber, "A constrained EM Algorithm for Independent Component Analysis", *Neural Computation*, **13**, 677-689 (2001).

AN HIGHER-ORDER MARKOV CHAIN MODEL FOR PREDICTION OF CATEGORICAL DATA SEQUENCES[*]

WAI KI CHING[†], ERIC S. FUNG and MICHAEL K. NG

Department of Mathematics,
University of Hong Kong,
Pokfulam Road, Hong Kong, CHINA
[†] *E-mail: wkc@maths.hku.hk*

In this paper we propose an higher-order Markov chain model for modeling categorical data sequences. We also propose an efficient estimation method based on solving a linear programming problem for the model parameters. Data sequences such as DNA and sales demand are used to illustrate the predicting power of our proposed models.

1. Introduction

Data sequences (or time series) occur frequently in many real world applications. The most important step in analyzing a data sequence (or time series) is the selection of an appropriate mathematical model for the data. Because it helps in predictions, hypothesis testing and rule discovery. A data sequence X can be logically represented as a vector

$$(X_1, X_2, \cdots, X_T),$$

where T is the length of the sequence, and $X_i \in \text{DOM}(A)$ ($1 \leq i \leq T$), associated with a defined semantic and a data type. In this paper, we consider two general data types, *numeric* and *categorical* and assume other types used can be mapped to one of these two types. The domains of attributes associated with these two types are called numeric and categorical respectively. A numeric domain consists of real numbers. A domain $DOM(A)$ is defined as categorical if it is finite and unordered, e.g., for any $a, b \in DOM(A)$, either $a = b$ or $a \neq b$, see for instance Gowda and Diday[5]. Numerical data sequences have been studied in detail, see for instance Brockwell and Davis[3]. Mathematical tools such as Fourier transform

---

[*]research support in part by hung hing ying physical sciences research fund, hku crcg grant nos. 10203408, 10203501, 10203907, 10203919.

and spectral analysis are employed frequently in the analysis of numerical data sequences. Different time sequences models are proposed and developed in the literature, see for instance Brockwell and Davis[3].

For categorical data sequences, there are many situations that one would like to employ higher-order Markov chain models as a mathematical tool, see for instance Adle[1], Huang et. al.[6], Li[7], Logan[8], MacDonald and Zucchini [9] and Raftery[10,11]. For example, in sales demand prediction, the sales demand of products can be classified into several states such as very high sales volume, high sales volume, standard, low sales volume, very low sales volume (categorical type: ordinal data). An higher-order Markov chain model is then used to fit the observed data. Alignment of sequences (categorical type: nominal data) is an important topic in DNA sequence analysis Waterman[12]. It involves searching of patterns in a DNA sequence of huge size. In these applications and many others, one would like to

(i) characterize categorical data sequences for the purpose of comparison and classification process; or

(ii) to model categorical data sequences and hence to make predictions in the control and planning process. It has been shown that higher-order Markov chain models are promising approach for these purposes Huang et. al.[6] and Waterman[12].

For simplicity in discussion, in the following we assume that each data point X_t in a categorical data sequence takes values in

$$\mathbf{M} \equiv \{1, 2, \cdots, m\}$$

and m is finite, i.e., it has m possible categories or states. The conventional model for an n-th order Markov chain has $(m-1)m^n$ states. The major problem in using such kind of model is that the number of parameters (transition probabilities) increases exponentially with respect to the order of the model. This large number of parameters discourages people from using an higher-order Markov chain directly. Raftery[10] proposed an higher-order Markov chain model which involves only one additional parameter for each extra lag. The model can be written as follows:

$$P(X_t = k_0 \mid X_{t-1} = k_1, \ldots, X_{t-n} = k_n) = \sum_{i=1}^{n} \lambda_i q_{k_0 k_i} \qquad (1)$$

where

$$\sum_{i=1}^{n} \lambda_i = 1$$

and $Q = [q_{ij}]$ is a transition matrix with column sums equal to one, such that

$$0 \leq \sum_{i=1}^{n} \lambda_i q_{k_0 k_i} \leq 1, \quad k_0, k_i \in \mathbf{M}. \tag{2}$$

Raftery proved that Eq. (1) is analogous to the standard AR(n) model in the sense that each additional lag, after the first is specified by a single parameter and the autocorrelations satisfy a system of linear equations similar to the Yule-Walker equations. Moreover, the parameters $q_{k_0 k_i}, \lambda_i$ can be estimated numerically by maximizing the log-likelihood of Eq. (1) subjected to the constraints Eq. (2). However, this approach involves solving an highly non-linear optimization problem (A coded program for solving the maximum log-likelihood problem can be found at http://lib.stat.cmu.edu/general/mtd). The proposed method neither guarantees convergence nor a global maximum. The main contribution of this paper is to generalize the Raftery model by allowing Q to vary with different lags. Numerical examples are given to demonstrate that our generalized model has a better prediction power than the Raftery model does. This means that our model is not over-parameterized in general. We also develop an efficient method to estimate the model parameters.

The rest of the paper is organized as follows. In Section 2, we propose our higher-order Markov chain models and discuss some properties of the proposed model. In Section 3, we propose an estimation method for the model parameters required in our higher-order Markov chain model. In Section 4, numerical examples on DNA sequence and the sales demand data are given to demonstrate the predicting power of our model. Finally, concluding remarks are given to conclude the paper in Section 5.

2. Higher-order Markov Chain Models

In this section we extend the Raftery model [10] to a more general higher-order Markov model by allowing Q to vary with different lags. We first notice that Eq. (1) can be re-written as

$$\mathbf{X}_{t+n+1} = \sum_{i=1}^{n} \lambda_i Q \mathbf{X}_{t+i} \tag{3}$$

where $\mathbf{X}_{t+i}$ is the state vector at time $(t + i)$. If the system is in state $j \in \mathbf{M}$ at time $(t + i)$ then

$$\mathbf{X}_{t+i} = (0, \ldots, 0, \underbrace{1}_{j\text{th entry}}, 0 \ldots, 0)^t.$$

The Raftery model in Eq. (3) can be generalized as follows:

$$\mathbf{X}_{t+n+1} = \sum_{i=1}^{n} \lambda_i Q_i \mathbf{X}_{t+n+1-i}. \tag{4}$$

We note that if $Q_1 = Q_2 = \ldots = Q_n$ then Eq. (4) is just the Raftery model in Eq. (3).

In our model we assume that $\mathbf{X}_{t+n+1}$ depends on $\mathbf{X}_{t+i}$ $(i = 1, 2, \ldots, n)$ via the matrix Q_i and weight λ_i. One may relate Q_i to the ith step transition matrix of the process and we will use this idea to estimate Q_i. Here we assume that each Q_i is an non-negative stochastic matrix with column sums equal to one. We also assume that the weight λ_i is non-negative such that $\sum_{i=1}^{n} \lambda_i = 1$. Before we present our estimation method for the model parameters we have the following theorem Ching et. al.[4].

Theorem 2.1. *If Q_i is irreducible, $\lambda_i > 0$ for $i = 1, 2, \ldots, n$ and $\sum_{i=1}^{n} \lambda_i = 1$ then the model in Eq. (4) has a stationary distribution $\bar{\mathbf{X}}$ when $t \to \infty$ independent of the initial state vectors $\mathbf{X}_0, \mathbf{X}_1, \ldots, \mathbf{X}_{n-1}$. The stationary distribution $\bar{\mathbf{X}}$ is the unique solution of the linear system of equations*

$$(I - \sum_{i=1}^{n} \lambda_i Q_i)\bar{\mathbf{X}} = 0 \quad and \quad \mathbf{1}^T \bar{\mathbf{X}} = 1 \tag{5}$$

where I is the m-by-m identity matrix (m is the number of possible states taken by each data point).

We remark that if some λ_i are equal to zero, we can rewrite the vector $\mathbf{Y}_{t+n+1}$ in terms of $\mathbf{X}_i$ where λ_i are nonzero. Then the model in Eq. (4) still has a stationary distribution $\bar{\mathbf{X}}$ when t goes to infinity independent of the initial state vectors, and the stationary distribution $\bar{\mathbf{X}}$ can be obtained by solving the corresponding linear system of equations with the normalization constraint.

3. Parameters Estimation

In this section we present an efficient method to estimate the parameters Q_i and λ_i for $i = 1, 2, \ldots, n$. To estimate Q_i, we regard Q_i as the ith step transition matrix of the categorical data sequence $\{X_t\}$. Given the categorical data sequence $\{X_t\}$, one can count the transition frequency $f_{jk}^{(i)}$ in the sequence from state j to state k in the ith step. Hence one can construct the ith step transition matrix for the sequence $\{X_t\}$ as follows:

$$F^{(i)} = \begin{pmatrix} f_{11}^{(i)} & \cdots\cdots & f_{m1}^{(i)} \\ f_{12}^{(i)} & \cdots\cdots & f_{m2}^{(i)} \\ \vdots & \vdots \;\; \vdots & \vdots \\ f_{1m}^{(i)} & \cdots\cdots & f_{mm}^{(i)} \end{pmatrix}. \tag{6}$$

From $F^{(i)}$, we get the estimates for $Q_i = [q_{kj}^{(i)}]$ as follows:

$$\hat{Q}_i = \begin{pmatrix} \hat{q}_{11}^{(i)} & \cdots\cdots & \hat{q}_{m1}^{(i)} \\ \hat{q}_{12}^{(i)} & \cdots\cdots & \hat{q}_{m2}^{(i)} \\ \vdots & \vdots \;\; \vdots & \vdots \\ \hat{q}_{1m}^{(i)} & \cdots\cdots & \hat{q}_{mm}^{(i)} \end{pmatrix} \tag{7}$$

where

$$\hat{q}_{kj}^{(i)} = \begin{cases} \dfrac{f_{kj}^{(i)}}{\displaystyle\sum_{j=1}^{m} f_{kj}^{(i)}} & \text{if } \displaystyle\sum_{j=1}^{m} f_{kj}^{(i)} \neq 0 \\[4mm] 0 & \text{otherwise.} \end{cases} \tag{8}$$

We have the following two theorems which state that the estimators are unbias.

Theorem 3.1. *The estimators in Eq.(8) can be obtained by the maximization of the following likelihood function*

$$L = \prod_{i=1}^{n} \prod_{j=1}^{m} \prod_{k=1}^{m} (q_{kj}^{(i)})^{f_{kj}^{(i)}}$$

subject to

$$\sum_{k=1}^{m} q_{kj}^{(i)} = 1, \quad \forall 1 \le i \le n,\ 1 \le j \le m.$$

Theorem 3.2. *The estimators in Eq. (8) satisfies* $E(f_{kj}^{(i)}) = q_{kj}^{(i)} E\left(\displaystyle\sum_{j=1}^{m} f_{kj}^{(i)}\right).$

3.1. *Linear Programming Formulation for Estimation of* λ_i

Theorem 2.1 gives a sufficient condition for the sequence $\mathbf{X}_t$ to converge to a stationary distribution $\mathbf{X}$. Suppose $\mathbf{X}_t \to \bar{\mathbf{X}}$ as t goes to infinity then $\bar{\mathbf{X}}$ can be estimated from the sequence $\{X_t\}$ by computing the proportion of the occurrence of each state in the sequence and let us denote it by $\hat{\mathbf{X}}$. From Eq. (5) one would expect

$$\sum_{i=1}^{n} \lambda_i \hat{Q}_i \hat{\mathbf{X}} \approx \hat{\mathbf{X}}. \tag{9}$$

This suggests one possible way to estimate the parameters $\lambda = (\lambda_1, \ldots, \lambda_n)$ as follows. We consider the following optimization problem:

$$\min_{\lambda} \max_{k} \left| \left[\sum_{i=1}^{n} \lambda_i \hat{Q}_i \hat{\mathbf{X}} - \hat{\mathbf{X}} \right]_k \right|$$

subject to

$$\sum_{i=1}^{n} \lambda_i = 1, \quad \text{and} \quad \lambda_i \geq 0, \quad \forall i.$$

Here $[\cdot]_k$ denotes the kth entry of the vector. The constraints in the optimization problem guarantee the existence of the stationary distribution $\mathbf{X}$. Next we see that the above optimization problem formulate a linear programming problem:

$$\min_{\lambda} \ w$$

subject to

$$\begin{pmatrix} w \\ w \\ \vdots \\ w \end{pmatrix} \geq \hat{\mathbf{X}} - \left[\hat{Q}_1 \hat{\mathbf{X}} \mid \hat{Q}_2 \hat{\mathbf{X}} \mid \cdots \mid \hat{Q}_n \hat{\mathbf{X}} \right] \begin{pmatrix} \lambda_1 \\ \lambda_2 \\ \vdots \\ \lambda_n \end{pmatrix},$$

$$\begin{pmatrix} w \\ w \\ \vdots \\ w \end{pmatrix} \geq -\hat{\mathbf{X}} + \left[\hat{Q}_1 \hat{\mathbf{X}} \mid \hat{Q}_2 \hat{\mathbf{X}} \mid \cdots \mid \hat{Q}_n \hat{\mathbf{X}} \right] \begin{pmatrix} \lambda_1 \\ \lambda_2 \\ \vdots \\ \lambda_n \end{pmatrix},$$

$$w \geq 0, \quad \sum_{i=1}^{n} \lambda_i = 1, \quad \text{and} \quad \lambda_i \geq 0, \quad \forall i.$$

We can solve the above linear programming problem efficiently and obtain the parameters λ_i. In the next subsection, we demonstrate the estimation method by a simple example.

Instead of solving an min-max problem, we remark that we can also formulate the following optimization problem:

$$\min_{\lambda} \sum_{k=1}^{n} \left| \left[\sum_{i=1}^{n} \lambda_i \hat{Q}_i \hat{\mathbf{X}} - \hat{\mathbf{X}} \right]_k \right|$$

subject to

$$\sum_{i=1}^{n} \lambda_i = 1, \quad \text{and} \quad \lambda_i \geq 0, \quad \forall i.$$

The corresponding linear programming problem is given as follows:

$$\min_{\lambda} \sum_{k=1}^{n} w_k$$

subject to

$$\begin{pmatrix} w_1 \\ w_2 \\ \vdots \\ w_n \end{pmatrix} \geq \hat{\mathbf{X}} - \left[\hat{Q}_1 \hat{\mathbf{X}} \mid \hat{Q}_2 \hat{\mathbf{X}} \mid \cdots \mid \hat{Q}_n \hat{\mathbf{X}} \right] \begin{pmatrix} \lambda_1 \\ \lambda_2 \\ \vdots \\ \lambda_n \end{pmatrix},$$

$$\begin{pmatrix} w_1 \\ w_2 \\ \vdots \\ w_n \end{pmatrix} \geq -\hat{\mathbf{X}} + \left[\hat{Q}_1 \hat{\mathbf{X}} \mid \hat{Q}_2 \hat{\mathbf{X}} \mid \cdots \mid \hat{Q}_n \hat{\mathbf{X}} \right] \begin{pmatrix} \lambda_1 \\ \lambda_2 \\ \vdots \\ \lambda_n \end{pmatrix},$$

$$w_i \geq 0, \quad \forall i, \quad \sum_{i=1}^{n} \lambda_i = 1, \quad \text{and} \quad \lambda_i \geq 0, \quad \forall i.$$

3.2. An Example

We consider a sequence $\{X_t\}$ of three states ($m = 3$) given by

$$\{1, 1, 2, 2, 1, 3, 2, 1, 2, 3, 1, 2, 3, 1, 2, 3, 1, 2, 1, 2\}. \tag{10}$$

The sequence $\{X_t\}$ can be written in vector form

$$\mathbf{X}_1 = (1, 0, 0)^T, \quad \mathbf{X}_3 = (0, 1, 0)^T, \quad \cdots \quad , \mathbf{X}_{20} = (0, 1, 0)^T.$$

We consider $n = 2$, then from Eq. (10) we have the transition frequency matrices

$$F^{(1)} = \begin{pmatrix} 1\,3\,3 \\ 6\,1\,1 \\ 1\,3\,0 \end{pmatrix} \quad \text{and} \quad F^{(2)} = \begin{pmatrix} 1\,4\,1 \\ 2\,2\,3 \\ 3\,1\,0 \end{pmatrix}. \tag{11}$$

Therefore from Eq. (11) we have the i-step transition matrices ($i = 1, 2$) as follows:

$$\hat{Q}_1 = \begin{pmatrix} 1/8\ 3/7\ 3/4 \\ 3/4\ 1/7\ 1/4 \\ 1/8\ 3/7\ \ 0 \end{pmatrix} \quad \text{and} \quad \hat{Q}_2 = \begin{pmatrix} 1/6\ 4/7\ 1/4 \\ 1/3\ 2/7\ 3/4 \\ 1/2\ 1/7\ \ 0 \end{pmatrix} \tag{12}$$

and

$$\hat{\mathbf{X}} = (\frac{2}{5}, \frac{2}{5}, \frac{1}{5})^T.$$

Hence we have

$$\hat{Q}_1\hat{\mathbf{X}} = (\frac{13}{35}, \frac{57}{140}, \frac{31}{140})^T, \quad \text{and} \quad \hat{Q}_2\hat{\mathbf{X}} = (\frac{29}{84}, \frac{167}{420}, \frac{9}{35})^T.$$

To estimate λ_i we consider the optimization problem:

$$\min_{\lambda_1, \lambda_2} w$$

subject to

$$\begin{cases} w \geq \dfrac{2}{5} - \dfrac{13}{35}\lambda_1 - \dfrac{29}{84}\lambda_2 \\ w \geq -\dfrac{2}{5} + \dfrac{13}{35}\lambda_1 + \dfrac{29}{84}\lambda_2 \\ w \geq \dfrac{2}{5} - \dfrac{57}{140}\lambda_1 - \dfrac{167}{420}\lambda_2 \\ w \geq -\dfrac{2}{5} + \dfrac{57}{140}\lambda_1 + \dfrac{167}{420}\lambda_2 \\ w \geq \dfrac{1}{5} - \dfrac{31}{140}\lambda_1 - \dfrac{9}{35}\lambda_2 \\ w \geq -\dfrac{1}{5} + \dfrac{31}{140}\lambda_1 + \dfrac{9}{35}\lambda_2 \\ w \geq 0, \quad \lambda_1 + \lambda_2 = 1, \quad \lambda_1, \lambda_2 \geq 0. \end{cases}$$

The optimal solution is

$$(\lambda_1^*, \lambda_2^*, w^*) = (1, 0, 0.0286),$$

and we have the model

$$\mathbf{X}_{n+1} = \hat{Q}_1\mathbf{X}_n. \tag{13}$$

We remark that if we do not specify the non-negativity of λ_1 and λ_2, the optimal solution becomes

$$(\lambda_1^{**}, \lambda_2^{**}, w^{**}) = (1.60, -0.60, 0.0129),$$

the corresponding model is

$$\mathbf{X}_{n+1} = 1.60\hat{Q}_1\mathbf{X}_n - 0.60\hat{Q}_2\mathbf{X}_{n-1}. \tag{14}$$

Although w^{**} is less than w^*, the model Eq. (14) is not suitable. It is easy to check that

$$1.60\hat{Q}_1 \begin{pmatrix} 1 \\ 0 \\ 0 \end{pmatrix} - 0.60\hat{Q}_2 \begin{pmatrix} 0 \\ 1 \\ 0 \end{pmatrix} = \begin{pmatrix} -0.1427 \\ 1.0285 \\ 0.1142 \end{pmatrix},$$

therefore λ_1^{**} and λ_2^{**} are not valid parameters.

We note that if we consider the optimization problem:

$$\min_{\lambda_1,\lambda_2} w_1 + w_2 + w_3$$

subject to

$$\begin{cases} w_1 \geq \dfrac{2}{5} - \dfrac{13}{35}\lambda_1 - \dfrac{29}{84}\lambda_2 \\ w_1 \geq -\dfrac{2}{5} + \dfrac{13}{35}\lambda_1 + \dfrac{29}{84}\lambda_2 \\ w_2 \geq \dfrac{2}{5} - \dfrac{57}{140}\lambda_1 - \dfrac{167}{420}\lambda_2 \\ w_2 \geq -\dfrac{2}{5} + \dfrac{57}{140}\lambda_1 + \dfrac{167}{420}\lambda_2 \\ w_3 \geq \dfrac{1}{5} - \dfrac{31}{140}\lambda_1 - \dfrac{9}{35}\lambda_2 \\ w_3 \geq -\dfrac{1}{5} + \dfrac{31}{140}\lambda_1 + \dfrac{9}{35}\lambda_2 \\ w_1, w_2, w_3 \geq 0, \quad \lambda_1 + \lambda_2 = 1, \quad \lambda_1, \lambda_2 \geq 0. \end{cases}$$

The optimal solution is the same as the previous min-max formulation and is equal to

$$(\lambda_1^*, \lambda_2^*, w_1^*, w_2^*, w_3^*) = (1, 0, 0.0286, 0.0071, 0.0214).$$

4. Some Practical Examples

In this section we apply our model to some examples data sequences. The data sequences are the DNA sequence and the sales demand data sequence. Given the state vectors $\mathbf{X}_i$, $i = t-n, t-n+1, \cdots, t-1$, the state probability distribution at time t can be estimated as follows:

$$\hat{\mathbf{X}}_t = \sum_{i=1}^{n} \lambda_i \hat{Q}_i \mathbf{X}_{t-i}.$$

In many applications, one would like to make use of the higher-order Markov models for the purpose of prediction. According to the this state probability distribution, the prediction of the next state $\hat{X}_t$ at time t can be taken as the state with the maximum probability, i.e.,

$$\hat{X}_t = j, \quad \text{if } [\hat{\mathbf{X}}_t]_i \leq [\hat{\mathbf{X}}_t]_j, \forall 1 \leq i \leq m.$$

To evaluate the performance and effectiveness of our higher-order Markov chain model, a prediction result is measured by the prediction accuracy r defined as

$$r = \frac{\sum_{t=n+1}^{T} \delta_t}{T},$$

where T is the length of the data sequence and

$$\delta_t = \begin{cases} 1, & \text{if } \hat{X}_t = X_t \\ 0, & \text{otherwise.} \end{cases}$$

Using the example in the previous section, there are two possible prediction rules:

$$\begin{cases} \hat{X}_{t+1} = 2, & \text{if } X_t = 1, \\ \hat{X}_{t+1} = 1, & \text{if } X_t = 2, \\ \hat{X}_{t+1} = 1, & \text{if } X_t = 3 \end{cases}$$

or

$$\begin{cases} \hat{X}_{t+1} = 2, & \text{if } X_t = 1, \\ \hat{X}_{t+1} = 3, & \text{if } X_t = 2, \\ \hat{X}_{t+1} = 1, & \text{if } X_t = 3. \end{cases}$$

The prediction accuracy r for the sequence in Eq. (10) is equal to $12/19$ for both prediction rules.

Next the test results on different data sequences are discussed. In the following tests, we solve min-max optimization problems to determine the parameters λ_i of higher-order Markov models. However, we remark that the results of using the 1-norm optimization problem as discussed in the previous section are about the same as that of using the min-max formulation. All the computations here are done by MATLAB with a PC.

4.1. The DNA Sequence

In order to determine whether certain short DNA sequence (a categorical data sequence of four possible categories) occurred more often than would be expected by chance, Avery[2] examined the Markovian structure of introns from several other genes in mice. Here we apply our model to the introns from the mouse αA-crystallin gene see for instance Raftery and Tavare[11]. We compare our second-order model with the Raftery second-order model. The model parameters of the model are given in Raftery and Tavare[11]. The results are reported in Table 1 below.

Table 1. Prediction Accuracy in the DNA Sequence.

	2-state model	3-state model	4-state model
New Model	0.57	0.49	0.33
Raftery's Model	0.57	0.47	0.31
Random Chosen	0.50	0.33	0.25

The comparison is made with different grouping of states as suggested in Raftery and Tavare[11]. In grouping states 1 and 3, and states 2 and 4 we have a 2-state model. Our model gives

$$\hat{Q}_1 = \begin{pmatrix} 0.5568 & 0.4182 \\ 0.4432 & 0.5818 \end{pmatrix}, \quad \hat{Q}_2 = \begin{pmatrix} 0.4550 & 0.5149 \\ 0.5450 & 0.4851 \end{pmatrix}$$

$$\hat{\mathbf{X}} = (0.4858, 0.5142)^T, \quad \lambda_1 = 0.7529 \quad \text{and} \quad \lambda_2 = 0.2471.$$

In grouping states 1 and 3 we have a 3-state model. Our model gives

$$\hat{Q}_1 = \begin{pmatrix} 0.5568 & 0.3573 & 0.4949 \\ 0.2571 & 0.3440 & 0.2795 \\ 0.1861 & 0.2987 & 0.2256 \end{pmatrix}, \quad \hat{Q}_2 = \begin{pmatrix} 0.4550 & 0.5467 & 0.4747 \\ 0.3286 & 0.2293 & 0.2727 \\ 0.2164 & 0.2240 & 0.2525 \end{pmatrix}$$

$$\hat{\mathbf{X}} = (0.4858, 0.2869, 0.2272)^T, \quad \lambda_1 = 1.0 \quad \text{and} \quad \lambda_2 = 0.0$$

If there is no grouping, we have a 4-state model. Our model gives

$$\hat{Q}_1 = \begin{pmatrix} 0.2268 & 0.2987 & 0.2274 & 0.1919 \\ 0.2492 & 0.3440 & 0.2648 & 0.2795 \\ 0.3450 & 0.0587 & 0.3146 & 0.3030 \\ 0.1789 & 0.2987 & 0.1931 & 0.2256 \end{pmatrix}, \quad \hat{Q}_2 = \begin{pmatrix} 0.1891 & 0.2907 & 0.2368 & 0.2323 \\ 0.3814 & 0.2293 & 0.2773 & 0.2727 \\ 0.2532 & 0.2560 & 0.2305 & 0.2424 \\ 0.1763 & 0.2240 & 0.2555 & 0.2525 \end{pmatrix}$$

$$\hat{\mathbf{X}} = (0.2395, 0.2869, 0.2464, 0.2272)^T, \quad \lambda_1 = 0.253 \quad \text{and} \quad \lambda_2 = 0.747.$$

When using the expected errors (assuming that the next state is randomly chosen with equal probability for all states) as a reference, the percentage gain in effectiveness of using higher-order Markov chain models is in the 3-state model. In this case, our model also gives a better estimation when compares with the Raftery's model.

4.2. *The Sales Demand Data*

A large soft-drink company in Hong Kong presently faces an in-house problem of production planning and inventory control. A pressing issue that stands out is the storage space of its central warehouse, which often finds itself in the state of overflow or near capacity. The Company is thus in urgent needs to study the interplay between the storage space requirement and the overall growing sales demand. There are product categories due to the sales volume. All products are labeled as either very fast-moving (very high sales volume), fast-moving, standard, slow-moving or very slow-moving (low sales volume). Such labeling are useful from both marketing and production planning points of view. Here we employ higher-order Markov models to predict categories of these four products. For our new model, we consider the second-order ($n = 2$) model and use the data to estimate $\hat{Q}_i$ and λ_i ($i = 1, 2$). The results are reported in Table 2. For comparison, we also study the first-order and the second-order full Markov chain model. Results shows the effectiveness of our new model.

Table 2. Prediction Accuracy in the Sales Demand Data.

	Product A	Product B	Product C	Product D
First-order Markov Model	0.76	0.70	0.39	0.74
Second-order Markov Model	0.79	0.78	0.51	0.83
New Model ($n = 2$)	0.78	0.76	0.43	0.78
Random Chosen	0.20	0.20	0.20	0.20

5. Concluding Remarks

In this paper we propose an higher-order Markov chain model for categorical data sequences. The number of model parameters increases linearly with respect to the number of lags. Efficient estimation methods for the model parameters are also proposed and designed by making use of the observed transition frequencies and the steady state distribution. The algorithm can be easily implemented in EXCEL environment. Numerical examples are given to demonstrate the predicting power of our model. The followings are some possible research directions for our model: It is well known that the hidden layer of a Hidden Markov model (HMM) is a first-order Markov chain model. It will be interesting to extend our idea to develop higher-order HMM, see for instance MacDonald and Zucchini[9]. In this paper we have not addressed the problem of statistical inference test for the model. Therefore this will be our future work.

References

1. S. Adke and D. Deshmukh, *Limit Distribution of a High Order Markov Chain*, J. R. Statist. Soc. B **50** 105–108 (1988).
2. P. Avery, *The Analysis of Intron Data and Their Use in the Detection od Short Signals*, J. Mol. Evoln. **26** 335–340 (1987).
3. P. Brockwell and R. Davis, *Time Series: Theory and Methods*, Springer-Verlag, New York (1991).
4. W. Ching, E. Fung and M. Ng, *Higher-order Markov Chain Models for Categorical Data Sequences*, preprint, (2002).
5. K. Gowda and E. Diday, *Symbolic Clustering Using a New Dissimilarity Measure*, Pattern Recognition, **24** 567–578 (1991).
6. J. Huang, M. Ng, W. Ching, D. Cheung, J. Ng, *A Cube Model for Web Access Sessions and Cluster Analysis*, WEBKDD 2001, Workshop on Mining Web Log Data Across All Customer Touch Points, The Seventh ACM SIGKDD International Conference on Knowledge Discovery and Data Mining, August, 47–58 (2001).
7. W. Li and M. Kwok, *Some Results on the Estimation of a Higher Order Markov Chain*, Comm. Statist. Simulation Comput. **19** 363–380 (1990).
8. J. Logan, *A Structural Model of the Higher-order Markov Process incorporating reversion effects*, J. Math. Sociol., **8** 75–89 (1981).
9. I. MacDonald and W. Zucchini, *Hidden Markov and Other Models for Discrete-valued Time Series*, Chapman & Hall, London (1997).
10. A. Raftery, *A Model for High-order Markov Chains*, J. R. Statist. Soc. B, **47** 528–539 (1985).
11. A. Raftery and S. Tavare, *Estimation and Modelling Repeated Patterns in High Order Markov Chains with the Mixture Transition Distribution Model*, Appl. Statist., **43** 179–99 (1994).
12. M. Waterman, *Introduction to Computational Biology*, Chapman & Hall, Cambridge (1995).

AN APPLICATION OF THE MIXTURE AUTOREGRESSIVE MODEL: A CASE STUDY OF MODELLING YEARLY SUNSPOT DATA

KIN FOON KEVIN WONG

Department of Mathematical Sciences,
College of Science, University of the Ryukyus,
Nishihara-cho 1, Okinawa 903-0213, Japan
E-mail: wong@math.u-ryukyu.ac.jp

CHUN SHAN WONG*

Department of Finance,
The Chinese University of Hong Kong,
Shatin, N.T., Hong Kong
E-mail: albertw@baf.msmail.cuhk.edu.hk

The mixture autoregressive (MAR) model has been introduced in the literature recently. The MAR model possesses certain nice features which other time series models do not enjoy. We apply the MAR models to the yearly sunspot numbers and made comparison with other competing models.

1. Introduction

Many nonlinear time series models have been proposed in the literature in the past two decades. Numerous successful applications of these models are reported. These models usually specify a nonlinear conditional mean and/or variance function and assume a Gaussian conditional distribution. Under the normality assumption, the marginal and/or conditional distributions of the time series are unimodal and symmetric. The unimodal limitation persists even the Gaussian distribution is replaced by a heavy-tailed distribution such as the Student t distribution. In some real-life examples, a multimodal conditional distribution may seem more appropriate than a unimodal conditional distribution.

The mixture distributions has a comparatively long history in the analysis of independent data. See, for example, Titterington et al.[1] Le et al.[2]

---

*Work partially supported by Direct Grant of the Research Grant Council of Hong Kong.

introduced the Gaussian mixture transition distribution (GMTD) models for modelling flat stretches, bursts and outliers in time series. The GMTD models allow a bit more flexibility in the shape of conditional distributions. However, these models cannot handle cyclical time series well because of the restrictions inherent in the models [3].

Recently, Wong and Li[3] generalized the idea of mixture distributions to the context of nonlinear time series. The proposed mixture autoregressive (MAR) model is actually a mixture of K Gaussian autoregressive models. The model has several nice features. First, various forms of stationarity results can be proven. It is possible that a mixture of a nonstationary autoregressive (AR) component and a stationary AR component results in a stationary process. Secondly, the autocorrelation functions can be easily derived. Thirdly, as a mixture model, the conditional distributions of the time series given the past history are changing over time. These distributions can be multimodal. It is also expected that the marginal distribution of the time series could be multimodal. Lastly, the MAR model is capable of modelling time series with heteroscedasticity. Wong and Li[3] have demonstrated the usefulness of the MAR model with the International Business Machines (IBM) stock prices data and the classical Canadian lynx data.

In this paper, we apply the MAR models to the yearly sunspot numbers [4]. We compare the MAR model with two other time series models, namely, the classical AR models and the self-exciting threshold autoregressive (SETAR) models, on the basis of the accuracy of the point predictions and the ability to describe predictive distributions. In Sec. 2, we briefly discuss the three time series models under consideration. The analysis of the yearly sunspot numbers is presented in Sec. 3. In Sec. 4, we discuss several extensions of the MAR model and outline some remaining problems.

2. The Models

An AR process of order p, AR(p), is defined by

$$y_t = \phi_0 + \phi_1 y_{t-1} + \cdots + \phi_p y_{t-p} + \epsilon_t, \qquad (1)$$

where y_t denotes the variable of interest at time t; and ϵ_t is the random error which follows a normal distribution with mean zero and variance σ^2. The conditional mean of y_t depends on its previous p observations. Statistical properties of the AR models can be founded in standard textbook on time series analysis, such as Brockwell and Davis[5].

Since its introduction two decades ago, the SETAR model has been widely used in different context for modelling nonlinear time series. The

SETAR model is basically a piecewise linear model with a threshold regime-switching mechanism. A SETAR$(K; p_1, \ldots, p_K)$ is defined by

$$y_t = \phi_{i0} + \phi_{i1} y_{t-1} + \cdots + \phi_{ip_i} y_{t-p_i} + \epsilon_{it}, \qquad \text{if } y_{t-d} \in D_i, \qquad (2)$$

where d is the delay parameter; D_i, $i = 1, 2, \ldots, K$, are some non-overlapping partition of the real line; and the random error ϵ_{it} is normally distributed with zero mean and variance σ_i^2. See Tong[6] for a comprehensive review of the SETAR model.

An MAR$(K; p_1, \ldots, p_K)$ model, proposed by Wong and Li[3] is defined by

$$y_t = \phi_{i0} + \phi_{i1} y_{t-1} + \cdots + \phi_{ip_i} y_{t-p_i} + \epsilon_{it}, \qquad \text{with probability } \alpha_i, \qquad (3)$$

for $i = 1, 2, \ldots, K$. Here, ϵ_{it}, the ith component's random error, is normally distributed with mean zero and variance σ_i^2; and α_i's are all positive and sum to one. Note that the AR model is a special case of MAR model when there is only one component. The conditional distribution function $F(.)$ is defined as

$$F(y_t | I_{t-1}) = \sum_{i=1}^{K} \alpha_i \Phi \left(\frac{y_t - \phi_{i0} - \phi_{i1} y_{t-1} - \cdots - \phi_{ip_i} y_{t-p_i}}{\sigma_i} \right),$$

where $\Phi(.)$ is the cumulative distribution of the standard normal distribution and I_{t-1} is the information set up to time $t - 1$.

Figure 1 shows the one-step ahead conditional density functions of the sunspot numbers from years 1921 to 1926, generated from the fitted MAR$(2; 2, 11)$ model in Sec. 3. The conditional density functions change from unimodal to bimodal because the conditional means of the components, which depend on the past values, change over time. The ability to handle the changing multi-modal conditional distribution is an attractive feature of the MAR model. However, there is no easy way to obtain the multi-step ahead conditional distribution, one has to rely on some Monte Carlo methods.

Wong and Li[3] proposed the use of the EM algorithm [7] for the parameter estimation. In the E-step, we take the conditional expectation of the unobserved random variables that indicate which components the variables y_t come from. And in the M-step, we maximize the log-likelihood function given the conditional expectation of the unobserved variables.

A Bayesian information criterion (BIC) can be used for the model selection of the MAR model. The BIC is defined as

$$\text{BIC} = -2l + \log(n - p_{\max}) \left(3K - 1 + \sum_{i=1}^{K} p_i \right),$$

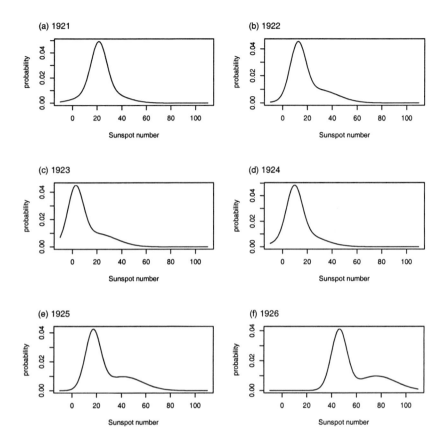

Figure 1. One-step conditional distributions of the sunspot numbers from years 1921 to 1926, generated from the fitted MAR(2;2,11) model.

$$l = \sum_{t=p_{\max}+1}^{n} \log f\left(y_t | I_{t-1}\right) = \sum_{t=p_{\max}+1}^{n} \log \left\{ \frac{d}{dy_t} F\left(y_t | I_{t-1}\right) \right\}.$$

Here, l denotes the maximized log-likelihood; n is the number of observations; and $p_{\max} = \max(p_1, \ldots, p_K)$ is the highest order among the K components. As illustrated in Wong and Li[3], the minimum BIC procedure performs very well in selecting the orders of the AR components, but performs rather poorly in selecting the number of components. The selection of the number of components for an MAR model is still an open problem.

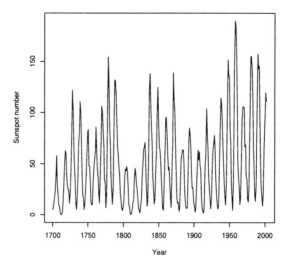

Figure 2. Sunspot numbers from years 1700 to 1999.

3. Sunspot Numbers

Sunspots are commonly known to be the places on the sun cooler than the rest of the sun's surface. As they are cooler, they appear to be darker than the rest of the sun. Scholars observed that the yearly record of the number of sunspots is cyclical with a period of roughly 11 years, which is called solar cycle, but hardly can we describe the reason for this phenomenon.

We adopt the yearly sunspot numbers from years 1700 to 1999 [4] for model fitting and comparison. Figures 2 and 3 show a time series plot and a histogram of the sunspot numbers respectively. The cyclical feature of the sunspot numbers is obvious from Fig. 2. And the marginal distribution of the sunspot numbers is skewed to the right from Fig. 3. These features suggest that a linear time series model such as AR model cannot handle the data well. The more sophisticated time series models should be considered.

In order to test the prediction power of individual models, we split the data into two parts. The training part, data in years 1700 to 1920, is used for model fitting and the test part, data in years 1921 to 1999, is reserved for the comparison of the forecasts derived from the AR, SETAR and MAR models.

The fitted AR(9) model, as suggested in Tong[6], for the sunspot data is

$$Y_t = 8.43 + 1.22Y_{t-1} - 0.47Y_{t-2} - 0.14Y_{t-3} + 0.16Y_{t-4} - 0.14Y_{t-5}$$
$$+0.06Y_{t-6} - 0.05Y_{t-7} + 0.07Y_{t-8} + 0.11Y_{t-9} + \epsilon_t, \qquad (5)$$

with the estimated variance $\hat{\sigma}^2 = 198.38$.

Tong[6] suggested a SETAR(2; 3, 11) model for the sunspot numbers cov-

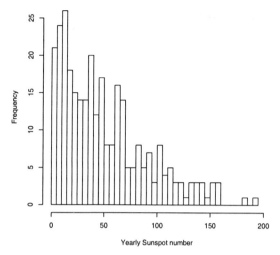

Figure 3. Histogram of sunspot numbers from years 1700 to 1999.

ered in the training part. The fitted $\text{SETAR}(2; 3, 11)$ is given by

$$
Y_t = \begin{cases}
\begin{aligned}
& 11.97 + 1.71Y_{t-1} - 1.26Y_{t-2} \\
& \quad +0.43Y_{t-3} + \epsilon_{1t}
\end{aligned} & \text{if } Y_{t-3} \leq 36.6, \\[2mm]
\begin{aligned}
& 7.84 + 0.73Y_{t-1} - 0.04Y_{t-2} - 0.20Y_{t-3} \\
& \quad +0.16Y_{t-4} - 0.22Y_{t-5} + 0.02Y_{t-6} \\
& \quad +0.15Y_{t-7} - 0.24Y_{t-8} + 0.31Y_{t-9} \\
& \quad -0.37Y_{t-10} + 0.38Y_{t-11} + \epsilon_{2t}
\end{aligned} & \text{if } Y_{t-3} > 36.6,
\end{cases} \tag{6}
$$

with the estimated variances $\hat{\sigma}_1^2 = 254.64$ and $\hat{\sigma}_2^2 = 66.80$.

We consider both two-component and three-component MAR models for the sunspot numbers. The best two-component MAR model, according to the minimum BIC criterion, is an $\text{MAR}(2;2,11)$ model with BIC = 1329.26. The fitted $\text{MAR}(2; 2, 11)$ is

$$
Y_t = \begin{cases}
19.76 + 1.60Y_{t-1} - 0.89Y_{t-2} + \epsilon_{it} & \text{with prob. } 0.3809, \\[2mm]
\begin{aligned}
& 6.13 + 0.70Y_{t-1} - 0.01Y_{t-2} - 0.18Y_{t-3} \\
& \quad +0.10Y_{t-4} - 0.14Y_{t-5} - 0.07Y_{t-6} \\
& \quad +0.23Y_{t-7} - 0.16Y_{t-8} - 0.03Y_{t-9} \\
& \quad +0.15Y_{t-10} + 0.15Y_{t-11} + \epsilon_{2t}
\end{aligned} & \text{with prob. } 0.6191,
\end{cases} \tag{7}
$$

with the estimated variances $\hat{\sigma}_1^2 = 244.26$ and $\hat{\sigma}_2^2 = 38.64$.

The best three-component MAR model is an $\text{MAR}(3; 1, 2, 7)$ model with

BIC = 1367.69. The fitted MAR(3;1,2,7) model is

$$Y_t = \begin{cases} -2.10 + 0.80Y_{t-1} + \epsilon_{1t} & \text{with prob. } 0.2219, \\ 23.89 + 1.67Y_{t-1} - 0.96Y_{t-2} + \epsilon_{2t} & \text{with prob. } 0.2989, \\ 9.27 + 1.10Y_{t-1} - 0.23Y_{t-2} - 0.24Y_{t-3} \\ \quad +0.19Y_{t-4} - 0.18Y_{t-5} - 0.20Y_{t-6} \\ \quad +0.25Y_{t-7} + \epsilon_{3t} & \text{with prob. } 0.4792, \end{cases} \tag{8}$$

with the estimated variances $\hat{\sigma}_1^2 = 20.82$, $\hat{\sigma}_2^2 = 218.36$ and $\hat{\sigma}_3^2 = 44.94$.

The comparison of the four fitted models is drawn in two dimensions: (i) out-sample forecast performance; and (ii) accuracy of the predictive distributions. We first work on the out-sample forecast. We generate one-step- to ten-step-ahead forecasts using each of the fitted models. Table 1 shows the root mean squared prediction errors of the multi-step ahead forecasts. From Table 1, the one-step-ahead forecasts generated from the SETAR model gives the smallest root mean squared prediction error. For larger lead time, the AR(9) model performs the best among the four models. On the other hand, the MAR models are relatively weaker in point prediction. As discussed in Wong and Li[3], the point forecasts generated by the MAR models may not be the best predictor of the futures values, as the conditional distribution of the time series can be multimodal.

Table 1. Root mean squared errors of the multi-step ahead point forecasts for the sunspot numbers in the test part.

Lead time	Model			
	SETAR(2;3,11)	AR(9)	MAR(2;2,11)	MAR(3;1,2,7)
1	17.13	17.95	20.88	21.08
2	29.45	27.29	34.45	36.20
3	37.90	32.85	41.84	46.39
4	42.07	34.80	43.91	51.17
5	43.29	35.32	44.25	53.10
6	42.66	35.42	44.48	53.57
7	43.07	35.63	45.14	53.60
8	43.48	35.25	45.52	53.52
9	43.32	35.26	45.81	53.67
10	43.46	35.53	45.98	53.51

We now compare the models based on their generated predictive distributions. Specifically, the one-step- and two-step-ahead predictive distributions, that is $F(Y_{t+1}|I_t)$ and $F(Y_{t+2}|I_t)$, are generated. The empirical coverages of the one-step- and two-step-ahead prediction intervals are shown in Table 2. From Table 2, the empirical coverages of the AR(9)-based and the MAR(3;1,2,7)-based one-step-ahead prediction intervals are closer to the nominal coverages than that generated by the SETAR and MAR(2;2,11) models. Consider the two-step-ahead prediction intervals, the MAR(3;1,2,7) model performs better than the other three models. Note that although the empirical coverages for the AR(9)-based two-step-ahead prediction intervals are close to the nominal coverages at high nominal levels, they are consistently higher than the nominal coverages at lower nominal levels.

Table 2. Empirical coverages (%) of the one-step- and two-step-ahead prediction intervals for the sunspot numbers in the test part.

Model	Theoretical coverage						
	95%	90%	85%	80%	70%	60%	50%
	One-step-ahead prediction intervals						
SETAR(2;3,11)	81.0%	75.9%	70.9%	69.6%	60.8%	49.4%	39.2%
AR(9)	87.3%	83.5%	77.2%	74.7%	65.8%	57.0%	50.6%
MAR(2;2,11)	84.8%	81.0%	79.7%	73.4%	64.6%	49.4%	44.3%
MAR(3;1,2,7)	87.3%	82.3%	79.7%	74.7%	64.6%	55.7%	45.6%
	Two-step-ahead prediction intervals						
SETAR(2;3,11)	84.8%	81.0%	78.5%	78.5%	73.4%	64.6%	54.4%
AR(9)	92.3%	87.2%	80.8%	79.5%	76.9%	75.6%	65.4%
MAR(2;2,11)	89.9%	78.5%	77.2%	73.4%	64.6%	54.4%	48.1%
MAR(3;1,2,7)	89.9%	83.5%	79.7%	77.2%	68.4%	60.8%	54.4%

We also compute the empirical coverages of the one-step- and two-step-ahead prediction intervals for the sunspot numbers in the training part. The results are shown in Table 3. The empirical coverages of the two MAR-based prediction intervals are closer to the nominal coverages than that generated by the other models. On the whole, the MAR(3;1,2,7) model is better than the other three models in describing the predictive distributions of the yearly sunspot numbers.

Note that, in generating the two-step predictive distributions, we use a Monte Carlo approach for the MAR and SETAR models. The Monte Carlo

Table 3. Empirical coverages (%) of the one-step- and two-step-ahead prediction intervals for the sunspot numbers in the training part.

Model	Theoretical coverage						
	95%	90%	85%	80%	70%	60%	50%
	One-step-ahead prediction intervals						
SETAR(2;3,11)	94.3%	92.9%	89.0%	83.3%	71.9%	64.8%	53.3%
AR(9)	94.8%	92.4%	86.2%	83.8%	76.2%	65.7%	56.2%
MAR(2;2,11)	96.7%	91.9%	87.6%	81.4%	71.4%	59.0%	50.0%
MAR(3;1,2,7)	96.2%	90.5%	87.1%	81.0%	71.0%	61.0%	50.5%
	Two-step-ahead prediction intervals						
SETAR(2;3,11)	95.2%	91.4%	89.0%	85.7%	77.6%	68.1%	53.8%
AR(9)	93.8%	91.0%	90.0%	86.3%	76.8%	66.8%	58.3%
MAR(2;2,11)	92.9%	90.0%	85.7%	80.0%	70.5%	61.4%	50.0%
MAR(3;1,2,7)	95.2%	92.9%	89.0%	81.0%	70.5%	61.0%	46.7%

approximation of the two-step predictive distribution is defined by

$$
F\left(y_{t+2}|I_t\right) = \frac{1}{N}\sum_{i=1}^{N} F\left(y_{t+2}\left|I_t, y_{t+1}^{(i)}\right.\right),
\tag{9}
$$

where $\left\{y_{t+1}^{(i)}\right\}$ are sampled from the one-step predictive distribution $F(y_{t+1}|I_t)$ and N is chosen to be 10,000.

4. Discussion

We have discussed the application of the MAR models via a case study of modelling yearly sunspot data. We have shown that the MAR models are potentiality useful in modelling nonlinear time series. The models allow much flexibility which other models do not enjoy.

Several extensions of the MAR models have been made in the literature. The mixture autoregressive conditional heteroscedastic (MAR-ARCH) models, proposed by Wong and Li[8], consist of a mixture of K autoregressive components with autoregressive conditional heteroscedasticity; that is, the conditional mean of the variable of interest follows a MAR process, whereas the conditional variance of the variable of interest follows a mixture ARCH process [9]. The usefulness of the MAR-ARCH models was illustrated with a chemical process temperature series and the Standard and Poor Composite 500 stock price index.

Wong and Li[10] proposed a logistic mixture autoregressive with exogenous variables (LMARX) model which consists of a mixture of two Gaussian transfer function models with the mixing probabilities, that is α_i in MAR model, changing over time. Applications of the LMARX model was illustrated with two examples, the riverflow data of River Jökulsá Eystri in Iceland and the Canadian lynx data.

Another extension of the MAR model is to relax the normality assumption in its AR components. Kam *et al.*[11] consider a mixture autoregressive model with a heavy-tailed conditional distribution for each AR component. This model has great potentials in estimating financial risk measures such as Value-at-Risk (VaR).

Problems for the mixture-type time series models remain open. As mentioned in Sec. 2, the estimation problem of the number of components in an MAR model requires further research. And the model diagnostic procedures for the MAR model has yet been developed.

As a conclusion, the mixture-type time series model is a promising alternative to the existing nonlinear time series models which deserves further investigation.

References

1. Titterington, D. M., Smith, A. F. M. and Makov, U. E. (1985) *Statistical Analysis of Finite Mixture Distributions*. New York: Wiley.
2. Le, N. D., Martin, R. D. and Raftery, A. E. (1996) Modeling flat stretches, bursts, and outliers in time series using mixture transition distribution models. *J. Am. Statist. Ass.*, **91**, 1504-1514.
3. Wong, C. S. and Li, W. K. (2000) On a mixture autoregressive model. *J. R. Statist. Soc. B*, **62**, 95-115.
4. SIDC (2002) *Sunspot Index Data Center*. http://sidc.oma.be/index.php3.
5. Brockwell, P. J. and Davis, R. A. (2002) *Introduction to Time Series and Forecasting*, New York: Springer.
6. Tong, H. (1990) *Non-linear Time Series*. New York: Oxford university Press.
7. Dempster, A. P., Laird, N. M. and Rubin, D. B. (1977) Maximum likelihood from incomplete data via the EM algorithm (with discussion). *J. R. Statist. Soc. B*, **39**, 1-38.
8. Wong, C. S. and Li, W. K. (2001) On a mixture autoregressive conditional heteroscedastic model. *J. Am. Statist. Ass.*, **96**, 982-995.
9. Engle, R. F. (1982) Autoregressive conditional heteroscedasticity with estimates of the variance of United Kingdom inflation. *Econometrica*, **50**, 987-1007.
10. Wong, C. S. and Li, W. K. (2001) On a logistic mixture autoregressive model. *Biometrika*, **88**, 833-846.
11. Kam, P. L., Chan, W. S. and Wong, C. S. (2002) Mixture autoregression with heavy-tailed conditional distribution. In progress.

BOND RISK AND RETURN IN THE SSE

LONGZHEN FAN
School of Management, Fudan University,
220 Handan Road,
Shanghai, 200433, P. R. China
E-mail: lzfan_fudan@hotmail.com

Abstract: The yield term structures implied in bond prices in the SSE are given, and two typical yield curves are found: inverted yield curves from January 1994 to March 1996, and rising yield curves from April 1996 to October 2001. Then traditional expectations hypothesis is tested and find that it does not hold in the SSE. With all the forward rates in the term structure, it is found that bond excess returns have strong predictability, and the predictability is absorbed by two predicting factors. Risk analysis finds that bond risk premia come from three risk sources: level factor, slope factor, and curvature factor.

1. Introduction

The identification of the factors that determine the time series and cross section behavior of the term structure of interest rate is a recurrent topic in finance literature. Most papers have focused on the U. S. bond market. Early empirical works like Fama (1984a, 1984b), Fama-Bliss (1987) have showed that traditional expectations hypothesis does not hold in the U.S. bond market, and they also provided evidence of rich patterns of variation in expected bond returns across time and maturities. Following the studies was a large literature that discussed the inconsistency of these patterns with the implications of the traditional expectations hypothesis. Examples are Campell, and Shiller (1991), Backus, Moumudar, and Wu(1997). They found that bond excess returns and yield curves have time-varying risk premia. Cochrane and Piazzesi (2002) made a study on predictability and risk premia of bond excess returns in the U. S. bond market. They found that a linear combination of yield term structure can catch the predictability of the bond excess returns. They also found a time-varying risk premium specification that can be used to explain the bond excess returns, and the specification is an AFFINE term structure.

Little is known about interest rates in China financial market. China now has a different financial system compared with west developed market. In China, most people consider bank saving interest rates specified by the Government as default free interest rates. When China treasury bonds are issued, usually the yield rates are a little higher than the saving rates. T-bond markets also are separated. One part of T- bonds are issued to household. If the holders want to sell the bonds before maturity, they have to sell them to the banks acting as the agency of the Government. Another part of T-bonds are issued to banks and some financial institutions, they are traded between them. All the above T-bonds lack liquidity. Many people or institutions buying them tend to hold them to maturity. The final part of T-bonds are the T-bonds that are issued and then traded in the exchanges-the Shanghai Stock Exchange and the Shenzhen Stock Exchange. This is a high liquid market. The implied interest rates of bond prices in this market can be considered as market interest rates. This paper studies the returns on T-bonds traded in the Shanghai Stock Exchange (the SSE), and their implied interest rates. The interests include: (1) whether expectations hypothesis holds or not; (2) whether bond excess returns can be forecasted or not; (3) how to model bond risk and risk premia in the SSE.

2. Yield Curve and Expectations Hypothesis Testing

2.1. *Notation*
First some Notations are introduced. We denote the log price of n-year zero-coupon bond with face value 1 at time t by $p_t^{(n)}$

$p_t^{(n)}$: log price at time t of n-year zero-coupon bond with face value 1
The log yield of the bond is

$$y_t^{(n)} = -\frac{1}{n} p_t^{(n)}$$

Log forward rate at time t implied by forward contracts between time t+n-1 and t+n is

$$f_t^{(n-1 \to n)} = p_t^{(n-1)} - p_t^{(n)}$$

Log holding period return from buying a n-year zero coupon bond at time t and sell it at time t+1 is

$$hpr_{t+1}^{(n)} = p_{t+1}^{(n-1)} - p_t^{(n)}$$

The excess return from holding a n-year zero coupon bond for one year is

$$hpx_{t+1}^{(n)} = hpr_{t+1}^{(n)} - y_t^{(1)}$$

2.2. *Yield Curve in the SSE*
In China, bond trading in the exchange began in 1991, but our study sample period is from January 1994. The reasons are: (1) number of bonds traded in the SSE is very small at the beginning, and to estimate interest rate curves with their prices may causes much error; (2) market is not much rational and efficient at the beginning. Yield curves are estimated with Nelson-Siegel (1987) model. The reason that it is used to estimate the yield curves is taking its advantage of only 4 parameters needed to estimate, and the number of bonds traded in the SSE is not

154

big. A yield curve is a group of yields of zero coupon bonds $(y_t^{(1)}, y_t^{(2)}, ..., y_t^{(n)})$. The yield curves are plotted in figure 1. Basic statistic characteristics are in Table 1.

Usually long-term yields are higher than short-term yields---a rising yield curve. But sometimes, short-term yields are higher than long-term yields---an inverted yield curve. The interest rates implied in the SSE show both two types. From January 1994 to March 1996, the yield curves in the SSE are inverted yield curves. From April 1996 to October 2001, the yield curves are rising yield curves. Basic statistics show that yields from January 1994 to March 1996 have obvious skewness and kurtosis. But from April 1996 to October 2001, yields have no obvious skewness.

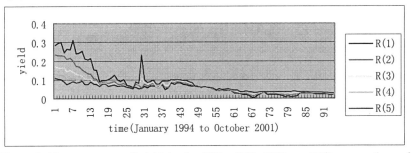

Figure 1. Term structure of yield in the SSE. R(1), R(2) ,...,R(5) are continuously-compounded yields of 1-year, 2-year,..., and 5-year zero coupon bonds respectively. The yields are estimated with Nelson-Siegel approach. Sample period: January 1994-October 2001

2.3. Expectations Hypothesis and Testing

Generally, we want to know the evolution of yields---the conditional expected value and variance next period. This is the central question for portfolio theory, hedging, derivative pricing, and economic explanation. The expectations hypothesis is the traditional benchmark for us to think about expected value of future yields.

The expectations hypothesis can be stated in three equivalent forms:

(1) The N period yield is the average of expected future one period yields

$$y_t^{(N)} = \frac{1}{N} E_t (y_t^{(1)} + y_{t+1}^{(1)} + y_{t+2}^{(1)} + y_{t+3}^{(1)} + \cdots + y_{t+N-1}^{(1)}) + risk\ premium \quad (1)$$

(2) The forward rate equals the expected future spot rate

$$f_t^{(N \to N+1)} = E_t (y_{t+N}^{(1)}) + (risk\ premium) \quad (2)$$

(3) The expected holding period returns are equal on bonds of all maturities.

Table 1. Basic properties of yield curves implied in the bond prices in the SSE

	$y^{(1)}$	$y^{(2)}$	$y^{(3)}$	$y^{(4)}$	$y^{(5)}$
		Table 1A (1994:01-1996:03)			
mean	0.149847	0.118714	0.099827	0.090167	0.08493
St. Deviation	0.014988	0.010206	0.005815	0.004141	0.00493
Median	0.102908	0.085496	0.088443	0.086438	0.07906
Skewness	-1.3561	-0.77252	-0.59074	2.104998	20.501
Kurtosis	0.529041	0.875031	0.80326	1.186684	4.02398
Min.	0.053028	0.055789	0.054186	0.053384	0.0529
Max.	0.310912	0.236051	0.170406	0.170876	0.23345
		Table 1B (1996:04-2001:10)			
mean	0.037503	0.042206	0.046364	0.049932	0.051326
St. Deviation	0.003017	0.002869	0.002893	0.00306	0.003072
Median	0.028305	0.032343	0.034764	0.036284	0.037728
Skewness	-0.84592	-0.25991	-0.07475	-0.27309	-0.06078
Kurtosis	0.606728	0.959818	1.114758	1.122987	1.200225
Min.	0.004069	0.014744	0.022943	0.027491	0.028859
Max.	0.084153	0.091369	0.09694	0.100787	0.102934

$$E_t(hprx_{t+1}^{(N)}) = y_t^{(1)} + (risk\ premium\ ) \qquad (3)$$

Based on equation (3), Fama and Bliss (1987) run a regression of one-year excess returns on long-term bonds against the forward-spot spread for the same maturity. The expectations hypothesis predicts a coefficient of zero---nothing should forecast bond excess returns. The "one-year returns" regression is

$$hprx_{t+1}^{(n)} = a + b(f_t^{(n-1 \to n)} - y_t^{(1)}) + \varepsilon_{t+1} \qquad (4)$$

With the interest rates in the SSE, we estimate equation (4) with LS estimation method. The results are in table 2. Table 2 indicates that the coefficient b are obviously not zero for all excess returns on the 4 zero coupon bonds, so it is concluded that forward-spot spread of the same maturity can be used to predict the excess returns on the bonds.

Fama-Bliss also run a regression of multi-year changes of one-year interest rate against forward-spot spreads. The change in $y^{(1}$ regression is

$$y_{t+n-1}^{(1)} - y_t^{(1)} = a + b(f_t^{(n-1 \to n)} - y_t^{(1)}) + \varepsilon_{t+n-1} \qquad (5)$$

The expectations hypothesis predicts the coefficients are 1 for all the regressions. The regression results are as table 3. Although the forward rates can predict future spot rates powerfully, the coefficient b are obviously not 1. So, table 3 show expectations hypothesis does not hold for the implied interest rate in the SSE.

Table 2. The "1 year returns" regression of Fama-Bliss's. The regression equation is $hprx_{t+1}^{(n)} = a + b(f_t^{(n-1 \to n)} - y_t^{(1)}) + \varepsilon_{t+1}$. Sample period: 1994:1-200:12

Maturity	1-year returns		
	b	$\sigma(b)$	R^2
2	0. 171589	0. 043341	0. 163825
3	0. 237435	0. 043079	0. 275217
4	0. 511031	0. 061005	0. 467278
5	0. 81857	0. 095317	0. 479679

Table 3. Change in $y^{(1)}$ regression. The regression equation is $y_{t+n-1}^{(1)} - y_t^{(1)} = a + b(f_t^{(n-1 \to n)} - y_t^{(1)}) + \varepsilon_{t+n-1}$. Sample period: 1994:1-200:12.

Maturity	Change in $y^{(1)}$		
	b	$\sigma(b)$	R^2
2	0. 828411	0. 043341	0. 820357
3	0. 679380	0. 033188	0. 860382
4	0. 679380	0. 033188	0. 791211
5	0. 462896	0. 031776	0. 791865

3. The Forecasting Factors of Bond Excess Returns

3.1. *Forecasting Bond Excess Returns with Term Structure*
The Fama-Bliss specification is most sensible for exploring the expectations hypothesis and its failures. Now we concern how to characterize bond excess returns. All the forward rates may be useful for forecasting bond expected returns. We adopt the following regression equation to forecast bond excess returns

$$hprx_{t+1}^{(n)} = \alpha + \beta_1 y_t^{(1)} + \beta_2 f_t^{(1 \to 2)} + \cdots + \beta_5 f_t^{(4 \to 5)} + \varepsilon_{t+1}^{(n)} \quad (6)$$

In equation (6), all the forward rates of the term structure are used as independent variables to explain bond excess returns. The regression results are in table 4. With all the forward rates as forecasting variables, we can improve predictability of the bond excess returns significantly. Comparing table 4 to table 2, R^2 rise from 0.16-0.47 to 0.55-0.63, and this is a great improvement of predictablity.

Table 4. Regression of one-year holding period returns on forward rates. Regression equation is $hprx_{t+1}^{(n)} = \alpha + \beta_1 y_t^{(1)} + \beta_2 f_t^{(1\to2)} + \cdots + \beta_5 f_t^{(4\to5)} + \varepsilon_{t+1}^{(n)}$. Sample period: 1994:1-200:12

n	α	$y^{(1)}$	$f^{(1\to2)}$	$f^{(2\to3)}$	$f^{(3\to4)}$	$f_t^{(4\to5)}$	R^2
			Coefficient				
2	0.003	-0.326	0.701	0.033	-0.034	-0.126	0.554
3	-0.014	-0.448	0.7444	0.461	0.077	-0.126	0.5381
4	-0.037	-0.568	0.8401	-0.305	1.245	-0.094	0.638
5	-0.057	-0.689	0.9746	-1.442	1.512	1.001	0.631
			Std. Error				
2	0.0059	0.042	0.104	0.229	0.111	0.0755	
3	0.010	0.072	0.179	0.393	0.190	0.129	
4	0.017	0.122	0.303	0.666	0.322	0.219	
5	0.0291	0.208	0.514	1.130	0.547	0.372	

3.2. Forecasting Short Rate with Term Structure

Now let us assume that all the information that is useful for forecasting future interest rate is current term structure. To forecast short rate change or short rate, we make following equation

$$y_{t+1}^{(1)} - y_t^{(1)} = \alpha + \beta_1 y_t^{(1)} + \beta_2 f_t^{(1\to2)} + \cdots + \beta_5 f_5^{(4\to5)} + \varepsilon_{t+1} \quad (7)$$

The regression results are in table 5. Compare table 5 to table 3,including all forward rates also improves the predictability of short rate change. Forward rates show much powerful to forecast short-term interest rate.

Table 5. One-period short rate forecast with all the forward rates. The regression equations is $y_{t+1}^{(1)} - y_t^{(1)} = \alpha + \beta_1 y_t^{(1)} + \beta_2 f_t^{(1\to2)} + \cdots + \beta_5 f_5^{(4\to5)} + \varepsilon_{t+1}$. Sample period: 1994:1-200:12.

	α	$y^{(1)}$	$f^{(1\to2)}$	$f^{(2\to3)}$	$f^{(3\to4)}$	$f^{(4\to5)}$	R^2
			Coefficient				
$y_{t+1}^{(1)} - y_t^{(1)}$	-0.003	-0.684	0.302	-0.033	0.034	0.126	0.90
			Std. Error				
$y_{t+1}^{(1)} - y_t^{(1)}$	0.006	0.042	0.105	0.2297	0.111	0.075	

Although the high predictability of short interest change is shown in table 5, it contains no information that is not contained in the holding period regression, it is perfectly implied in the two-year bond excess return regression. Mathematically,

$$hprx_t^{(2)} = p_{t+1}^{(1)} - p_t^{(2)} - y_t^{(1)} = -y_{t+1}^{(1)} + f_t^{(1\to2)} \quad (8)$$

$$E_t(y_{t+1}^{(1)} - y_t^{(1)}) = f_t^{(1\to2)} - y_t^{(1)} - E_t(hprx_{t+1}^{(2)}) \quad (9)$$

3.3. Principal Component Analysis

If we want to know how many factors are needed to determine the change of the interest rates, principal component analysis is a simple way to answer this question. We use principal component analysis approach to analyze principle components of the yield curve. Because forward rates are just the linear combinations of yields, it is equivalent to analyze the forward rates. The correlations of the yields $y_t^{(1)}, y_t^{(2)}, y_t^{(3)}, y_t^{(4)}, y_t^{(5)}$ are shown in table 6.

Table 6. The correlations of the yields $y_t^{(1)}, y_t^{(2)}, y_t^{(3)}, y_t^{(4)}, y_t^{(5)}$. Sample period :January 1994-October 2001.

	$y_t^{(1)}$	$y_t^{(2)}$	$y_t^{(3)}$	$y_t^{(4)}$	$y_t^{(5)}$
$y_t^{(1)}$	1				
$y_t^{(2)}$	0.977026	1			
$y_t^{(3)}$	0.921942	0.968433	1		
$y_t^{(4)}$	0.753757	0.815693	0.929621	1	
$y_t^{(5)}$	0.525939	0.590812	0.764518	0.938089	1

With the decomposition of the covariance matrix of yield curves, five components' cumulative proportions of variance and the loadings of the five components are in Table 7. From the loadings of the five components, we see the first component can be interpreted as the level of interest rates, the second components as the slope of the interest rates, the third as curvature. We need not to mention the last two components, because their total contribution is less than 0.1%. So generally, we say interest rates in the SSE is driven by two factors, at most three factors.

Table 7. Five components' cumulative proportions of variance and their coefficients as the linear combinations of the yields. Sample period: January 1994-October 2001.

	Comp. 1	Comp. 2	Comp. 3	Comp. 4	Comp. 5
Cumulative Proportion	0.912	0.991	0.999	0.999	1.000
	Coefficients of every component				
$y_t^{(1)}$	0.727	-0.399	0.550	0.000	0.000
$y_t^{(2)}$	0.511	0.000	-0.639	-0.262	-0.504
$y_t^{(3)}$	0.343	0.231	-0.398	0.000	0.819
$y_t^{(4)}$	0.244	0.507	0.000	0.791	-0.239
$y_t^{(5)}$	0.184	0.723	0.360	-0.549	-0.114

3.4. A Single Factor for Forecasting Bond Expected Returns

From the results in principle components analysis, the change in yield curve is described by two or three principle components. Although the factors that represent the changes of interest rates are different from the forecasting factors, we hope we can find as few as possible factors to forecast the interest rates.

First, we try to find one factor to maximize the predictability of excess returns with the forward rates. We adopt the approach of Chochrane and Piazzesi (2001). Let the factor be a linear combination of forward interest rates

$$f_{1t} = \gamma_1 y_t^{(1)} + \gamma_2 f_t^{(1\to2)} + \cdots + \gamma_5 f^{(4\to5)}$$

Excess returns of bonds relate the factor with the following equation

$$Hprx_{t+1}^{(n)} = a_n + b_n(\gamma_1 y_t^{(1)} + \gamma_2 f_t^{(1\to2)} + \cdots + \gamma_5 f^{(4\to5)}) + \varepsilon_{t+1}^{(n)} \quad n=2,3,4,5 \quad (10)$$

We normalized the coefficients by imposing that the average value of b_n is one

$$\frac{1}{4}(\sum_{n=2}^{5} b_n) = 1$$

We can fit the equation above in two stages. First, we estimate $\gamma_1, \gamma_2, ..., \gamma_5$ by running the regression

$$\frac{1}{4}\sum_{n=2}^{5} Hprx_{t+1}^{(n)} = \bar{a} + (\gamma_1 y_t^{(1)} + \gamma_2 f_t^{(1\to2)} + \cdots + \gamma_5 f_t^{(4\to5)}) + \varepsilon_{t+1}^{(n)} \quad (11)$$

$$= \bar{a} + f_{1t} + \bar{\varepsilon}_{t+1}$$

Then we can estimate the b_n's by running the four regressions

$$Hprx_{t+1}^{(n)} = a_n + b_n f_{1t} + \varepsilon^{(n)}_{t+1}, \quad n=2,3,4,5 \quad (12)$$

With regression equation (11), we estimate values of $\gamma_1, \gamma_2, ..., \gamma_5$, the results are in table 8. From equation (12), we determine the forecasting power of the factor, and results are in table 9. We see that the factor can forecast excess returns of 3, 4, 5 year bonds very well, but not so powerful as all the forward rates that show in Table 4. Surprisingly, the factor shows no forecasting ability for excess return of two-year bond. So we conclude that a single factor cannot explain the expected excess returns on the four zero coupon bonds. We have to add other factors to do so.

Table 8. The single factor that is constructed to explain bond returns. The regression equation is $\frac{1}{4}\sum_{n=2}^{5} Hprx_t^{(n)} = \bar{a} + (\gamma_1 y_t^{(1)} + \gamma_2 f_t^{(1\to2)} + \cdots + \gamma_5 f_t^{(4\to5)}) + \varepsilon_{t+1}^{(n)}$

	$\bar{a}$	γ_1	γ_2	γ_3	γ_4	γ_5	R^2
Estimate	−0.026	−0.505	0.814	−0.313	0.699	0.163	0.59
Std. error	0.014	0.103	0.256	0.563	0.273	0.185	

Table 9. Estimate of each excess return's loading on the single return-forecasting factor. The regression equation is $Hprx_{t+1}^{(n)} = a_n + b_n f_{1t} + \varepsilon^{(n)}_{t+1}$, n=2,3,4,5, where $f_{1t} = \gamma_1 y_t^{(1)} + \gamma_2 f_t^{(1 \to 2)} + \cdots + \gamma_5 f^{(4 \to 5)}$, the values of $\gamma_1, \gamma_2, ..., \gamma_5$ are in table 8.

Maturity	a_n (Std. error)	b_n (Std error)	R^2
2	0. 00813 (0. 00370)	0. 1092 (0. 0549)	
3	-0. 00378 (0. 00492)	0. 5407 (0. 0729)	0. 0471
4	-0. 0344 (0. 0075)	1. 2807 (0. 11129)	0. 4072
5	-0. 0754 (0. 01336)	2. 0693 (0. 19828)	0. 6234
			0. 5765

3.4 Two factors for Forecasting Bond Expected Returns

Because one factor cannot explain $hprx_{t+1}^{(2)}$ at all, so we need at least another factor to forecast bond expected returns. Comparing Table 4 to Table 9, we find that the forecaster of $hprx_{t+1}^{(2)}$ in Table 4 is the suitable factor, so we choose the second factor as

$$f_{2t} = -0.316 y_t^{(1)} + 0.698 f_t^{(1 \to 2)} + 0.033 f_t^{(2 \to 3)} - 0.034 f_t^{(3 \to 4)} - 0.126 f_t^{(4 \to 5)}$$

Then we estimate the $b_1^{(n)}, b_2^{(n)}$ by running the four regressions

$$Hprx_{t+1}^{(n)} = a^{(n)} + b_1^{(n)} f_{1t} + b_2^{(n)} f_{2t} + \varepsilon^{(n)}_{t+1} \quad \text{n=2,3,4,5} \quad (14)$$

The estimation results are in table 10. Comparing Table 4 to Table 10, it is found that two factors catch all the linear predicting power of the forward rates. With the two factors to forecast bond excess returns, we have almost the same R^2 as the 5 factors ($y^{(1)}, f^{(1 \to 2)}, f^{(2 \to 3)}, f^{(3 \to 4)}, f^{(4 \to 5)}$). The basic statistics of the two factors are shown in table 11.

Table 10. Estimates of each excess return's loadings on the two return-forecasting factors. The regression equation is $Hprx_{t+1}^{(n)} = a^{(n)} + b_1^{(n)} f_{1t} + b_2^{(n)} f_{2t} + \varepsilon^{(n)}_{t+1}$, n=2,3,4,5, with $f_{1t} = \gamma_1 y_t^{(1)} + \gamma_2 f_t^{(1\to 2)} + \cdots + \gamma_5 f^{(4\to 5)}$, coefficients $\gamma_1, \gamma_2, ..., \gamma_5$ are given in Table 8, and $f_{2t} = -0.316 y_t^{(1)} + 0.698 f_t^{(1\to 2)} + 0.033 f_t^{(2\to 3)} - 0.034 f_t^{(3\to 4)} - 0.126 f_t^{(4\to 5)}$

Maturity	a_n (Std. error)	b_{1n} (Std. error)	b_{2n} (Std. error)	R^2
2			0. 03955	
	0. 00269	1	(9. 54E−16)	
	(0. 00261)	(0. 1056)		
3				0. 5539
	−0. 00818	0. 80907	0. 45226	
	(0. 00454)	(0. 18344)	(0. 06873)	
4				0. 5243
	0. 00773	−0. 1386		
	(−0. 0337)	(0. 31211)	1. 29588	
			(0. 11694)	
5				0. 6243
	−0. 0663	−1. 6705	2. 25185	
	(0. 01297)	(0. 52407)	(0. 19635)	
				0. 6248

Table 11. Means and covariance of the two factors

	f_1	f_2
Mean	0. 01046	0. 04494
Covariance		
f_1	0. 00029	
f_2	0. 00023	0. 00209

4. Risk Premia

Having set a pattern to expected returns, we naturally want to relate that pattern to covariance. In finance theory, the expected excess returns on financial assets are explained by their risk. The general formula that explains expected excess returns on financial assets with their risks is

$$E_t(hprx_{t+1}) = \text{cov}_t(hprx_{t+1}, \varepsilon_{t+1}')\lambda_t - \frac{1}{2}\sigma_t^2(hprx_{t+1}) \tag{14}$$

where hpx_{t+1} denote the (4×1) vector of excess log returns, ε_{t+1} is a vector of shocks to pricing factors, and λ_t is a vector of factor risk premia or market prices of risk (see Cocharane and Piazzesi, 2001).

4.1. Calculating Market Price of Risk
Let C denote the covariance matrix of returns with shocks

$$C = \text{cov}_t(hprx_{t+1}, \varepsilon_{t+1}')$$

We can obtain market price of risk by solving the equation,

$$\lambda_t = (C'C)^{-1}C'[E_t(hprx_{t+1}) + \frac{1}{2}\sigma_t^2(hprx_{t+1})] \tag{15}$$

If we have more shocks than returns, the solution is not unique.

We have a model for expected returns,

$$E_t(hprx^{(n)}_{t+1}) = a^{(n)} + b_1^{(n)}f_{1t} + b_2^{(n)}f_{2t} \tag{16}$$

where

$$a = (a^{(2)}, a^{(3)}, a^{(4)}, a^{(5)})', \; b_1 = (b_1^{(2)}, b_1^{(3)}, b_1^{(4)}, b_1^{(5)})', \; b_2 = (b_2^{(2)}, b_2^{(3)}, b_2^{(4)}, b_2^{(5)})'$$

We assume that $\varepsilon_t, hprx_{t+1}$ have constant conditional variances and covariance.

With equation (15) and (16), we can calculate the risk premia λ_t by

$$\lambda_t = C'(CC')^{-1}[a + b_1f_{1t} + b_2f_{2t}] + C'(CC')^{-1}\frac{1}{2}\sigma_t^2(hprx_{t+1}) \tag{17}$$

or compactly,

$$\lambda_t = \lambda_0 + \delta\begin{pmatrix} f_{1t} \\ f_{2t} \end{pmatrix}$$

$$\lambda_0 = C'(CC')^{-1}(a + \frac{1}{2}\sigma_t^2(hprx_{t+1}))$$

$$\delta = C'(CC')^{-1}(b_1, b_2)$$

4.2. Yield Curve Shocks
Equation (14)-(17) tell us how to calculate market prices of risks λ_t, all the remains is to choose an interesting set of shocks ε_{t+1}, it is an interesting step to assume that all the shocks are shocks that cause unexpected changes of yields.

So let's find shocks from unexpected changes of yield structures. Start with a VAR representation for zero-coupon bond yields

$$y_{t+1} = \mu_y + \Phi_y y_t + v_{t+1}^y \tag{18}$$

where $y_t = [y_t^{(1)}, y_t^{(2)}, \cdots, y_t^{(5)}]'$.

We want to define an interesting set of yield shocks η_{t+1} by choosing an orthogonalization matrix $\sum_y$ $v_{t+1}^y = \Sigma_y \eta_{t+1}^y$ $\tag{19}$

we normalized the shocks η_{t+1} to be orthogonal and unit variance, $E(\eta^y \eta^{y\prime}) = I$. We can define the shocks η_{t+1} by an eigenvalue decomposition of the covariance matrix of the yield innovations

$$E(v_{t+1}^y v_{t+1}^y{}') = \Sigma_y \Sigma_y{}' = Q\Lambda Q'$$
$$\Sigma_y = Q\Lambda^{1/2} \tag{20}$$

Where Q satisfy $Q' = Q^{-1}$, and Λ is diagonal.

Next, we have to find the covariance of holding period return shocks with these yield shocks. From the definition of holding period excess returns, we have

$$hprx_{t+1}^{(n)} = p_{t+1}^{(n-1)} - p_t^{(n)} - y_t^{(1)}$$
$$= -(n-1)y_{t+1}^{(n-1)} + ny_t^{(n)} - y_t^{(1)} \tag{21}$$

We obtain

$$\text{cov}_t(hprx_{t+1}^{(n)}, \eta_{t+1}^y{}') = -(n-1)\text{cov}_t(y_{t+1}^{(n-1)}, \eta_{t+1}^y{}') \tag{22}$$

and thus

$$C = \text{cov}_t(hprx_{t+1}, \eta_{t+1}^y{}') = -A\Sigma_y = -AQ\Lambda^{1/2} \tag{23}$$

where

$$A = \begin{bmatrix} 1 & 0 & 0 & 0 & 0 \\ 0 & 2 & 0 & 0 & 0 \\ 0 & 0 & 3 & 0 & 0 \\ 0 & 0 & 0 & 4 & 0 \end{bmatrix}$$

4.3. Empirical Results
From equation (18), the yield innovations have the covariance matrix of table (12).

Table 12. Covariance matrix of yield innovations. First, auto regression $y_{t+1} = \mu_y + \Phi_y y_t + v_{t+1}^y$ is done for yield curves y_t, and then the covariance matrix of the regression residuals $v_{t+1}^{(y)}$ is computed.

	$v^{y_1}_{t+1}$	$v^{y_2}_{t+1}$	$v^{y_3}_{t+1}$	$v^{y_4}_{t+1}$	$v^{y_5}_{t+1}$
$v^{y_1}_{t+1}$	0. 00026846				
$v^{y_2}_{t+1}$	0. 00019414	0. 00019667			
$v^{y_3}_{t+1}$	0. 00017051	0. 00020356	0. 000250863		
$v^{y_4}_{t+1}$	0. 00016247	0. 00020975	0. 000298677	0. 00040622	
$v^{y_5}_{t+1}$	0. 00015819	0. 00021665	0. 000347059	0. 00049403	0. 00064348

Figure 2 presents the eigenvalue decomposition of the yield VAR innovation covariance matrix, $Q\Lambda^{1/2}$. Each line represents how much each yield rises in response to one of the orthogonalized unit variance shocks η^{y}_{t+1}. We see that yield unexpected changes are caused mainly by three shocks. The first shock is "level" shock, loadings to the level shock rise slowly with time to maturity. The second shock has a sharp slope, it influences the short maturity bonds with negative loadings and long-term bonds with positive loadings, it lower short-term yields, and raises long-term yields. The third shock is like the curvature, it rises mid-term yields of 2, 3 years bond, and lower the short-term 1 year bond, and 5 year long-term bond. The other two shocks have little influences on the unexpected yield changes of bonds.

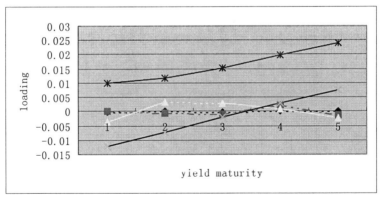

Figure 2. The eigenvalue decomposition of the yield innovation covariance matrix. The graph presents the columns of $Q\Lambda^{1/2}$ from the eigenvalue decomposition. Each line represents how a unit standard deviation movement in each orthogonalized shock affects yields of various maturities.

Table 13 presents results about these shocks. The table starts by presenting the square root of the eigenvalues. This tells us how important each factor is to the conditional covariance matrix of yields. The next four rows of table 13 presents the C matrix, they are the loadings of bond unexpected returns on the shocks. From level column, we conclude a level positive shock gives increasingly negative returns across the term structure. A slope shock gives positive returns of short-term bond returns at one hand and negative returns of long-term bond at other hand. The curvature shock gives larger negative returns on mid-term bonds than short-term and long-term bonds. $\lambda_0, \delta_1, \delta_2$ of table 13 show our estimates of factor risk premia. Time variations in the factor premia are generated by the coefficients δ_1, δ_2, these coefficients are very big, so we conclude that time variations of premia are significant.

Table 13. Factor risk premia in bond returns. From covariance matrix of table 12, we find the shocks by an eigenvalue decomposition of the yield shock covariance matrix, $\Sigma\Sigma' = Q\Lambda Q'$, and $\Sigma = Q\Lambda^{1/2}$. λ_t are the market prices of risks defined by

$$E_t(hprx_{t+1}) = \text{cov}_t(hprx_{t+1}, \eta^{y'}_{t+1})\lambda_t - \frac{1}{2}\sigma^2_t(hprx_{t+1}) .$$

	Level	Slope	Curvature	Shock 4	Shock 5
$100\times std.\ Dev.$ $(\Lambda^{1/2})$	3.80	1.66	0.63	0.27	0.04
	$100\times C$: how returns load on shocks				
$hprx^{(2)}_{t+1}$	-1.01	1.23	0.37	-0.02	0.01
$hprx^{(3)}_{t+1}$	-2.32	1.44	-0.64	0.09	-0.05
$hprx^{(4)}_{t+1}$	-4.61	0.64	-0.91	0.23	0.08
$hprx^{(5)}_{t+1}$	-7.92	-1.17	-0.26	-0.90	0.001
	Factor risk premia				
λ_0	2.7812	8.3485	1.9242	-0.3762	-0.1572
δ_1	9.3	81.6963	22.8812	-8.7874	-4.5298
δ_2	-28.0958	-17.6983	-6.1801	21.9118	7.7269
$\lambda_0 + \delta_1 Ef_{1t} + \delta_2 Ef_{2t}$	1.61575	8.407465	1.885739	0.516683	0.142697

5. Concluding Remarks

With the data of traded bond prices in the SSE, we obtain the yield curves implied in the bond prices, test the traditional expectations hypothesis, and study the predictability of bond excess returns with the yields, and the relation between risks and risk premia. The following conclusions are drawn from the empirical results:

(a) The yield term structures implied in the SSE show two types. From January

1994 to March 1996, the yield curves in the SSE are inverted yield curves. From April 1996 to October 2001, the yield curves are rising yield curves. Yields from January 1994 to March 1996 have obvious skewness and kurtosis. But from April 1996 to October 2001, yields have no obvious skewness.

(b) Bond excess returns have strong predictability with yield curves. And such predictability can be absorbed by two forecasting factors.

(c) Bond risk premia come from three resources: level factor, slope factor, and curvature factor. They all have explanation ability for the risk premia of bond returns. The risk premia also changes with time obviously.

References

1. D. Backus, S. Foresi, A. Mozumdar, and L.Wu , Predictable changes in yields and forward rates, *Working Paper*, New York University, (1997).

2. J. Cochrane, and M.Piazzesi, Bond risk pemia, *NBER Working paper*, No. W9178, (2002).

3. J. Campell, Understanding risk and returns, *Journal of Political Economy*, **104**, 298 (1996).

4. E. Fama, Forward rates as predictors of future spot rates, *Journal of Financial Economics,* **3**, 361 (1976).

5. E. Fama, The information in the term structure, *Journal of Financial Economics* , **13**, 509 (1984a).

6. E. Fama, The information in the term structure, *Journal of Political Economics*, **13**, 529 (1984b).

7. E. Fama, and R.Bliss. The information in long-maturity forwards rates, *American Economic Review*, **77**, 680(1987).

8. C. Nelson, and A. Siegel, Parsimonious modeling of yield curve, *Journal of Business*, **60**, 473(1987).

9. N. Anderson, J. Sleath, New estimates of the UK real and nominal yield curves, *Bank of Eangland Quartly Bulletin*, **54**, 384 (1999).

MINING LOYAL CUSTOMERS: A PRACTICAL USE OF THE REPEAT BUYING THEORY

H.P. LO* AND Z. NG

Department of Management Sciences
City University of Hong Kong
China
E-mail: mshplo@cityu.edu.hk

X.L. LU

Department of Statistics
Nankai University
China

E-retailing and database marketing are two emerging industries that require strong support from the customer relationship management (CRM) system. For a website, it is important to keep customers interested and come back frequently to visit. Who will come again? What percentage of transactions is accounted for by repeat-visitors? What characteristics do repeat-visitors have? These are important questions to be answered. As for a database marketing company, the selection of potential customers to mail an offer or catalog is of key importance. Who should receive which catalogs and when to send out the catalogs are difficult questions constantly challenging the management.

As web data and direct marketing data are available in huge volumes, data mining is an important and popular tool for both industries to develop good CRM systems to target loyal customers. Since most of these data are genuine purchasing data, one could even go one step further to develop models to describe and predict behaviors of customers. In this paper, two statistical models from the theory of repeat buying, the logarithmic series distribution and the negative binomial distribution, are used to fit the data from two large databases: One is obtained from a popular website in Hong Kong and the other is a publicly available database from a direct marketing company. Both models provide very good fit to the data and useful predictions are obtained.

1. Introduction

Loyal customers are those who make repeated purchases of a product/service. As the CEO of one major direct marketing company in the United States has put it: "I only consider a customer who has made more than one purchase in my company as a genuine customer". The reason for targeting loyal customers is very obvious. Every manager knows that loyal customers contribute the highest

---

* Corresponding author. Tel.: +852-2788-8647; fax: +852-2788-8560;
E-mail: mshplo@cityu.edu.hk

profits and it costs more to recruit a new customer than retaining a current customer. How to target loyal customers based on customers' personal characteristics and purchase behaviors has become an important issue to be solved by every marketing manager of a company.

Using data mining techniques to mine loyal customers is a logical answer to the above question for large companies. This is because huge amount of data relating to a company's customers are involved. These data include customers' opinions, perceptions, purchase behaviors and day-to-day transactions. Two emerging industries particularly require the use of data mining in this area. They are the e-retaining web-sites and the new direct marketing companies.

Among all data generators, no one would dispute that the Web is leading others in producing huge amount of data. The volume of data captured from the Web is increasing exponentially. According to San Diego, California-based consulting firm, the WebSideStory's StatMarket Division, which tracks activities of more than 100,000 Web sites worldwide, on March 23, 2001 (StatMarket 2001) alone, there were 53.7 million surfers to its monitored sites. As this company monitors about 25% of the daily Internet audiences, the total number of surfers per day could be well over 200 millions. The growth is expected to be even more dramatic in e-commerce. International Data Corporation projected that the worldwide Internet commerce revenue for B to B transactions will increase to 500 billion US dollars in 2002 (Mena 1999). This creates many opportunities and challenges for data mining. The opportunities arise from the sheer volume of data because websites can keep track of much more information; every mouse clicked, and every page viewed are noted in the web-log. The challenges are due to the incredible speed at which the data is generated. And yet, as estimated by the Gartner Group (Mena 1999), only 2% of the existing online data is currently being analyzed.

The need to mine loyal customers is vital for companies that are involved in e-retailing. These companies, whether large or small, are in an "information-intensive" and "ultra-competitive" mode. "Information-intensive" is because the Web log file could provide detailed information on every browse, visit, and transaction on the Web and it is an ideal environment for personal marketing. The pages, topics, keywords, sections one selects over time, together with some personal information obtained during registration, can be used to create a profile for the customer. This profile can be used to cross-sell new products and services to the Web user. On the other hand, e-customers are becoming accustomed to getting timely and useful product information based on their preferences and personalized features and they are used to obtaining quick and useful information from the Web. They are always well informed. If a website does not provide a user with the type of content that interests him, he will, with a click of the mouse, switch to a competitor who will. So it is "ultra-competitive". To stay competitive in such an environment, the most popular approach taken is to personalize their customers' online experience by providing customized products, services, and content so as to retain them as long as possible.

Another emerging commercial industry that is also a major data generator and requires the use of data mining to target their loyal customers is the new direct mailing industry (Shepard 1999). This new direct marketing is an information-driven marketing process, made possible by database and data mining technology, that enables marketers to develop, test, implement, measure, and appropriately modify customized marketing programs and strategies. With the help of data mining, direct marketers are now analyzing more relevant and timely customer-level information and use customers' attitude, lifestyle, and purchase behavior to develop customized marketing strategies.

The selection of potential customers to mail an offer or catalog is of key importance to direct marketers and catalogers. Who should receive which catalogs and when to send out the catalogs are difficult questions constantly challenging the management of direct marketing companies. Catalogs are never mailed out at random. They are always mailed to a list deliberately chosen in order to achieve some purposes. Since the databases of customers of these companies are usually very large, different data mining tools have been proposed to develop the mailing list. The most commonly used method in this industry is the RFM, the Recency, Frequency, Monetary segmentation.

There are many more data mining tools that can be used to develop marketing strategies. For example, one may use the collaborative filtering in market basket analysis, decision tree in customer segmentation and classification, neural network or k-means method in clustering, etc. Most of these techniques are data-driven and lack theoretical support. These techniques are perfectly appropriate in most cases if no attempts are made to study the effect of marketing factors, or to predict how customers behave when the values of the marketing factors change. Otherwise, theoretical models such as logistic regression are needed to describe the observed patterns and generalize them into future customer behaviors. Furthermore, in order to target loyal customers, models that study customers' purchasing behaviors in more than one period are required. The repeat buying theory developed by Ehrenberg (1988) is a possible solution.

This paper describes an application of the repeat buying theory in analyzing the behaviors of web visitors and direct mailing customers. We explain how the theoretical models can be used to derive useful marketing information and develop marketing strategies. In section 2, two commonly used statistical models in repeat buying are described. In sections 3 and 4, we demonstrate how these models can be used in web mining and direct mining respectively. A conclusion is given in Section 5.

2. Two Models for Repeat Buying

The main reason for identifying appropriate models is for prediction purpose. Many marketing and business information can be predicted if a model can be identified and provide good fit to the data. Since a website and a catalog can be treated as fast moving consumable goods (FMCG), many distributions discussed in Ehrenberg (1988) can be candidates for the repeat buying models. The most popular statistical models of this kind of data are the Poisson, negative binomial and the logarithmic series distributions. The Poisson distribution is often an appropriate model for describing the frequency of purchase of a FMCG during a fixed period in a homogeneous population since the assumptions of a Poisson process can be satisfied in general. For heterogeneous population where the mean number of purchases varies across the population, the negative binomial distribution has been shown to be a better alternative. And when the customers who made no purchase during the study period are removed, the logarithmic series distribution can often be used as a simplified version of the negative binomial distribution. Ehrenberg (1988) provides a good explanation of the theoretical background and Wani and Lo (1983) and Lo and Wani (1983) discuss statistical properties and parameter estimations of these three distributions.

The followings are the probability functions of the three models:

Poisson distribution:

$$\Pr[X = x] = \frac{e^{-\lambda}\lambda^x}{x!} \quad x = 0,1,\ldots \tag{1}$$

Negative binomial distribution (NBD):

$$\Pr[X=x] = (1+a)^{-k} \frac{\Gamma(k+x)}{\Gamma(x+1)\Gamma(k)}\left(\frac{a}{1+a}\right)^x \quad x = 0, 1, \ldots \tag{2}$$

Logarithmic series distribution (LSD):

$$\Pr[X = x] = \frac{\theta^x}{x[-\ln(1-\theta)]} \quad x = 1, 2, 3, \ldots \text{ and } 0 < \theta < 1 \tag{3}$$

Wani and Lo (1986) describe several graphical methods for the identification of a suitable candidate for fitting this kind of data. For demonstration, we use the U_r plot here. The plot is a simple scatter diagram of $U_r = (r*f_r)/f_{r-1}$ against the value of r. If the points, especially the first few points, resemble a straight line, one of the following distributions: Poisson, negative binomial, and the logarithmic series, is a good candidate for fitting the data. Furthermore, if the straight line has a positive slope and a negative intercept of similar magnitude, the logarithmic series distribution is the best candidate. But if the straight line has a smaller negative intercept, the negative binomial distribution is a better solution. Straight lines with horizontal slope indicate that the Poisson distribution could be used.

When one of the above models fits the data, many interesting conclusion related to purchasing behaviors of customers can be established using the repeat buying theory. In the next two sections, we demonstrate the applications of these models to the databases of a web site and a direct marketing company.

3. Two Models for Repeat Buying

ACITYJOB.com *(A pseudo name is used to keep the anonymity of the web-site)* is a very popular website for job-seekers in Hong Kong. It has many years' experience of recruiting candidates for best jobs. ACITYJOB offers information on many posts available from companies in Hong Kong. It also provides job-seekers with career guidance and up-to-date salary trends. ACITYJOB.com receives on average over several thousand visitors per day. It is useful to study the characteristics of the browsers of the ACITYJOB.com site, and their web behaviors through the use its web log files.

The most time-consuming part of mining website involves the capturing, extraction, aggregation, and preparation of server log data for analysis. We started with three types of data files: web log files; subscriber profiles; and job profiles.

The largest file is the web log file. This is where every transaction between the server and browsers is recorded with a date and time, the IP address of the server making the request for each page, the status of that request, and the number of bytes transferred to that requester etc. Each day, on average, there could be up to hundreds of mega bytes of data collected from the ACITYJOB Web.

Not all the information contained in the log file is useful. A large proportion of the log file is related to graphics, pictures etc that constitute the pages and provide no information on the usage of the website. For example, on a particular day, out of the million entries to the website, only 30% entries are requests for pages (asp). When the log file is read into the database system, only these pages are retained.

The second file is the subscriber profiles – A visitor to the ACITYJOB.com is required to register with the ACITYJOB.com. The file contains personal information such as age, gender, type of present job etc. on all the subscribers.

The third data file is the job profiles - Details of all the jobs advertised in the ACITYJOB.com are included in this data file. It contains information on job title, job type and job industry, qualification, etc.

The study period covers the last week of 2000 and first seven weeks of 2001. Due to the size of the data files, it is impossible to use EXCEL, ACCESS or other simple commercial software to clean the data files and prepare the database. The statistical software SAS is used to handle these large data files. SAS Macros were written to conduct the following tasks:

A. Reading the web log file – The web log file of the ACITYJOB.com was created by Microsoft Internet Information Server 4.0 using the Extended Log Format (ELF). Macros were used to capture each useful field.

B. Cleaning the data files – only entries that request for a page were captured; time spent on a page less than 1 second or more than 1800 seconds were removed.

C. Creating new variables – to create variables for the time spent on a page; total time spent on the website; dummy variables for categorical data; etc.

D. Merging the data files – to identify the job requested and the identity of the visitor; relevant information were attached to the entries in the log files and a database was developed.

E. Preparing different data files – to facilitate data analysis and data mining, several data files were prepared from the database. These files include a user file with number of visits and time spent and a job file with number of hits for each job.

These data files in SAS format are very large, many of them are more than 500 mega bytes in size and one of them requires two full size CD ROMs to store the data.

When the three data files are merged together, the so-called "webographic" information for ACITY.COM is created.

While there are many interesting findings that can be observed from the webographic information, this paper concentrates on the repeat-visiting patterns of the subscribers. The following table shows the distribution of subscribers grouped by number of visits to the websites during the study period.

Table 1: Distribution of subscribers according to number of visits

Number of Visits (r)	% of Subscribers(f_r)	Number of Visits (r)	% of Subscribers(f_r)

0	88.79	9	0.13
1	5.10	10	0.08
2	2.27	11	0.10
3	1.22	12	0.06
4	0.73	13	0.05
5	0.46	14	0.05
6	0.32	15	0.05
7	0.21	16	0.03
8	0.17	> 16	0.18

The U_r plot of the data is shown in the following figure:

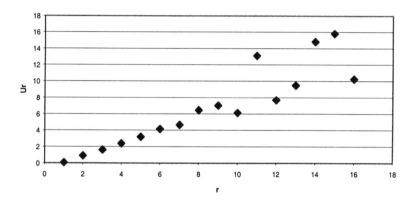

Fig. 1. U_r plot for number of visits

It is clear that the U_r plot suggests that the logarithmic series distribution (LSD) can be a good candidate for fitting the data.

In order to test whether the logarithmic series distribution fits the data well or not, a 5% simple random sample is first selected from the data file of all subscribers. These close to 4000 subscribers are then grouped together according to the number of visits to the website. The sample mean for this sample is 3.0472 and the maximum likelihood estimator of θ is 0.8545. Chi-squared goodness of fit test is used. The test statistic has a value of 13.57 with 10 d.f. and a p-value >0.15. The test is not significant, meaning that the logarithmic series distribution can be used to fit the data.

There are many interesting implications once we can establish that the logarithmic series distribution of $\theta = 0.8522$ fits the visiting pattern (Ehrenberg 1988). The followings are just some examples:

a. 85% (θ) of the visits to the websites will be from repeat-visitors.

b.   About 68% $(1+[\ln(1+\theta)/\ln(1-\theta)])$ of the visitors will be repeat-visitors.

c.   The average number of visits to the website by new subscribers is forecasted to be 1.38 $(\theta/\ln[1+\theta])$.

d.   The percentages of sessions accounted for by repeat-visitors who will visit the website at least r times is θ^{r-1}. For example, 62% of the sessions will be from subscribers who visit the site for at least four times.

The number of subscribers who will visit the website r times is monotonically decreasing.

4. Targeting Loyal Customers for Direct Marketing

Database marketing is growing more and more popular and the problem of selecting the loyal customers to mail an offer is of key interest to the direct marketers. Since customers differ in terms of their behaviors (responding, buying, returning, staying or leaving and so on), direct marketers use various methods to partition them into groups, or homogeneous market segments and choose the highly valued segments to mail in order to get a maximum profit.

Weinstein (1994) discusses the use of various dimensions such as geography, socioeconomic, psycho graphic, product usage, and benefits for customer segmentation. Previous purchase behavior is often considered as the most powerful predictors and this idea is used in the segmentation process by means of Recency, Frequency, and Monetary (RFM) variables (Shepard, 1999). Statistical methods such as factor and cluster analysis are another approach (Shepard, 1999).

Yet the most interesting methods are those that develop models for studying the relationship between dependent variables (dollars spent or response rate) and independent variables (demographic variables and history purchase behavior). Many different functional forms for the relationship have been proposed. Perhaps the most commonly used are the regression models, both linear and logistics. Malthouse (1999) proposes the use of ridge regression to develop the model. It could also be a tree-based model. Haughton and Oulabi (1997) compare the performance of CART and CHAID on a case study. Zahavi and Levin (1995, 1997) investigate the use of neural networks. These scoring models will assign each customer a score by predicting their response rate or the dollars spent.

The performance of such scoring models can be evaluated by a "gains chart" (Banslaben, 1992), or sometimes called a "gains table" (Jackson and Wang, 1994) or a "decile analysis" (Shepard, 1999). The gains chart is computed by sorting the data in descending order of scores and customers with similar score values are divided into groups of equal size (usually deciles). Then average and cumulative average dollar amounts or response rates per group are calculated.

When using direct mail as a medium for communicating with potential buyers, deciding how many customers to mail is a complicated decision in the context of a broader business plan. The common practice is send mail to those people in the mailing list, whose expected returns exceed the marginal costs of the mailing. Or when deciles are used, to send mails to all people that belong to the deciles with average expected returns larger than the marginal costs. Bult and Wansbeek (1995) further refine the selection procedure by using maximized expected profit. Colombo and Jiang (1999) suggest a stochastic RFM model to carry out this task. In practice, the most commonly used is the gains chart.

While there are many scoring models developed in the literature for targeting profitable customers, there are very few studies that are based on the theory of repeat buying. As the chance of making a further purchase is obviously related to the loyalty of a customer, we believe that the purchase behaviors of new buyers and repeat buyers could be different and therefore propose to estimate separately the proportions of buyers for these two groups of customers.

A publicly available large dataset, 02DMEF, supplied by the Direct Marketing Educational Foundation (DMEF 2002) is used for the demonstration. 02DMEF contains data from a business with multiple divisions, each mailing different catalogs to a unified customer base that consists of 96,551 customers. The file contains information on the life to date (LTD) orders, dollars, and items for total business and major divisions (A, C, D, F, H, K, L, M, and T); orders and dollars in the most recent 12, 24 and 36 months for total business and each major division; recency of first and latest purchases for total business and each major division; payment method; and demographic information (gender, age, and zip code etc.).

Since the data contains transaction records of more than four years, four consecutive purchase periods can be defined as follows: the most recent 12 months is defined as period IV, the most recent 12 months before period IV is period III, the most recent 12 months before period III is period II, and the whole period before period II is defined as period I (period I is longer than one year). By subtracting the orders and dollars in the most recent 36, 24, 12 months from the orders and dollars life to date and the orders and dollars in the most recent 36, 24 months, we obtain each customer's orders and dollars in the four periods, I to IV, for total business and for each major division respectively.

Among the many product divisions included in the data file, we choose division H for demonstration and customers of division H constitute the sample. Among the 96,551 customers in the data file, 9,812 persons have bought the products of Division H at least once. Since the duration of Period I for a customer varies according to the time the customer placed the first order, our discussions will concentrate on Periods II to IV, whose durations are all equal to

12 months. The following table shows the distribution of customers grouped by the number of purchases made during the Period II to IV.

Table 2: Frequency of Purchases for Division H

No. of Purchases	No. of customers in P. II	No. of customers in P. III	No. of customers in P. IV
0	93852	93920	94260
1	1939	1819	1435
2	517	552	603
3	142	163	144
4	62	51	48
5	20	24	38
6	9	13	13
7	4	6	5
8	2	1	2
9	2	2	1
10	1	0	0
11	0	0	0
12	0	0	0
13	0	0	2
14	1	0	0

Period II is used as an example to demonstrate the application of repeat-buying theory. Figure 2 below shows the U_r plot of the data in Period II.

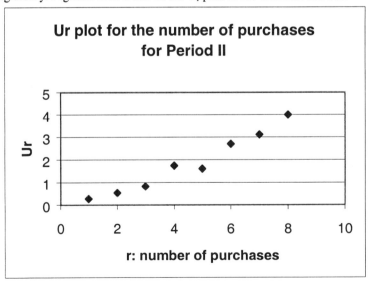

Figure 2: U_r plot for numbers of purchases

It is clear that the points in the U_r plot resemble a straight line with positive slope. The intercept is negative indicating the NBD could be a candidate distribution to fit the data. To develop the NBD, we have to estimate the parameters m and k (or a) from the empirical data. The best estimator of m is simply the observed mean which is the unbiased maximum likelihood estimator. The estimation of the second parameter k (or a) is less straightforward and various ways of estimation have been proposed. An estimating procedure common in statistics is the method of moments, which here means estimating a by equating the observed sample variance to its expected value $m(1+a)$. This is however not particularly efficient statistically for the NBD. An alternative method utilizes the number of non-buyers by equating the observed proportion of customers with zero purchase p_0 to its expected value, i.e.

$$p_0 = (1+m/k)^{-k}, \text{ or } (1+a)^{-m/a}. \tag{4}$$

This equation does not have a closed form solution but numerical method can be used to estimate the parameters.

Using the data in Period II, the parameters are estimated as follows:

m = 0.04026, a = 0.9437, and k = 0.04266 .

Chi-squared goodness of fit test is used to validate the appropriateness of the model. Eight classes are used as customers who made more than six purchases are grouped into one class due to their small expected frequencies. The test statistic has a value of 5.7473 with 5 d.f. and a p-value of 0.3316. The test is not significant. The negative binomial distribution fits the data well. The following table compares the observed and expected frequencies for different r. It is interesting to note that even for such a large data base, the frequencies as predicted by the NBD are so close to the real situation. This confirms that the repeat buying theory can be applied to direct marketing industry.

Table 3: Observed and expected numbers of customers who made r purchases

Number of purchases (r)	Observed number of customers(f_{ro})	Expected number of customers(f_{re})
0	93852	93852.05
1	1939	1943.89
2	517	492.03
3	142	162.66
4	62	60.07
5	20	23.58

6	9	9.62
> 6	10	7.09

Since the NBD fits the data well, many useful information from the repeat buying theory can be used to predict the purchasing behaviors of customers in future periods. To demonstrate, we consider the prediction of two important statistics in the coming period (Period III).

Using Period II as base period, a customer who has made at least one purchase in Period II is defined as a repeat buyer if he also makes purchases in Period III. A customer who has made no purchase in Period II but makes at least one purchase in Period III is called a new buyer.

Let r_R denote the proportion of buyers in Period II who will be repeat buyers in Period III and r_N denotes the proportion of non-buyers in Period II who will be new buyers in Period III. According to repeat buying theory (Ehrenberg 1988), we have:

$$r_R = 1 + \frac{(1+2a)^{-k} - (1+a)^{-k}}{1-(1+a)^{-k}} \quad \text{and}$$

$$r_N = 1 - \frac{(1+2a)^{-k}}{(1+a)^{-k}} .$$

As we have estimated a = 0.9437, and k = 0.04266 in Period II, we have
$r_R = 0.4178$ and $r_N = 0.01674$.

Since there are 2699 buyers and 93,852 non-buyers in Period II, the predictions for the numbers of repeat buyers and new buyers in Period III are respectively 1128 and 1571.

As in fact the data base 02DMEF has the purchase history of customers in Period III, we may check the accuracy of the predictions by finding the actual numbers of repeat and new buyers in Period III. The observed values are 958 repeat buyers and 1673 new buyers. It is interesting to note that using such simple model, we are able to achieve an average forecast error rate of less than 12%. Management may use these formulae to determine the number of customers to approach in future periods.

Another piece of information that should be useful to the direct marketers is the expected number of purchases by the customers in a future period. According to repeat buying theory, given a customer has made x purchases in a Period, the expected number of purchases in the next period is $(x+k)(\frac{a}{1+a})$. Hence, the following table can be produced:

Table 4: Predicted and observed average number of purchases made in Period III

No. of purchases made in Period II	Predicted average no. of purchases in Period III	Observed average no. of purchases in Period III
0	0.0209	0.0241
1	0.5094	0.4544
2	0.9979	0.7369
3	1.4864	1.1056
4	1.9749	1.5968
5	2.4634	2.4500
6	2.9519	3.3333
> 6	3.4404	2.3000

It can be seen from Table 4 that the predicted values are quite close to the observed values. The following figure also illustrates the accuracy of the predictions.

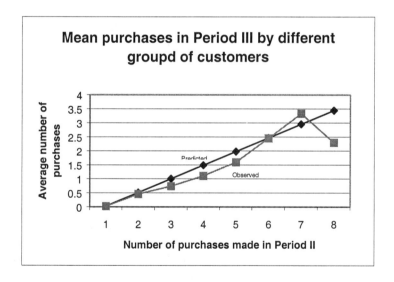

Figure 3: Average number of purchases in Period III

5. Conclusion

Data mining has become a very popular tool due to the enormous amount of data produced, collected, and stored everyday in all walks of life. The huge volumes of data involved in web mining and direct marketing certainly warrant the use of data mining. But people should not miss a more important issue: Data collected from the Web and direct marketing provide a much more accurate and detailed factual information about their customers. Not only that we can use the cross selling and decision tree types of approach that are purely data driven to develop CRM systems, we could even dig deeper into the data and develop models that have predictive power, and models that have theoretical support for a more general use. Through these models, we should be able to examine the relationships among different factors and the dependent variable; evaluate the consequences if values of some factors are changed. These models also have the generalization power so that we can use them in other situations and formulate future marketing strategies. In marketing, there is already a full spectrum of literatures on consumer behavior but many of them rely on interview or panel data, which could have data quality problem. As web data and direct marketing data are actual customer behaviors and they are available in huge volumes, it is now a golden opportunity to apply and adapt some of the results in marketing research and statistics to web mining and direct marketing data and develop suitable new models. In fact, we were quite surprised by the very good fit of the logarithmic series distribution and the negative binomial distribution to the web data and the direct marketing data. We have tried several data sets, used different study periods, but all confirm the theory developed by Ehrenberg (1988). We are also encouraged to note the simplicity of the model and the rich amount of implications that can be concluded from the model. An obvious extension of the study is to investigate how marketing variables affect the parameters, k and a of the NBD and θ of the LSD. The findings could have significant financial implications to companies involved in e-commerce and direct marketing. Further study in this direction has already been started.

References

1. J. Banslaben, Predictive Modeling. In E. Nash (Ed.). *The Direct Marketing Handbook*. New York: McGraw-Hill (1992).
2. J.R. Bult and T. Wansbeek, Optimal Selection for Direct Mail. *Marketing Science*, **14 (4)**, 378-394 (1995).
3. R. Colombo, and W. Jiang, A Stochastic RFM Model. *Journal of Interactive Marketing*. **13 (3)**, 2-12 (1999).
4. Direct Marketing Educational Foundation (2002), The DMEF Data Set Library – 02DMEF, http://www.aimannual.com/dmef/dmefdset.shtml, November 2002.
5. A.S.C. Ehrenberg, *Repeat Buying, 2nd ed.,* New York: Oxford University Press (1988).
6. D. Haughton and S. Oulabi, Direct Marketing Modeling with CART and CHAID. *Journal of Direct Marketing*, **11 (4)**, 42-52 (1997).

7. R. Jackson and P. Wang, *Strategic Database Marketing*. Lincolnwood, IL: NTC (1994).
8. H.P. Lo and J.K. Wani Maximum Likelihood Estimation of the Parameters of the Invariant Abundance Distributions. *Biometrics*, **39**, pp 977-986 (1983).
9. E.C. Malthouse, Ridge Regression and Direct Marketing Scoring Models. *Journal of Interactive Marketing*, **13 (4)**, 10-23 (1999).
10. J. Mena, Data Mining Your Website. *Digital Press* (1999).
11. D. Shepard, *The new Direct Marketing, 3rd ed.,* New York: McGraw-Hill (1998).
12. StatMarket: http://www.statmarket.com/#, 19 May 2001.
13. J.K. Wani and H.P. Lo, A Characterization of Invariant Power Series Abundance Distributions. *The Canadian Journal of Statistics*, **11(4)**, pp 317-323 (1983).
14. J.K. Wani and H.P. Lo, Selecting a Power-Series Distribution for Goodness of Fit. *The Canadian Journal of Statistics*, **14(4)**, pp 347-353 (1986).
15. A. Weinstein, *Market Segmentation.* New York: Irwin Professional Publishing (1994).
16. J. Zahavi and N. Levin, Issues and Problems in Applying Neural Computing to Target Marketing. *Journal of Direct Marketing*, **9 (3)**, 33-45 (1995).
17. J. Zahavi and N. Levin, Applying Neural Computing to Target Marketing. *Journal of Direct Marketing*, **11 (1)**, 5-22 (1997).